Presbyterian Pluralism

COMPETITION IN A PROTESTANT HOUSE

WILLIAM J. WESTON

The University of Tennessee Press / Knoxville

Portions of this book appeared in an earlier version as "Princeton and Union: The Dialogue of Pluralism" in *USQR* (Union Seminary Quarterly Review), vol. 54, nos. 3–4 (1991): 155–76. Reprinted by permission of the publisher.

Sections of chapters 8, 9, and 10 appeared in an earlier version as "The Presbyterian Controversy: The Triumph of the Loyalist Center" in *Beyond Two Parties: Reclaiming a Nonpartisan History of American Protestantism,* edited by William Trollinger and Douglas Jacobsen (Grand Rapids, Mich.: Wm. B. Eerdmans Publishing Co., 1997). Reprinted by permission of the publisher.

Library of Congress Cataloging-in-Publication Data

Weston, William J., 1960–
Presbyterian pluralism : competition in a Protestant house /
William J. Weston.—1st ed.
p. cm.
Includes bibliographical references and index
ISBN 0-87049-982-3 (cloth: alk. paper)
1. Religious pluralism—Presbyterian Church in the U.S.A. 2. Religious pluralism—United States. 3. Presbyterian Church in the U.S.A.—History—19th century. 4. Presbyterian Church in the U.S.A.—History—20th century. 5. Presbyterian Church—United States—History—19th century. 6. Presbyterian Church—United States—History—20th century. 7. United States—Church history—19th century. 8. United States—Church history—20th century. I. Title.
BX8937.W47 1997
285'.132—dc21   96-51236
                                                                       CIP

To Susan

CONTENTS

Acknowledgments

I am indebted to the people and collections of the following libraries and repositories for the data of this study: Centre College, Danville, Kentucky; Department of History, Presbyterian Church (U.S.A.), Philadelphia; Lancaster Theological Seminary, Lancaster, Pennsylvania; Princeton Theological Seminary, Princeton, New Jersey; Union Theological Seminary, New York City; Westminster Theological Seminary, Philadelphia; and Yale University, New Haven, Connecticut. The photographs are courtesy of Susan Sullivan at the Presbyterian Department of History, Cynthia Frame at Union Theological Seminary, and Grace Mullin at Westminster Theological Seminary.

I thank the following for discussing the ideas of this book: Darryl Hart and Mark Massa, who shared their dissertations-in-progress with me; Nancy Ammerman; Matthew Arneson; Peter Berkowitz; John Burgess; James Carper; Robert Handy; Dean Hoge (from whom the subtitle is borrowed); Joy Kauffman; Sally Kilgore; Jenny Weston Kittrix; Miles Lackey; Martin Marty; Brock Miller; Margaret Coulling Miller; Joseph Moorhead; Braulio Muñoz; Roger Nemeth; Joseph Small; Raymond Sun; and William, Jean, and Lila Weston.

I am especially grateful to the following for reading and commenting on portions of this text: Cameron Afzal, Fritz Bogar, Jackson Carroll, Kai Erikson, Margaret Farley, Juan J. Linz, Donald Luidens, R. Stephen Warner, an anonymous reader, Meredith Morris-Babb and the folks at the University of Tennessee Press, and (most of all) Susan Perkins Weston.

Beau Weston
Danville, Kentucky
Independence Day, 1996

INTRODUCTION

The world is diverse; we can accept diversity or reject it. Accept it, and you get endless dialogue which convinces neither side and leads nowhere. Reject it, and you get endless conflict which eliminates neither side or leads to oblivion. On the one hand, the dangling conversation; on the other, culture wars.

There is an alternative, though, which allows for both tolerance and action: competition. Competition is the kind of pluralism that we actually find and that actually works. When we start looking for competition, we find that many customary polarities turn out to involve not two parties going head-to-head, but three: the two public opponents—call them "liberals" and "conservatives"—and the vast mass whom they are trying to win over. Jack Rogers, in an analysis similar to this one, estimates that in the Presbyterian Church the liberals comprise perhaps 10 percent and the conservatives 15, while the center makes up fully 75 percent of the church membership.[1]

When this competition goes on within an institution, such as a church, the liberals and conservatives do compete, but ultimately the decisive actions lie with the central party of denominational loyalists. The loyalists are not ambivalent "moderates" in the middle of a liberal-to-conservative spectrum, but a party with a distinctive interest in advancing the traditional order of the church as it is.[2] What is at stake for the loyalists is not simply institutional survival, but their theological and ecclesiological vision of the church. Loyalists are the group least likely to exit the organization and therefore most likely to voice their position when forced to the conclusion that their organization is failing.[3]

The vision of competition proposed here stands in contrast to one of the proposals most visible in the sociology of religion today: the "culture wars" argument. Robert Wuthnow and James Davison Hunter argue that the "restructuring of American religion" is creating a new polarization which cuts across old denominational lines. This notion was outlined earlier for the Presbyterian Church by Dean Hoge. Reconceptualizing the problem not as a two-party conflict but as a three-party competition provides a more nuanced (and hopeful) analysis of the struggle. Loyalists within each denomination are the principal bulwark against a culture war which would rip the denominations apart. If the loyalists fail, then three-party competition may degenerate into a two-party culture war, but that has not yet occurred. Understanding competitive pluralism may be the best bet to keep the shooting from starting.[4]

This competitive vision came to me as a result of studying how pluralism came to be accepted in the Presbyterian Church, U.S.A. (the "northern Presbyterians") early in this century. The Presbyterian Church is a good case for pluralism because it is a creedal church, believing in orthodoxy—that is, believing that there is a *right* way to understand the most important things. The Presbyterian Church should be the hardest case for pluralism. Yet, while the Presbyterian Church upholds an ideal of one orthodoxy, within it a variety of views always have coexisted.

Help in solving this puzzle comes from the recent body of sociological work which argues that the United States as a whole always has been characterized by competition in a pluralistic religious market. This theoretical position has been outlined by R. Stephen Warner; compared cross-culturally by Laurence Iannaccone, Mark Chaves, and David Cann; and applied most thoroughly to explain American religious history by Roger Finke and Rodney Stark.[5] Still, this line of work has been confined to competition among denominations, not within them.[6]

The resolution of the problem of intradenominational diversity emerged from attending more closely to one explicit element of a creedal church that often is implicit in discussions of American religion as a whole: the church's constitution. The constitution is both the procedural foundation of the church as an organization, and the body of precedent and practice developed around the written text by the church as a living institution. In this, the constitution of the Presbyterian Church resembles the Constitution of the United States. The church constitution, though, also articulates its theological standards. The struggle in the Presbyterian Church was over the meaning of these theological standards, and the form of this struggle was a competition within the bounds of the church's constitution. The result of this particular competition was important historically and theoretically, because it did more than deal with one instance of diversity. It also created a specific kind of pluralism: a competitive pluralism, to be guided by the church's constitution.

This is the history of that competition. The liberals and the conservatives competed for the support of the central "loyalist" majority. At first the liberals, represented by Charles Briggs, tried to make the whole church liberal, and they lost. Then they switched their arguments from liberalism to tolerance and gradually won over the loyalists, represented by the Special Commission of 1925. Thereafter, the conservatives, represented by J. Gresham Machen, pressed their position so exclusively that they lost. The triumph of constitutional tolerance made competitive pluralism the policy of the Presbyterian Church.

There has been continuous historical interest in the turn-of-the-century developments in the Presbyterian Church in the U.S.A., treated most influentially by Lefferts Loetscher in *The Broadening Church* (1954).[7] More recently have appeared Mark Massa's study of Charles Briggs,[8] Bradley Longfield's treatment of the fundamentalist/modernist controversy,[9] and Darryl Hart's biography of J. Gresham Machen.[10] The liberal version of the story, as the broadening of the church, is captured in Loetscher's title; this version sees Briggs as ill-used early on, only to have his vision triumph later.[11] The conservative account, in contrast, sees Machen and other "defenders of the faith" as badly treated by the liberals and driven from the church.

Yet both kinds of standard accounts err. First, they usually separate the events of the Briggs case in the 1890s from the Machen struggles of the 1920s and 1930s, missing the narrative of competition which connects them. Second, both liberals and conservatives tell the story as a conflict of liberals and conservatives, missing the decisive and distinctive role of the much larger loyalist body within the church. Third, the usual focus on the stories of particular historical individuals obscures the way in which this case also can be understood as a struggle of general sociological types, institutions, and structures, as they are approximated and represented by real people and agencies in the Presbyterian Church. I focus on the particular individuals and institutions chosen here because they were, in fact, the most important representatives of these ideal types. If these people had not existed, however, the story likely would have been similar, with, say, Arthur McGiffert substituted for Briggs, Carl McIntyre for Machen, and any number of denominational leaders for the loyalist Special Commission of 1925.

This book has an unusual structure. In effect, it tells the same story four times, delving deeper each time. Part 1 is a brief narrative of the northern Presbyterian Church competition, from the Briggs case in the 1890s to the Machen controversies of the 1920s and 1930s, sketching the parts which are elaborated in later sections.

Part 2 returns to the actors and structures creating and underlying this story. The chapters in this part go deeper into the structure underlying the narrative of competition in the Presbyterian Church. In a sense, they recapitulate this story three more times, each time uncovering a more general and enduring layer of the living organization of Presbyterianism.

The first layer, explored in chapters 8, 9, and 10, is that of the primary actors at the critical points in the story of pluralism, namely, Charles A. Briggs, J. Gresham Machen, and the Special Commission of 1925. In addition to being vital participants in the Presbyterian conflict, each of these actors well represents a liberal, conservative, or loyalist position, respectively, in the competition.

The second layer, probed in chapter 11, is that of the principal institutions that carry the opposing positions on pluralism. The stories of Princeton Theological Seminary, of Princeton, New Jersey, and Union Theological Seminary in New York, are told as a dialogue about pluralism, from their beginnings as antitheses of one another, through a century of conflict, to their mutual accommodation on a new and quite different common ground.

Chapter 12 examines the third and deepest layer of this competitive struggle, the party structure of the church. The three great parties—liberal, loyalist, and conservative—form the enduring contours of the church. The party structure of the church shapes the conflicts of individuals and of institutions, yet it persists beyond them. The deep party structure of the Presbyterian Church was not unaffected by the conflict over pluralism, however; the result of the struggle was to *legitimize the party structure itself* in the eyes of the church.

Part 3 elaborates upon the theory of competitive pluralism that the historical case illustrates. The final chapter is a postscript about recent developments in pluralism in the Presbyterian Church (U.S.A.).

Part I

The Narrative

Chapter 1

THE PRESBYTERIAN CHURCH
IN THE U.S.A. BEFORE
THE BRIGGS CASE

*B*y the time of the Briggs case in the 1890s, the Presbyterian Church had a history of more than two centuries of development on American soil. It was planted principally by Presbyterians from Scotland and northern Ireland, and by English Puritans and a smattering of Reformed Protestants from the European continent. The Scotch-Irish element was strongest in Philadelphia and the areas to its west and south, while the "English" element was strongest in New York and New England. The Scotch-Irish tended to insist strictly on the creed of the church and the forms of Presbyterian religion, while the other group was less insistent on the Presbyterian distinctives and more concerned with the promotion, in collaboration with other churches, of vital piety. While the ethnic character of these distinctions became diluted over the years, these different tendencies, in broad outline, remained. From the beginning, then, some diversity characterized the American Presbyterian Church.[1]

The Presbyterian Church is organized in a hierarchy of courts, in which clergy, representing the pastoral ministry, and elders, representing the laity, are represented equally. Each congregation has a "session," which sends representatives to the area "presbytery." Presbyteries are represented in a "synod," and all the synods are represented in the national "general assembly." The American Presbyterian denomination organized a presbytery in Philadelphia in 1706, and a synod in 1717. The General Assembly for the new national church was created after the American Revolution in 1788.[2] The constitution of the church consisted of the Westminster Standards: the Confession of Faith, the Larger and Shorter Catechisms, the Directory of Worship, and the Plan of Government and Order, as modified by the church. The constitution established what had to be believed and done in the church, and the organization of the church as a system of courts meant that these constitutional standards of faith and practice would be enforced.

In 1729, a crucial debate took place between the Philadelphia and New York groups over how strictly ministers should be bound to the Westminster Confession. The Philadelphia group argued for strict subscription to every article, while the northern members opposed being bound to any creed created by humans, preferring to accept only the Bible as the rule for the church. In the "Adopting Act," a compromise was worked out by institutional loyalists, according to which ministers would subscribe to the Westminster Confession "as containing the system of doctrine" found in the Bible; if a candidate had scruples about any part of the Confession, it was left up to the presbytery to decide if these scruples posed a bar to ordination, subject to review by the higher courts.[3]

The Adopting Act compromise brought out the three parties that are always found in the church (and, perhaps, in any organization): conservatives who favor a strict and exclusive confessional position, liberals who favor a broad reading of the church's position, and loyalists who want to conserve the denomination.[4]

The Adopting Act allowed enough room for interpretation that each presbytery could establish standards somewhat different from those adhered to by the others. The strict presbyteries got stricter, and the broad ones got broader. These differences sometimes grew into schisms. In the mid-eighteenth century, there was a seventeen-year separation (1741 to 1758) between the revivalistic, New York–oriented New Side and the confessional, Philadelphia-based Old Side. At the beginning of the nineteenth century, the revivalistic Cumberland Presbyterians, who did not hold the strict Westminster Confession view of predestination, separated from the rest of the church. In 1837, a separation occurred between the ecumenical, New York–oriented New School and the confessional, Philadelphia-based Old School. By the time of the Civil War, each of these schools had divided into northern and southern churches over questions of slavery, union, and the political role of the church.[5]

The southern Old and New schools reunited in 1865 to form the Presbyterian Church in the United States (PCUS), and the two schools in the north united in 1870 to form the Presbyterian Church in the United States of America (PCUSA). The southern and northern churches remained apart until 1983. While parallel developments were occurring in both denominations, the more dramatic struggles occurred in the northern branch.[6] The struggle over pluralism in the northern branch of the Presbyterian Church (the PCUSA) from 1890 to 1940 is the story we shall trace here.

During the separation of Old and New schools in the North, Princeton Theological Seminary became the leading intellectual institution of the Old School, and Union Theological Seminary in New York became the leading intellectual institution of the New School. Princeton was controlled directly by the denomination, while Union was formally independent but effectively Presbyterian. With the reunion of the two schools in the North in 1870, each side recognized the orthodoxy of the other, and the Westminster Confession was retained in the constitution of the new church. In the reunited church, Philadelphia and Princeton remained conservative centers, while New York and Union provided leading liberals. The leading loyalists generally were found outside the northeastern base of the two extreme parties.[7]

At the time of the reunion, the General Assembly was given a veto over the appointment of professors at all the Presbyterian seminaries, including Union and Princeton. This put all these institutions on the same footing. For Union, this meant giving up some of the independence that it had enjoyed— a major concession by the seminary to promote denominational unity. For Princeton, on the other hand, this arrangement gave the seminary more freedom than it had had before. The General Assembly's veto power would be tested for the first time in the case of Charles Briggs.[8]

Chapter 2

1890s: The Briggs Case
and Its Aftermath

*C*harles Augustus Briggs was the leading liberal in the Presbyterian Church in the U.S.A. in the years before his suspension from the ministry in 1893. He was an important professor of the Bible at Union Theological Seminary in New York, which then was one of the foremost seminaries in the nation. Conservatives opposed him for teaching the "Higher Criticism" of the Bible, treating Scripture as the product of a progressive historical process that colored the text with the historically conditioned consciousness of the people who brought it forth.

After his trials and suspension, Briggs remained at Union and continued to have a liberalizing effect on the church, especially by promoting church union. Briggs was not much worried about the differences of doctrine and practice in the various denominations. He was confident that they could be comprehended and overcome over the long haul, in a continuing historical process. He was not concerned about the fact that, at any given moment, the church likely would encompass a wide diversity of views and practices. Nor was he daunted by the prospect of profound changes in the church that future developments might bring. The essence of Christianity would be preserved, he believed, and the future historical church would be better for its comprehensiveness.

The Trials of Charles A. Briggs

In 1880, Union Theological Seminary and Princeton Theological Seminary began work on the *Presbyterian Review*, a theological journal designed to cement the recently healed breach between the New School and the Old School among the northern Presbyterians. Charles A. Briggs, already an accomplished liberal Biblical scholar at Union, was coeditor of this journal, representing the former New School, and he worked with several Princeton professors over the years. Due to tension between the liberals and conservatives in the church, the *Review* ceased publication in 1889. As a result of his writings and editorial work concerning the controversies in the church in the 1880s, Briggs became the recognized leader of the liberal wing of the denomination.[1]

The biggest struggle within the Presbyterian church in this period was the attempt to revise the Westminster Confession of Faith, the church's creed. Briggs led those calling for a new and simpler creed as a step on the way to a broad union of all Presbyterian denominations, and perhaps of all Christian churches.[2] The opponents of revision saw the effort as an attempt to undermine the distinctive Calvinist doctrines of historical Presbyterianism, especially predestination, and to reduce the church to the "least common denominator" in the interests of Christian unity. A coalition of centrists loyal to denominational traditions and conservatives loyal to specific doctrines won this first battle in what was to become a long and bitter struggle between Briggs and the conservatives. Briggs thought that his later trials for his use of Higher Criticism were designed chiefly to divert attention from the revision question.[3]

The fight began in earnest in 1891, when Briggs was transferred to a newly created chair in biblical theology at Union. In January of that year, he delivered his inaugural address, entitled "The Authority of Holy Scripture." In this address he defended the authority and supernatural inspiration of the Bible, as well as the authority of the church and of "reason" (by which he meant experience and conscience, as well as reasoning). At the same time, he attacked "Bibliolatry" and scholastic versions of Calvinism. He used and defended the methods of Higher Criticism, claiming on this basis that the Pentateuch was not written by Moses and that more than half of the Book of Isaiah was not written by that prophet. He emphasized God's immanence in the world and proclaimed that there has been an evolution in religious understanding.[4] Although this was not the first time Briggs had published his views, the inaugural address was widely publicized, especially by alarmed conservatives.

Conservatives considered these ideas, especially Higher Critical views of the Bible, to be heretical, and they demanded an investigation. In April 1891, they convinced the Presbytery of New York, of which Briggs was a member, to conduct a trial.[5] Following an investigation in October and November of that year, the Presbytery voted that the charges were not sustained, and Briggs was acquitted.[6] The prosecuting committee, however, took the matter to the denomination's General Assembly, meeting in Portland, Oregon, in May 1892. Briggs claimed that the prosecuting committee had no authority to continue after the presbytery had dismissed it, but the General Assembly allowed the committee to proceed. This assembly, which was under conservative control, remanded the Briggs case to New York Presbytery for a new trial "on the merits." To make its own convictions clear, the assembly also issued the "Portland Deliverance," which asserted, against Higher Critical views, the "inerrancy" of the (now unavailable) original autograph manuscripts of the Bible, a theory championed at Princeton Seminary. Briggs and others questioned the constitutional authority of the General Assembly to make such a declaration on behalf of the church without seeking the concurrence of the presbyteries.[7]

In December 1892, Briggs again was tried in New York Presbytery and again was acquitted of all charges. The prosecuting committee then took its case back to the General Assembly, this time asking for an appellate trial by the entire assembly. In so doing, they bypassed the normal court of appeal, the Synod of New York. Briggs contested this, as well as again challenging the standing of the prosecuting committee after the case had been dismissed by the presbytery. Nevertheless, the assembly agreed to entertain the appeal, which it heard at the end of May 1893. Despite impassioned speeches on his behalf by other liberals, as well as Briggs's own erudite defense of his position, his victory in the lower court was overturned by a large margin. On June 1, 1893, Charles Briggs was suspended from the Presbyterian ministry. At this same assembly, the creed revision proposals that Briggs had championed went down in defeat. Briggs saw this result as confirming his suspicion that his trial and the anti-revision effort were connected.[8]

The actions of the General Assembly of 1893 brought to a head a dispute between the denomination and Union Seminary. As part of the reunion of the New and Old schools in 1870, the seminary had agreed to allow the General Assembly to have veto power over the appointment of professors. The General Assembly of 1891 exercised this veto over Briggs's transfer to the new chair. Union Seminary contended that the right of veto applied only to new appointments, not to the transfer of existing faculty. The seminary denied the authority of the veto and abrogated the agreement of 1870. This issue was being discussed concurrently with the Briggs trials. After Briggs's suspension in 1893, however, the victorious conservatives demanded the capitulation of the seminary and the firing of Briggs. The seminary refused this demand and returned to its original condition of independence from the General Assembly, retaining Briggs on the faculty.[9]

Briggs devoted the remainder of his life to promoting church union, a cause that long had engaged him, and he became an acknowledged leader of the movement for organic union of all churches. He remained on the Union faculty until his death in 1913. In 1899, as a step on the path to a larger, united church, he was ordained in the Protestant Episcopal Church, thereby becoming the first non-Presbyterian on the Union faculty. This move elicited some pressure for him to resign, but he was supported by liberals and ecumenists on Union's board of directors. Briggs remained a champion of the liberal Protestant church and was one of the few Protestants with close ties to liberals in the Roman Catholic Church.[10]

Briggs promoted a variety of federal and comprehensive schemes for church union and specialized in the study of Christian symbols or creeds. When he died, he had a reputation for rigorous scholarship and careful argument, as well as for self-assured combativeness. His literary output had been enormous, and he also had been a great collector for the Union library. After his death, two further books were arranged for publication, and his papers were collected by his daughter, Emilie Grace Briggs, the first woman to graduate from Union Theological Seminary.[11]

AFTERMATH OF THE BRIGGS CASE

The rules of the church require that "when any matter is determined by a major[ity] vote, every member shall either actively concur with, or passively submit to such determination; or, if his conscience permit him to do neither, after sufficient liberty modestly to reason and remonstrate, peaceably withdraw from our communion, without attempting to make any schism."[12] When the majority decision went against him, even though he thought he had been railroaded and denied due process, Briggs did indeed withdraw quietly. Briggs himself remained in the Presbyterian Church for several more years before his ordination in the Episcopal Church. Somewhat less quiet were two other liberal scholars, Henry Preserved Smith and Arthur C. McGiffert, who also were forced out of the Presbyterian ministry in the aftermath of the Briggs trials; but they, too, did not attempt schism.

Henry Preserved Smith was a professor at the church's Lane Theological Seminary in Cincinnati, Ohio. He was an ardent defender of Briggs within the church, and when Briggs went down, Smith went down with him. Smith was tried by the Presbytery of Cincinnati in 1892 for denying the inerrancy of the Bible, and was suspended from the ministry. He appealed to the Synod of Ohio in 1893 and lost; then he appealed to the General Assembly of 1894. Having suspended Briggs on largely the same charges the previous year, this assembly had no difficulty deciding what it thought of Smith's case. Smith lost by an even larger vote than Briggs had. Henry Preserved Smith joined the Congregational Church in 1899 and in 1913 came to Union Seminary as librarian.[13]

Arthur Cushman McGiffert had been a supporter of Smith's on the Lane faculty. After Smith's suspension, McGiffert became the professor of church history at Union Seminary in 1893. In 1897, he published *A History of Christianity in the Apostolic Age,* which drew the charge from conservatives that he was irreverent and naturalistic in handling the Bible. When the matter came to the General Assembly in 1898, the church leadership attempted to avoid another divisive heresy trial and encouraged McGiffert to withdraw quietly. McGiffert refused, denying that he had violated any essential Presbyterian doctrine. The Assembly of 1899 condemned views which McGiffert seemed to espouse but held back from naming him by name. In 1900, George Birch, Briggs's old prosecutor, brought charges in New York Presbytery against McGiffert. The presbytery condemned certain errors in his teaching but thought McGiffert faithful to the church. Birch appealed to the General Assembly, where McGiffert was certain of condemnation and suspension. Before the trial, and on the advice of his colleague Briggs, McGiffert resigned from the Presbyterian ministry. He later joined the Congregational Church and, still later, became president of Union Seminary.[14]

The greatest long-term effect of the Briggs case on the development of the Presbyterian Church was that Union Seminary was freed from denominational control to become a leading center of liberal religious thought. This independence initially was brought about by the seminary's abrogation of the assembly's veto power, but it became part of the culture of the seminary with the addition of Henry P. Smith and Arthur C. McGiffert to the faculty, as well as the movement, begun by Briggs, to make the faculty multidenominational. Although they remained separate, Union Seminary and the Presbyterian Church continued to have important effects upon each other.

The removal of these three liberal scholars from the ministry and the defeat of the movement to revise the Confession made the 1890s a very successful decade for the conservatives. They also counted the separation of Union Seminary from the denomination and the removal of the liberal voices at Lane Seminary as gains. These latter events, however, would come back to haunt the conservatives, as thereafter they had no direct leverage on the liberal intellectual centers. For their part, the liberal leadership was chastened by the disasters of the 1890s. They learned greater respect for compromise and for the constitution of the church. For this reason, they had much greater success in broadening the institutional base of the church in the decade of the 1900s. Ultimately, the ability of liberals to compromise with the loyalists—and the rejection of accommodation by the conservatives—would mean the triumph of pluralism in the Presbyterian Church.

Chapter 3

1900s: Broadening the Base

*I*f the 1890s were a decade of conservative successes in the church, the first decade of the 1900s proved better for the liberals. Through compromise with the loyalist center, the liberals got the church to revise the Confession in 1903, to reunite with the Cumberland Presbyterians in 1906, and to help create the Federal Council of Churches in 1908. The liberal leaders established themselves as loyal churchmen, team players willing to compromise. As a result, they succeeded in effectively broadening the institutional base of the church, while affirming an evangelical Presbyterian piety. By giving up any insistence on the liberal doctrine or program, they won a practical measure of tolerance for themselves and their new allies.

Reinterpreting the Creed, 1903

Although the conservative Calvinists fought hard against it, the Westminster Confession was revised when the liberals gave up on the idea of a new creed and instead compromised with the loyalist center on a reinterpretation of the Confession. This revision, which took a step away from Westminster Calvinism, became the basis for reunion with the more Arminian ("free will") Cumberland Presbyterian Church. The opposition to the revision, and to the Cumberland reunion, was led by Princeton's B. B. Warfield, one of Briggs's coeditors on the failed *Presbyterian Review* and a leading conservative thinker within the church.[1]

The attempted creedal revision in the 1890s had demonstrated support for some change but gave no specific mandate. The poll of the church conducted in 1889 revealed, for example, that fifty-five presbyteries, out of more than four hundred responding, wanted to drop the section of the Westminster Confession which called the pope "anti-Christ."[2] Many Presbyterians, to take another example, had qualms about the section that suggested that there were some who died as infants who would not be saved.[3]

The most heated controversy, however, was over revision of the distinctive Calvinist doctrine of predestination: the view that, by God's eternal decree, some were elected to salvation and the rest were elected to damnation.[4] Conservative Presbyterians thought this doctrine to be essential to the idea of God's complete sovereignty over the world. They were determined to fight any revision (even revision of texts unrelated to predestination), in order to defend what they regarded as an essential Presbyterian belief. At the other end of the spectrum were those who thought that this high doctrine of predestination was offensive both to the idea of human free will and to the idea of God's mercy. The conservatives contended that change would damage the distinctive witness of Presbyterianism and drive away those devoted to the denomination. Their opponents claimed that revision would hold those of tender conscience who rebelled against this harsh portrayal of God's character and, at the same time, draw in those who were repelled by the church's seeming negation of human reason and freedom.

At the turn of the century, the General Assembly, responding to many requests to do something about revising the creed, asked the presbyteries to make specific proposals to revise the Westminster Confession. While many specific proposals came back, there was no unified direction. The committee of the 1902 General Assembly charged with assessing these returns could not extract a specific plan of revision but saw in the replies a general mandate for change.

Three strategies for revision were available: to send down a set of overtures, each proposing a specific revision of the text; to send down a new, simplified, summary creed; or to send down an overture containing a declaratory statement, to be appended to the Confession without changing the text of the creed, explaining the interpretation that the church put on the difficult chapters. The committee convinced the General Assembly to do all three. In 1903, the votes came back from the presbyteries. The summary of the creed went down to defeat. The specific textual changes were approved, such as dropping the charge that the pope was anti-Christ. Most importantly, the

"Declaratory Statement" was approved.[5] The conservatives saw this result as watering down the doctrine of the church and made it a grievance for decades to come.[6]

The "Declaratory Statement" is a carefully crafted piece of committee writing, deliberately ambiguous on the contested point. The statement explains that it is not a revision, but a "disavowal . . . of certain inferences drawn from . . . the Confession of Faith," inferences drawn by parties unnamed. The crucial lines read:

> concerning those who are saved in Christ, the doctrine of God's eternal decree is held in harmony with the doctrine of his love to all mankind, . . . ; that concerning those who perish, the doctrine of God's eternal decree is held in harmony with the doctrine that God desires not the death of any sinner, but has provided in Christ a salvation sufficient for all, . . . freely offered in the gospel to all; [and] that men are fully responsible for their treatment of God's gracious offer.[7]

It is not explained how these doctrines may be "held in harmony."[8]

The critical difference between the failed attempt at revision in the 1890s and the successful try in the 1900s was that, in the latter, revision was disentangled from any larger scheme of church union or ecumenical cooperation. The liberals had learned a lesson: the Presbyterian Church could be changed, but only on the basis of distinctively Presbyterian arguments. The center of the denomination would not be moved to support revision by, for example, the prospect of a merger with the Episcopalians or even the Cumberland Presbyterians; the loyalists could be swayed, however, by the thought that the bald statements of the Confession might be read in a way that impeached the evangelical Presbyterian belief in God's mercy. The liberals had to offer the denominational loyalists some argument that revision was necessary to preserve, rather than undermine, distinctive Presbyterianism.

CUMBERLAND REUNION, 1906

Attempts had been made for almost a century to heal the breach with the Cumberland Presbyterian Church, but it was the creed revisions that made this reunion possible. This merger brought into the PCUSA a sizable number of ministers and lay members who were loyalists or liberals. Conservatives in the PCUSA, in the main, had opposed the reunion and were suspicious of the former Cumberlanders. Naturally enough, given this guarded reception as well as their own theological positions, the former Cumberlanders tended to vote with the loyalist-to-liberal group in the reunited church.[9]

The Cumberland church had grown out of the frontier revivals in Tennessee and Kentucky at the beginning of the nineteenth century. The revivals developed powerful, emotional techniques to convince people of their sinfulness and of their need to make a choice for (or against) Christ. The Presbyterians, who taught that the elect were predestined for salvation, had rejected this emphasis on choice on the part of the sinner, as it seemed to limit God's sovereign power to choose to save. Revivals often were conducted by fervent preachers who scorned seminary training—which Presbyterians prided themselves on—as deadening to the spirit. In fact, eastern Presbyterians found revivals offensive to their bourgeois aesthetics, as much as to their theology. As a result of their qualms about revivals, in the decades after the American Revolution the Presbyterian Church lost its position as the largest denomination to the Baptists and Methodists, who conducted revivals on the basis of this Arminian (free will) doctrine. These revivals were especially powerful in the Cumberland Valley, and Presbyterians there accepted Arminianism and a clergy with less education. Eastern Presbyterians rejected both accommodations, and the two groups split in 1810.

Church union had been at the top of the liberal agenda in the 1890s, and Briggs himself was a leading proponent of organic union of the Christian churches on the broadest basis. This project disquieted both the Calvinist conservatives and the denominationally oriented loyalists in the church, who feared that the liberals were willing to "sell out" Presbyterianism in order to achieve a unified liberal church. Learning from the failures of the 1890s, liberal leaders in the new century followed a more careful course of church union. They pursued organic union with closely related denominations, one merger at a time; at the same time, they tried to establish a limited federal union with other evangelical Protestant denominations for certain service works. This two-pronged approach won the support of the Presbyterian center, a group that eventually would provide the strongest supporters of ecumenism.

The Cumberland reunion was the natural outgrowth of the first component of this strategy. The two denominations had the same historical roots, were very similar in theology, complemented one another geographically, and had not (unlike the northern and southern Presbyterian Churches) been divided by the bitter issues of the Civil War. Nevertheless, the conservatives opposed the reunion on the same grounds that had made for schism a century before. The opponents of reunion overlapped considerably with the opponents of the Confession revision. By the same token, the "center-left" alliance created by the revision struggle was even more strongly in favor of reunion, and this group eventually carried the day. The northern Presbyterian Church voted solidly for reunion, 194 presbyteries out of 241. A large, more conservative minority of the Cumberland Church chose to remain apart, but the PCUSA did not divide over the issue.[10] In 1906, the new church was larger, stronger—and broader.

FEDERAL COUNCIL OF CHURCHES, 1908

The second component of the ecumenical strategy resulted in the creation of the Federal Council of Churches in 1908. The experience of Briggs and others had convinced the "inclusivist" liberal leaders that immediate organic union of the evangelical churches was out of the question. Therefore, they began to work on a project of federal union, which would not interfere with the "sovereignty" of any member church but would allow for a united Protestant voice and more efficient Protestant action. This unity seemed increasingly necessary in the face of the large non-Protestant immigration, which was swelling rapidly at this time.[11]

The Federal Council was not a very strong organization, but its creation was a liberal victory and a first step toward realizing an ambitious plan for organic union. This plan would bear fruit a decade later. The principal work of the council was in coordinating mission work, and it was from missionary cooperation that the later ecumenical leadership would emerge.

The four decades after the reunion of the New and Old schools in 1870 had produced a new church. The passing of the older generation, the trials, the creed revision, and the Cumberland reunion had altered the character of the church significantly. The new generation of leaders, especially among the loyalists, were not bound by either school. The schools were dying—indeed, they were dead. This point never was grasped completely by some of the conservatives. This was especially true of the intellectual leaders of the right wing of the church at Princeton Seminary. From the 1890s on, when Briggs's sparring partner, B. B. Warfield, led the faculty, the Princeton conservatives withdrew from active leadership in the church, becoming an increasingly isolated body of intellectuals. The conservatives never were fully successful competitors in the church, because they were fighting the wrong enemy. They were trying to convince the loyalists of the dangers of the New School, when in fact the New School was dead—and its descendants now *were* the loyalists. Even in the 1930s—two generations after the reunion—the conservatives still were trying to fight for the Old School against the New. But the New School was gone, and the new church had gone beyond the struggles of previous generations.

Chapter 4

1910s: RHETORICAL FUNDAMENTALISM

*T*he second decade of the twentieth century was marked by conservative reaction, which attempted to narrow church doctrine in response to the broadening of the preceding decade. The greatest achievement of this ideological retrenchment was the articulation by the General Assembly of 1910 of what were known as the "five points," and their affirmation by the General Assembly of 1916. These steps mark the appearance of a "fundamentalism" in the Presbyterian Church.[1] In the long run, however, these rhetorical successes were no match for the institutional changes brought about by the earlier broadening of the church.

The "five points" became the central symbolic weapon of the church's conservative wing. In the five points, the General Assembly proclaimed that the inerrancy of Scripture, the virgin birth of Christ, his vicarious atonement, his bodily resurrection, and his miracles all were essential and necessary beliefs for Presbyterian ministers. These all were points that had been contested by "scientific" and historically oriented scholars, including some Presbyterians, who had a growing popular following. These doctrines, the conservatives thought, were the fundamentals of supernatural Christianity which had to be defended against an increasingly militant secular "naturalism."

In proclaiming the five points, the Presbyterian Church took a step away from its traditional apologetic defense of distinctively Presbyterian doctrines, moving instead toward a defense of the fundamentals of Christianity in general. This change created tension in the right wing of the church between the traditional, confessional conservatives (that is, the loyalists) and the new, militant fundamentalists.[2] Although individual Presbyterians, since the 1870s, had been involved intimately in what later was called "fundamentalism," their actions generally had been carried on outside the denomination, especially in Bible conferences. Strictly speaking, there were very few "fundamentalists" or "modernists" within the northern Presbyterian Church, although many fundamentalist leaders did come out of the PCUSA. Transdenominational fundamentalism eventually was to split the right wing of the church off from the denominationally-oriented center, in the same way that transdenominational modernism earlier had split off the left wing of the church from the center.

Liberals fought the five points. While they may have been motivated by disagreement with the doctrines themselves, the liberal leaders based their case on the argument that it was unconstitutional for the General Assembly to proclaim essential doctrine without the concurrence of the presbyteries. This, the liberals argued, created a new test of orthodoxy in an unconstitutional, un-Presbyterian way. The proponents of the five points countered that there was nothing new in them, only a reasonable inference from the traditional standards of the church and, indeed, from the teachings of any evangelical Christian body. Liberals contrasted the unilateral proclamation of the five points with the carefully constitutional procedures they had had to follow in making their creedal revisions and initiatives in the preceding decade.

Princeton Seminary took a leading role in promoting and defending all of the five points and, to a degree, came to revel in its isolation from the "modern" currents of university culture. Nevertheless, changes in that seminary began in these years which would break the center-right alliance that had ruled the church for a generation. J. Gresham Machen had joined the faculty in 1906, and in the new decade, he started to achieve prominence as an articulate young conservative. J. Ross Stevenson, already an eminent churchman and a leader of the loyalists in the denomination, became president of the seminary in 1913. The two became leaders in an intense struggle that in the 1920s led to the removal of Machen and his party from the seminary. Ironically, in later years, Machen was to lead a schismatic movement that, in its turn, also was torn apart by the tension between Presbyterianism and fundamentalism.

World War I marks a shift in the emergence of fundamentalism in the church. In 1918, at the height of the American participation in the war, the liberals worked with the loyalists to retake the initiative in the denomination by proposing a grand organic union of all the evangelical Protestant churches.

A leading Presbyterian proponent of this union was loyalist Princeton Seminary President J. Ross Stevenson. Stevenson, as vice-chairman of the Committee on Church Cooperation and Union, brought the union proposal to the General Assembly.[3] The conservatives and fundamentalists, including a majority of the Princeton Seminary faculty, mobilized against this proposal, with J. Gresham Machen emerging as the Presbyterian leader of this group.[4] The conservatives convinced a majority of the presbyteries that organic union was a threat to the distinctive tradition and constitutional heritage of the Presbyterian church, and the proposal was soundly defeated, as it was in other churches. The liberals had overplayed their transdenominational commitments and lost.[5]

The conservatives convinced the loyalist majority because they had an argument that was based on what the loyalists, rather than the conservatives themselves, thought was most important. The lasting effects of this battle would be to return the ecumenical movement to federal—and narrowly constitutional—channels, and to hearten the conservatives to take action against what they considered to be liberal abuses. When the liberals later learned to cast their argument for ecumenism in Presbyterian, rather than progressive or interdenominational terms, they won the competition of arguments. The loyalist center of the Presbyterian Church came to provide strong leaders for the ecumenical movement, one of the foremost of whom was J. Ross Stevenson.

The immediate consequence of the "grand union" battle, however, was that the conflict within Princeton Seminary was brought out into the open. Hereafter, the conservative Machen "majority" would engage in a civil but quite serious struggle with the loyalist Stevenson "minority" for the control of the seminary and, ultimately, for the whole Presbyterian Church.[6]

Chapter 5

1920s: Fundamentalists and Modernists Fight for the Center

*I*n the 1920s, the struggle between the liberals and the conservatives in the Presbyterian Church came to a head. On the whole, the liberals won. The conservatives had an early success in removing the liberal Baptist Harry Emerson Fosdick from a Presbyterian pulpit. However, when the liberals countered with the widely distributed "Auburn Affirmation," a plea for toleration and constitutional process in the church, the conservatives failed to press their advantage and try them in the church courts. The tide began to turn against the conservatives when the Special Commission of 1925 recommended toleration and unity in the face of disorder in the Presbyterian Church.

The Fosdick Case, 1922–1924

The first great struggle of the twenties was over the preaching of Harry Emerson Fosdick. Fosdick, a liberal northern Baptist, was one of the most eminent and successful preachers of his time. He also was a professor of preaching at Union Theological Seminary in New York when the First Presbyterian Church of New York City called him to be an associate pastor.[1] Since Fosdick was not a Presbyterian, this was highly irregular; by calling a non-Presbyterian, the liberals supporting Fosdick showed that they were not primarily denominational loyalists. New York Presbytery was generally tolerant of experiments, however, and the church was allowed to proceed. In 1922, though, Fosdick preached a sermon entitled "Shall the Fundamentalists Win?" Without Fosdick's consent, this was reprinted and circulated widely. It provoked the conservatives in the Presbyterian Church to action. Clarence Macartney, who, with the assistance of

Machen and others, led the opposition, published a reply sermon entitled "Shall Unbelief Win?"[2]

Macartney and the conservative majority in Philadelphia Presbytery sent an overture to the General Assembly of 1923, demanding action against Fosdick.[3] The anti-Fosdick forces lost the first committee vote on their overture; but, with impassioned speeches by Macartney and leadership by William Jennings Bryan, the prominent Democratic party leader and a fundamentalist, they won the vote on the floor. The assembly ordered New York Presbytery to deal with Fosdick; and then, in a move that angered many liberals, the body seemed to prejudice the case by expressing its "profound sorrow that doctrines contrary to the standards of the Presbyterian Church" were proclaimed from the First Church pulpit, doctrines which had caused "controversy and division" in the church. Eighty-five commissioners to the assembly, led by the liberal New York minister William P. Merrill, filed an official protest.[4]

To make their point even clearer, the conservatives succeeded in having the General Assembly adopt the "five points"—the inerrancy of Scripture, the virgin birth of Christ, his vicarious atonement, his bodily resurrection, and his miracles—for the third time. Since this was only a declaration of a General Assembly, it did not automatically become part of the constitution of the church to remain in force thereafter. Technically, each General Assembly was free to undo the work of any previous assembly, although this rarely occurred. For this reason, it was not out of order for the conservatives to reiterate the five points each time they wanted a show of strength, and the practice would remain in order until and unless this declaration was sent down to the presbyteries for ratification. It never was.

The conservatives, especially the fundamentalists among them, were looking for a showdown over doctrine, and the Fosdick case seemed to provide the perfect opportunity. While the Fosdick investigation was going on, however, the liberals were coming up with an innovative reply.

THE AUBURN AFFIRMATION, 1924

Liberals and some loyalists in the church had complained about the "five points" since the latter's first proclamation in 1910. Some objected to the content, but more doubted that the General Assembly could, without the concurrence of the presbyteries, unilaterally enact what the critics called a new test of orthodoxy for the church. The reiteration of the "five points" by the General Assembly of 1923 brought these questions to the fore again. When coupled with what was thought to be the prejudicial way in which Fosdick and the First Church pulpit had been treated by that same assembly, these liberal and loyalist elements were moved to produce a public plea for liberty in the church. The result was the Auburn Affirmation.

In early 1924, "An Affirmation designed to safeguard the unity and liberty of the Presbyterian Church in the United States of America" was published from Auburn, New York. Part of the text was a protest against the treatment of Fosdick. The greater part, however, was about the "five points." The affirmation questioned the constitutionality of the unilateral declaration of these points by the General Assembly. More importantly, it said that the points themselves were only one set of theories about the essential doctrines of Christianity. The document stated that, while some of the signers did in fact agree with those theories, all affirmed the liberty of interpretation that the Presbyterian Church traditionally had allowed on such matters.

From its first appearance, the Auburn Affirmation has been misunderstood. It was taken to be an affirmation of liberal theology. In fact, it was an affirmation of Presbyterian constitutional order. In the affirmation, the liberals did not force liberalism upon the conservatives; rather, the liberals made major concessions to the loyalists. In other words, the liberals subordinated their own theological position in order to compete for the allegiance of the loyalists; after a close struggle, they won. Unlike Briggs or Machen, the affirmationists competed successfully in the Presbyterian Church, because they understood the true social and political structure of the institution. The victory of the affirmationists was a victory for competition in the Presbyterian Church—and a victory for pluralism.

According to J. Gresham Machen, the Auburn Affirmation contended that the five points asserted by the General Assembly were "only theories" and not beliefs necessary for Presbyterian ministers.[5] The virgin birth of Christ, Machen would pronounce, is either a fact or not a fact, and it is not possible to assert that one believed the Gospel and yet treat its contents, such as the story of the virgin birth, as only a theory. The affirmationists, Machen asserted, therefore were liberals of an extreme sort, blatantly professing their unbelief. Worse, by not disciplining them when it had the chance, the General Assembly acquiesced in this heresy.

In fact, however, the Auburn Affirmation did not draw a simple distinction between fact and theory; rather, it made distinctions among fact, doctrine, and theory. Speaking of the subjects addressed in the five points, the signers clearly stated: "We all hold most earnestly to these great facts and doctrines." They go on to say:

> Some of us regard the particular theories contained in the deliverance of the General Assembly of 1923 [that is, the five points] as satisfactory explanations of these facts and doctrines. But we are united in believing that these are not the only theories allowed by the Scriptures and our standards as explanations of these facts and doctrines of our religion, and that all who hold to these facts and doctrines, whatever theories they may employ to explain them, are worthy of all confidence and fellowship.[6]

It is not only the facts, therefore, that a Presbyterian must believe, but also the doctrines contained in the Scripture and the Westminster standards.

What is the relationship between a fact and a doctrine? This, it turns out, was a favorite topic of Machen himself. His usual illustration was this: "'Christ died'—that is history; 'Christ died for our sins'—that is doctrine."[7] A doctrine, in other words, explains the value of a fact. A Christian, Machen held, must believe both the fact and the doctrine. And the affirmationists agreed.

Accepting a fact and a particular interpretation of its value, though, still leaves a question of just how both fact and doctrine work, how they can be true. What is needed is a theory to explain the conditions of the world that make a particular fact and doctrine possible. To take Machen's example, the fact that Christ died and the doctrine that Christ died for our sins does not explain just how Christ's death can atone for our sins. One theory, the theory expressed in the five points, is that God accepted the crucifixion of Christ as a vicarious substitute for the sins of humanity. Some signers of the Auburn Affirmation also accepted this theory. This is not, however, the only theory, as the history of heated debates in the church over Christ's saving action testify.[8]

The real argument of the Auburn Affirmation, though, was not about facts or doctrines. The argument was not even about theories. Instead, it was about the constitution of the Presbyterian Church. Specifically, the affirmation contended that "the constitution of our church provides that its doctrine shall be declared only by concurrent action of the General Assembly and the presbyteries. . . . From this provision of our constitution, it is evident that neither in one General Assembly nor in many, without concurrent action of the presbyteries, is there authority to declare what the Presbyterian Church in the United States of America believes and teaches."[9] This concurrence of the presbyteries never was obtained—or even sought—by any of the General Assemblies that asserted the "certain theories" contained in the five points. Under the constitution, the affirmationists argued, a Presbyterian had the liberty to choose among several theories to explain the necessary facts and doctrines unless and until the Presbyterian Church judged among those theories in a constitutional manner. This position was hardly a wild liberal innovation; Charles Hodge himself had made this argument against the original "Portland Deliverance."[10]

The appeal to unity and constitutional liberty was a shrewd move on the part of the liberals. By convincing the loyalists that the conservatives posed a threat to the loyalist constitutional position, the liberals formed an alliance that also removed a threat to their own position. This is not to say that the liberals were here disingenuous in their profession of loyalty to the constitution. Rather, they were prudent in assessing the position of the Presbyterian Church at that moment. They stood a better chance of winning a case for liberalism under constitutional procedures than in a no-holds-barred fight. In other words, they stood to gain more by competition than by conflict. In the long run, they were proved right.

The Auburn Affirmation appeared in early 1924, over the signatures of 150 Presbyterian ministers. By the time of the General Assembly of that year, nearly 1,300, out of some 10,000 ministers of the church, had signed it. Most of the liberals of the church signed, including its two principal authors, Robert Hastings Nichols of Auburn Seminary and Henry Sloane Coffin of Union Seminary. The signers, who represented almost every synod and the vast majority of presbyteries in the church, were less likely than the average minister to have come originally from other denominations, and were disproportionately pastors of congregations—the largest and wealthiest congregations at that. Moreover, while the liberal Auburn and Union seminaries provided the single largest group of signers, 14 percent of the total were graduates of loyalist McCormick Seminary of Chicago, and a further 10 percent came from Princeton Seminary itself.[11]

THE GENERAL ASSEMBLY OF 1924

The appearance of the Auburn Affirmation guaranteed that the General Assembly of 1924 would be a lively one. In retrospect, it appears to have been one of the pivotal meetings of the church in the past century. For the conservatives, the Auburn Affirmation was a red flag of apostasy. Overtures were sent up from the Cincinnati and Chester presbyteries, demanding action against the affirmationists. Another overture came from Philadelphia Presbytery, raising the "five points" to be tests of orthodoxy for officers of the General Assembly. Finally, there was to be the further disposition of the Fosdick case, which the previous General Assembly had sent back to New York Presbytery for further treatment.[12]

The conservatives were organizing a campaign for moderator of the assembly, with Clarence Macartney as their candidate. The liberals did not run a candidate of their own, but quietly voted for the loyalists' standard-bearer, Charles Erdman. Henry Sloane Coffin, the leading liberal, even sought publicly to distance the liberals from Erdman, in order that Erdman not be "tainted" in the eyes of conservatives.[13] Erdman was a professor at Princeton Seminary and a theological conservative. Also, however, he was a man with wide experience in the Presbyterian Church, devoted to missions and church cooperation, and an ally of J. Ross Stevenson, the president of Princeton Seminary. In the seminary, Machen led the faculty "majority" in opposing the candidacy of his colleague Erdman for the moderatorship.

The election of the moderator, the first important action of any assembly, was a close one, but Macartney won. The principal committees chosen under his moderatorship had conservative majorities. Maitland Alexander, a strong Machen ally, chaired the important Bills and Overtures Committee, which decided where and how overtures should be treated. This committee had in hand the Chester overture to take action against the Auburn Affirmationists.

The assembly of 1923 had ordered New York Presbytery to treat with Fosdick. The presbytery had done so but had found him to be sufficiently orthodox and useful to the church to retain the First Presbyterian pulpit. Incensed, the conservatives returned to the General Assembly of 1924, demanding Fosdick's removal. The assembly was stymied by the fact that Fosdick was not actually a member of New York Presbytery and therefore was not subject to Presbyterian disciplinary action. Before it could address the doctrinal question, therefore, the ecclesiastical issue had to be settled. To that end, the General Assembly sent down an order to ask Fosdick to either join the Presbyterian Church or resign his First Presbyterian pulpit.[14] When faced with this choice, the Baptist Fosdick said he could not affirm any creed devised by humans, including the Westminster Confession; therefore First Presbyterian was obliged, reluctantly, to let him go.[15] The conservatives won the battle, but in the assembly they were outmaneuvered on the organizational question and therefore failed to provoke a conclusive fight over doctrine.

The Philadelphia overture elevating the "five points" was sent to the assembly's Permanent Judicial Commission. This body ruled that the overture was unconstitutional because it attempted to make a new test of ministerial subscription without the concurrence of the presbyteries. The conservatives lost again.[16] Finally, even though conservatives, including William Jennings Bryan, controlled the Bills and Overtures Committee, which held the overtures against the Auburn Affirmationists, the committee recommended that no action be taken.[17]

The inaction of the General Assembly of 1924 against the Auburn Affirmationists is something the conservatives later came to rue and that students of the church have regarded as a great puzzle.[18] Machen reportedly wanted to press heresy charges against the affirmationists, but he was discouraged by his allies, who did not think that they had the votes to win in a public confrontation.[19] Quirk, the most thorough historian of the affirmation, calls this failure an "enigma." He attributes it to a failure of nerve on the part of certain strategically placed conservative ministers; even though they had been willing to discipline Presbyterian professors such as Briggs, McGiffert, or Henry Preserved Smith, or non-Presbyterian ministers such as Fosdick, they were squeamish about disciplining other Presbyterian ministers.[20]

It seems more likely that the conservative leaders realized that, if they proceeded with the overture against the affirmationists, they would lose in the assembly, just as they had lost on the Fosdick case and on the Philadelphia "five points" overture. They would lose not because the assembly agreed with liberal theology, nor even because it agreed with the plea for liberty. The General Assembly was likely to reject this attack on the affirmationists because it was out of order. "Do all things decently and in order" is traditionally one of the favorite Scripture texts of Presbyterians. The conservatives, attempting to go straight to the substantive point that they wished to establish, did not always attend to all the church's rules of proper procedure. They failed to see that, for liberals and loyalists alike, the protection that these rules gave to liberty in the church *was* the substantive issue.

In the affirmationist case, the conservatives lost an important opportunity to press their doctrinal point when they bypassed that central pillar of disciplinary order in the Presbyterian Church, the presbytery. Had the conservatives, instead of trying to act directly through the General Assembly, brought charges against individual affirmationists within their presbyteries, according to the usual order, they well might have won the substantive battle against liberal theology in the Presbyterian Church.

In spite of these losses, it appeared to many that conservatives and their allies still held a dominant position in the denomination. Several observers, at both extremes in the church, thought that the liberals, rather than the conservatives, would be forced to withdraw.[21] This estimate was especially popular before the Scopes trial of 1925, when fundamentalism was still a growing movement within the established churches, including the Presbyterian Church. To the surprise of many, though, it was the conservatives who eventually felt obliged to withdraw.

THE SPECIAL COMMISSION OF 1925

In retrospect, the General Assembly of 1924 seems to have been the high-water mark of conservative strength in the Presbyterian Church. The following year, 1925, was the year of the Scopes trial and a turning point for fundamentalism nationally. Within the Presbyterian Church, it was a year when forward movement for the conservative program in the church was checked. While the church was very far from becoming liberal, it did begin to move in the direction of toleration and breadth.

The first test of strength at the General Assembly of 1925 was the election of the moderator. Charles Erdman of Princeton Seminary once again was the candidate of the loyalists and liberals, and this time he won a solid victory. The conservatives then won a point, when the Judicial Commission ruled that New York Presbytery had acted improperly in licensing ministerial candidates who would not affirm the doctrine of the virgin birth of Christ. At this point, the liberals appeared ready to walk out. To head off further acrimony, Erdman proposed from the floor that a special commission be set up to study the causes of the unrest in the church. They were to report to the next General Assembly "to the end that the purity, peace, unity and progress of the Church may be assured." This proposal was seconded by both Henry Sloane Coffin of Union Seminary, a leading liberal, and by William Jennings Bryan, the conservative standard-bearer, who soon was to represent the fundamentalist side in the Scopes trial. The motion was unanimously approved by the assembly. Erdman then appointed a "Committee of Fifteen," made up mostly of respected loyalists.[22]

The Special Commission of 1925 returned its report to the General Assembly of 1926. Taking a historical view of controversy in the church, the report concluded that toleration would do more to settle the disputed issues than would schism. The limits of this toleration, however, would not be left up to individuals, but would be set by the church acting according to its constitution. The commission took a middle path between liberal claims for extreme toleration and the contention of conservatives, led by Machen, that two distinct religions existed within the church and that they should be separated from one another.[23] The report was adopted by a sizable majority and, according to one commentator, "satisfied all but the most extreme Fundamentalists."[24] The Special Commission asked for an extension, so as to bring in their final report in 1927.

THE TURNING OF THE TIDE

The General Assembly of 1927 began with an unusual event, one that signaled the revulsion of the center of the church at the prospect of division: the election of the moderator by acclamation. Dr. Robert Speer was a highly respected loyalist who for years had run the foreign mission enterprises of the church. Under his moderatorship, the 1927 assembly was one of the most united in many years. When the Special Commission of 1925, of which Speer was a member, brought in its second and final report, the assembly was ready for unity. The report retained the tolerant, conciliatory tone sounded the previous year. It emphasized the necessity of strict constitutional order in the church and for that reason rejected the basis upon which the "five points" had been declared. The commission's report was adopted unanimously, without debate.[25]

After adoption of the Special Commission's report, after the Scopes trial and its humiliation of Presbyterian conservative leader William Jennings Bryan, and after the General Assembly of 1927, it was clear that the tide had turned against the conservatives. Now the coalition of loyalists and extreme conservatives—which had, in the main, run the church since the Briggs trial—came apart. This splintering occurred not over theological doctrine, but over church policy. The conservatives had adopted a policy of doctrinal purity that did not fully reflect the diversity that always had existed within the Presbyterian Church. Perhaps more important, the conservative position was out of accord with the constitutional safeguards protecting that diversity. The constitutional tradition, including the liberty that it allowed, was a defining aspect of the Presbyterian Church and, by the same token, part of the identity of those in the center of the church. The liberals had learned to respect the constitutional tradition; if they did not, there would be no protection for the liberty that made their (minority) position in the church possible. When the conservatives took the extraordinary step of attacking and undermining that constitutional tradition—initially in the five points and Auburn Affirmation struggle, conclusively in the later Independent Board of Foreign Missions fight—they lost the competition for the hearts and minds of the centrists.

After 1927, the center of action in the Presbyterian struggle shifted from a fight between liberals and conservatives to a conflict between the center and the right. The most important battles of this struggle were fought in and about Princeton Theological Seminary. In these battles, the loyalists ultimately would bring to bear the weight of the church, and the conservatives would withdraw from the seminary at the end of the 1920s. After a protracted struggle in the 1930s, this extreme movement would shatter, dividing and dividing again.

Chapter 6

1929: THE BATTLE FOR
PRINCETON SEMINARY

With the triumph of the Special Commission of 1925, the loyalist majority in the Presbyterian Church embraced toleration as an idea enshrined in Presbyterian tradition. The conflict in the church then shifted from being a fight between conservatives and liberals to being one between conservatives and loyalists. The site—and the prize—of this new battle would be Princeton Seminary itself.

Ironically, when the conservatives failed in the "five points" fight to eliminate from the whole Presbyterian Church the doctrine they opposed, they themselves began arguing for a kind of pluralism in the church. They claimed a right to be tolerated themselves, demanded control of a least one seminary (Princeton), and insisted that their position deserved to be accorded legitimacy within the diverse Presbyterian Church.

DIVISIONS WITHIN PRINCETON SEMINARY

For the Presbyterian Church as a whole, the division between Old School and New School officially had ended with the reunion of 1869. At Princeton Theological Seminary, however, many continued to believe that the consistent Calvinism of the Old School, the "Princeton Theology" that had made the seminary the leading conservative institution in America by the end of the nineteenth century, was right. Moreover, some at the seminary believed that at Princeton Seminary, if nowhere else, *only* the Old School theological position should be propagated.[1] At the end of the 1920s, these exclusive conservatives constituted a slim majority of the faculty.

J. Ross Stevenson, who was inaugurated as president of Princeton Theological Seminary in 1913, thought differently. Stevenson thought that Princeton Seminary should represent the entire Presbyterian Church and not a "particular theological faction."[2] The "Charter and Plan" of the seminary, he noted, states: "As this institution derives its origin from the General Assembly, so that body is to be considered at all times its patron, and the fountain of its powers. The Assembly shall, accordingly, ultimately sanction all its laws, direct its instructions and appoint its principal officers."[3] If Princeton was to be the agent of the General Assembly of the whole church, Stevenson argued, it must be at least as broad as the General Assembly is. By the late 1920s, Stevenson had drawn nearly, but not quite, half of the faculty to this loyalist, inclusively conservative position.

The conservative "majority" of the faculty saw themselves as the defenders of the grand tradition of Princeton Theology, the successors of Charles Hodge and B. B. Warfield, who faced all comers in the cause of consistent Calvinism. They were led by J. Gresham Machen, a professor of the New Testament and a vigorous polemicist against modernism in the church. Machen charged that President Stevenson and his allies were trying to tear Princeton away from its historic defense of traditional Presbyterianism.[4]

The loyalist "minority" of the faculty was led by President Stevenson and Charles R. Erdman. Stevenson was an experienced pastor and a former moderator of the General Assembly who remained active in its works. Erdman was very conservative theologically—in fact, he is the only member of the Princeton faculty who actually contributed to *The Fundamentals,* from which "fundamentalism" gets its name. Moreover, he had been the moderator of the 1925 General Assembly who had appointed the Special Commission. Stevenson, for his part, contended that it was the faculty majority who threatened Princeton's Presbyterianism. With a vehemence unusual for him, President Stevenson charged that Machen and his allies were trying to make Princeton into "an interdenominational seminary for Bible School–premillenial–secession fundamentalism."[5]

Both the "majority" and the "minority" were very small, and the bitterness of the fight was due, in part, to the fact that just a few changes would tip the balance. The minority, composed of men with pastoral experience who taught in the seminary's practical fields, consisted of Stevenson, Erdman, professor of preaching J. Ritchie Smith, and the historian Frederick Loetscher. Against these four votes, the majority, with little pastoral experience, had at most seven, consisting of Machen, his close friend William Park Armstrong, William Greene, Geerhardus Vos, Robert Dick Wilson, Oswald Allis, and Caspar Wistar Hodge, grandson of Charles Hodge. John Davis, the Old Testament professor, usually voted with the minority until his death in 1926. In addition, the minority could usually count on the support of Paul Martin, who, as secretary of the faculty, attended all meetings but did not have a vote.[6]

All parties to the dispute agree that, theologically, all the members of the Princeton Seminary faculty were conservative Presbyterians. The Stevenson loyalists favored more practical training for ministers, were more involved with the variety of life in the church, and were more tolerant of its diversity. The loyalist minority was loyal to the denomination and conceived of the church as a living, historical institution that governed itself under its constitution. The majority, in contrast, were loyal to a doctrine and conceived of the church as a voluntary association for the propagation of that doctrine. The loyalists could, practically speaking, find a way to live with doctrinal diversity in the church, if it were established constitutionally. The exclusive conservatives, on the other hand, defined the church by its doctrine and therefore had no place for diversity of doctrine within the church. The loyalists saw themselves as conservative Presbyterians, but they were attacked by Machen's party as "indifferentists."

THE FIGHT ON THE RIGHT AT PRINCETON

The first item on Stevenson's agenda was a revision of the seminary curriculum, to give the students more practical training. Erdman and the others with pastoral experience supported this change, as did most students. B. B. Warfield, the long-time head of the conservative group in the faculty and the leading light of the conservative "Princeton Theology" in the church at large, led the opposition.[7] Most of the revisions carried, however, when Machen, in order to save the Greek requirement, compromised with the loyalists (a rarity in his career). Warfield, dismayed by the revision and disappointed in his former student Machen, ceased attending faculty meetings and effectively ceded the leadership of the conservatives in the seminary and in the denomination to others.[8] As a result, when a similar accommodation could not be reached in the next major seminary battle, Machen emerged as the pivotal voice for the conservative position.

The first public breach within the seminary faculty came in 1918, over the proposed organic union of several Protestant denominations.[9] Erdman favored this Grand Union, and Stevenson headed the committee that brought the proposal to the Presbyterian Church. The faculty (and church) majority opposed it, on the grounds that the doctrinal basis of the union was too vague to preserve the distinctive beliefs of evangelical Christianity. Machen was particularly prominent in opposing the plan—and in opposing his Princeton colleagues who supported it—in both the religious and the secular press.[10] Although the conservatives won that fight, in later years they often brought up the plan of union in arguments against the minority.

In 1924, a majority of the seminary students, with the support of the faculty majority, withdrew from the Middle Atlantic Association of Theological Schools because they thought the organization too liberal. They then joined with students at fundamentalist seminaries to create the League of Evangelical Students. President Stevenson opposed this step because it separated Princeton from all the other Presbyterian seminaries. Charles Erdman was the advisor to the student body at that time and very conservative in his own theology, but he also was devoted to the denomination and agreed with Stevenson in opposing the formation of the league. For this reason, Erdman was removed from the position of student advisor and replaced by a member of the league-supporting majority.[11]

At the same time, a minor incident involving Machen and Erdman became the occasion for wide publicity about tensions within the seminary. In 1924, Machen was the temporary "stated supply" preacher of the First Presbyterian Church in Princeton, where he often attacked modernism and liberalism in his sermons. This offended Henry Van Dyke, a professor at Princeton University and a prominent Presbyterian liberal who had chaired the 1903 Creed Revision Committee. Van Dyke publicly announced that he was giving up his pew in the church until Machen stopped preaching there.[12] The following year, Machen gave up that pulpit to devote himself to teaching and was succeeded by Erdman. Van Dyke then returned to his pew in First Presbyterian.

The *Philadelphia Presbyterian,* a conservative magazine, speculated that Van Dyke had returned because he found Erdman's preaching to be an aid to "rationalism." Incensed, Erdman responded with a letter to the magazine that blamed the ill will at Princeton Seminary on the abusive spirits of those members of the faculty who also were editors of the *Presbyterian*. Machen was the only person serving both the *Presbyterian* and Princeton at that time, and he was outraged in his turn.[13] It later came out that Erdman had meant another Princeton faculty member, Oswald Allis, whom he mistakenly had thought was still an editor of the *Presbyterian*.[14] Erdman apologized to Machen and regretted his conduct, but the tension in the seminary unalterably had been made public.

In 1924, Machen led the opposition to his colleague Erdman for the moderatorship of the General Assembly. This further strained relations between the two, although both tried to keep their personal conflicts out of the public eye. Machen again opposed Erdman's candidacy for the moderatorship in 1925, this time without success. Stevenson, who had been a moderator himself, supported Erdman. Stevenson also supported Erdman's proposal for the Special Commission of 1925.

Machen opposed Erdman not because he was a liberal, but because he tolerated liberals in the church. In Machen's view, Christianity and liberalism believed two different doctrines and therefore were two different religions; thus they could not be contained in the same organization. Anyone who tolerated liberals in the church must, by this reckoning, be indifferent to the importance of doctrine; Machen mounted his opposition to Erdman and Stevenson thereafter because they were, in his estimation, "indifferentists."

In 1926, the year in which the Special Commission delivered its report, Machen was to be considered for promotion to the apologetics chair at Princeton. The General Assembly, as had been demonstrated in the Briggs case, had veto power over the appointment of professors in its seminaries, although it rarely exercised this power. Stevenson and Erdman, in a highly unusual move, urged the directors of the seminary not to promote Machen to the apologetics chair, on the grounds that Machen was "temperamentally unfit."[15] Stevenson said that he opposed Machen for the chair because the latter was determined upon a divisive policy, and because Machen's "implacable hostility . . . would make brotherly cooperation . . . utterly impossible."[16] When the matter came before the assembly, Stevenson urged that it and all other Princeton appointments be held up until a special committee could be sent by the assembly to investigate conditions "subversive of Christian fellowship" at Princeton Seminary.[17] The assembly, which had had enough of the festering divisions so publicly displayed at the denomination's leading seminary, agreed to this proposal.

The moderator of the assembly, William O. Thompson, the president of Ohio State University and a member of the (ongoing) Special Commission of 1925, himself headed up the investigating committee. The Thompson Committee, which was composed of prominent loyalists, held interviews with all the groups at Princeton Seminary. They discovered that the faculty divisions were repeated among the boards of directors and trustees, the director majority siding with the faculty majority, the trustee majority siding with Stevenson. The directors, who had charge of running the seminary, had been created by the General Assembly, while the trustees were a secular corporation that managed the seminary's property.[18] For several years, the two boards had clashed over the running of the school.

The Thompson Committee found a wide divergence in the faculty about what the problem at the seminary was, as well as about its solution. The faculty majority held that there were doctrinal differences between the two faculty groups, that "no peace between them is either possible or desirable," and that therefore the majority "must by every means in its power seek to secure its rightful control of the life of the institution."[19] The faculty minority, on the other hand, held that there was no difference on doctrine and wished to work with all parties for reconciliation.

The Thompson Committee faced a difficult problem in trying to end the tension at Princeton. Machen insisted that the root issue was doctrinal, but the minority insisted that there was no difference among them on doctrine. Machen said that Stevenson was indifferent to doctrine, which Stevenson hotly denied.[20] The right wing of the church was splitting apart not directly over doctrine, on which they agreed, but on the importance of doctrinal agreement for the health of the church.

The issue on which the two sides were fundamentally at odds was whether the "Theological Seminary of the Presbyterian Church in the U.S.A.," as Princeton officially was known, should represent the whole church or only the part of it that had been in control at the time of the reunion of the Old and New schools. Ultimately, the Thompson Committee, which itself represented the whole Presbyterian Church, concluded that "the drift of Seminary control seems to be away from the proper service of the Church and toward an aggressive defense of the policy of a group" and came down on the side of Stevenson's representative vision of Princeton Seminary.[21]

This finding still did not settle how the tension was to be reduced at Princeton. Even if the committee had wanted to remove either faction (which it did not), such an effort, in and of itself, would have defeated the attempt to make the seminary representative. Instead, the committee settled on the "administrative" (rather than doctrinal) solution of merging the two opposing boards of control and delaying the professors' promotions until that merger was accomplished. They reasoned that the division between the boards was what had perpetuated the seminary's other divisions.[22] Merging the boards would force all sides to come to some sort of accommodation. This solution also would allow everyone to save face by avoiding any question concerning the genuine orthodoxy of either party.

The administrative solution proposed by the Thompson Committee seemed to satisfy most of those concerned, but it deeply offended Machen and some of his group. They did not, it seems, want face saving and accommodation; they wanted a showdown. Even when conservative leader Clarence Macartney tried to arrange a compromise whereby the promotions of Machen and another professor would go through in exchange for the conservative directors' acceptance of the seminary's reorganization, it was Machen who opposed any compromise. The extreme conservatives in the seminary vowed to fight.[23]

The Thompson Committee's report to the General Assembly of 1927 was well received. The committee then asked to be continued and expanded, so that it might settle the question of how, exactly, to accomplish the merger of the boards. In 1928, the expanded Thompson Committee brought in its report on how to merge the two boards. When it appeared that Stevenson and the loyalists would be favored by the merged board, the Princeton board of directors asked for another year to settle things among themselves at the seminary, before any changes were made. Their request was granted. Machen's promotion, as well as some other appointments, again were delayed, and eventually Machen withdrew his name from consideration.[24] By this time, he may have seen the handwriting on the wall and been anticipating that he would not wish to remain at Princeton Seminary.

By the General Assembly of 1929, the directors had not been able to compose their differences, and the Thompson Committee's plan to merge the boards was voted in. Machen mounted a challenge to this plan on the basis of certain technicalities, but he lost.[25] The new board, with a loyalist, pro-Stevenson majority, took control in the spring of 1929.

Machen thereupon withdrew from the seminary, taking with him four members of the faculty and some fifty students. He already had been raising money to start a new seminary, independent of denominational control. In the fall of 1929, Westminster Theological Seminary opened its doors in Philadelphia, its mission being to perpetuate the old Princeton Theology.[26]

The struggle for Princeton Seminary had pitted an exclusive, conservative view of the Presbyterian Church against another view, and the exclusive position had lost. The view that prevailed was not the liberal view, but a loyalist, traditional, denominationally-oriented conception. While there were liberals in the church, including some who would accept just about any doctrine, no liberals had been party to the Princeton dispute. Instead, this conflict had pitted loyalist conservatives against extreme conservatives; and the former, who probably always are in the majority in the church, asserted their dominance. The institutional loyalists beat the doctrinal loyalists in an institutional fight. The degree of tolerance and inclusivity that they established was limited by what the church as a whole, through its corporate representatives and constitutional procedure, thought just. This was in line with the position of the Special Commission of 1925: not individual choice, but liberty within the constitution.

In Machen's view, that way lay apostasy.

Chapter 7

1930s: Machen and the Conservative Separation

he conservatives fought an increasingly bitter fight with the loyalists in the Presbyterian Church throughout the 1930s. While they struggled about many issues, the central battle was over the control of foreign missions. Machen raised the stakes in a series of conflicts, until, by the end of the decade, the most extreme group of conservatives had created not one but two new denominations. By that time, too, the remaining right wing of the Presbyterian Church in the U.S.A. was in disarray, and Machen himself was dead.

The first skirmish concerned a proposed merger between the Presbyterian Church in the U.S.A. and the United Presbyterian Church of North America, the latter being the successor to several dissenting Scottish churches. Machen opposed this merger, much as B. B. Warfield before him had opposed the Cumberland reunion. The merger failed because the United Presbyterians did not approve it, but not before a majority of the Presbyterian Church in the U.S.A. had voted for the union. Machen became further convinced of the doctrinal laxity of the leaders of the church and showed no willingness to compromise with them.[1]

Battling for Foreign Missions

In 1932, a study entitled *Re-Thinking Missions: A Laymen's Inquiry after One Hundred Years* was published by an independent group funded by John D. Rockefeller. The Presbyterian Church, along with several other mainline denominations, initially had endorsed the idea of such an inquiry. However, when the liberal group that produced this report, led by Harvard professor William Hocking, contemplated the idea that Christian missions should cease because the other world religions were the equal of Christianity in truth and spiritual value, the Presbyterian leadership repudiated *Re-Thinking Missions*. Robert Speer, the senior secretary of the Presbyterian Board of Foreign Missions (PBFM), himself wrote a pamphlet criticizing the report.

The conservatives, however, found their church's denunciations of *Re-Thinking Missions* too weak, and they remained suspicious of liberalism among the church's missionaries.[2] Their suspicions seemed confirmed when novelist and Presbyterian missionary Pearl S. Buck praised the report and endorsed its conclusions. Conservatives protested strongly, and Buck was obliged to cut her ties with the PBFM.

In 1933, Machen proposed an overture in New Brunswick Presbytery to make the PBFM reform itself and stop propagating error. No specifications of error were contained in the overture. The presbytery invited Machen and Robert Speer to discuss the soundness of the overture. This was not the first time these men had tangled on this point; as early as 1926, Speer had asked Machen to substantiate his attacks on missionaries, but "knowing that he could not prove his contention, Machen backed down."[3] In their 1933 encounter, the presbytery, after hearing both men make their cases, declined to approve the overture and instead sent one "affirming its confidence" in the PBFM.[4]

Machen's allies in Philadelphia Presbytery had passed the same overture critical of the PBFM, however, and thus it was sent to the General Assembly.[5] At that assembly, Machen was invited to address the Committee on Foreign Missions when it considered the Philadelphia overture. This was highly unusual, because Machen was not a delegate to the assembly, no delegate from Philadelphia would speak to the committee in favor of its own overture, and Machen's own presbytery, New Brunswick, had repudiated this same proposal. The church's official account of this fight, printed in the minutes of the General Assembly without an indication of the author, reports that "[i]t was also known, as Dr. Machen himself later stated to the committee, that he would accept neither the judgment of the committee nor the decisions of the General Assembly if it did not conform to his view."[6] Machen was given an official hearing on his charges, while a representative of the PBFM "answered each point that he made one by one."[7]

Once again, an official—and generally loyalist—body of the church was unconvinced by Machen's charges. In fact, the committee reported that both the PBFM and the missionaries deserved the "whole-hearted, unequivocal, enthusiastic and affectionate commendation of the church at large."[8] The committee went on to say that, while everyone in the church had a right to criticize the church's representatives, it

> deplores the dissemination of propaganda calculated to break down faith in the sincerity of such representatives . . . [and reminds] every constituent of the Church that there are orderly methods of procedure whereby through the established courts all such representations ought to be made. The Assembly disapproves all methods of approach which would contravene such orderly methods, but would remind the Church that . . . a man must be held innocent until he is proven guilty of any charge; and that suspicion of motives is not adequate evidence against any man and certainly ought not to be used in the Christian Church.[9]

The full assembly adopted this commendation, and the Philadelphia overture failed. Machen had taken his case directly to the top and lost.

THE INDEPENDENT BOARD OF PRESBYTERIAN FOREIGN MISSIONS

At that point Machen could have begun again, this time using the "orderly methods and procedures" that the committee wrote of to bring disciplinary action against specific missionaries for specific offenses.[10] His principal concern, however, was not with orderly procedure but with pure doctrine. For this reason, when he lost the fight to keep Princeton Seminary true to Old School doctrine, he declared the whole institution unsound and withdrew to create his own pure organization. It is not surprising, then, that when Machen failed to convince the church to purify its foreign missions, he pursued the same course.

At the same General Assembly of 1933, Machen's allies on the Committee on Foreign Missions had proposed an alternate slate of members for the PBFM. When their slate was rejected by the General Assembly, this group immediately declared itself to be the "Independent Board of Presbyterian Foreign Missions" (IBPFM), with J. Gresham Machen as president.[11] The church's official account summed up this action this way: "In other words, the very persons who had asked the General Assembly to be given charge of the work of foreign missions and to whom the General Assembly had refused to entrust this work refused to accept the authority of the Assembly and proceeded to constitute themselves, in contempt of the Assembly's action, an Independent Board for Presbyterian Foreign Missions."[12] Denominational leaders were particularly irked that the new organization was created immediately, while the General Assembly was still meeting, evidently according to a premeditated plan.[13]

Since missions create new churches, the creation of a mission board independent of the denomination seemed to many to be schismatic and hence to require disciplinary action. While the church had come to accept independent seminaries, such as Westminster, it specifically had rejected the practice of working with independent mission agencies, after long experience with them in the nineteenth century. The "deliverance" of the General Assembly of 1934 on the IBPFM noted that the Presbyterian Church had tried outside missionary agencies for fifty years but that "experience had clearly demonstrated the inefficacy of such agencies under a Presbyterian form of government." An exception was made for "certain interdenominational work" which the church could not do alone and which the General Assembly had "approve[d] in specific deliverances." The IBPFM met neither criterion.[14] Ironically, it was precisely the desire to repudiate independent mission agencies that had led the Old School, of which Machen and his group claimed to be the only true descendants, to separate from the New School a century before.

In 1934, the Judicial Commission charged with interpreting the constitution took up the question, and ruled that the IBPFM undermined the good order of the Presbyterian Church. The General Assembly, in considering how to act on this ruling, was particularly irritated by the attempt of the IBPFM to get local congregations to divert their mission offerings from the official agencies of the church, already hard pressed by the Depression, to this new board. Based on this judgment and evidence, the General Assembly of 1934 declared that officers of the Presbyterian Church in the U.S.A. must resign from the IBPFM or risk suspension.[15]

When the IBPFM members refused to comply with the directive of the General Assembly, proceedings were begun against them in their respective presbyteries. In 1934 and 1935, Machen was tried in New Brunswick Presbytery on several administrative charges, such as disobeying the orders of the General Assembly, advocating "rebellion" in the church, and refusing to abide by his ministerial vows, in which he had promised "subjection to his brethren in the Lord." The prosecution denied that there was any doctrinal issue in the case and affirmed its own belief in the "five points." Machen, on the other hand, charged that the real issues were not administrative but doctrinal, and he challenged every charge and every judge against him, losing almost every point.[16]

In March 1935, Machen had his day in court in the Presbytery of New Brunswick. Speaking through counsel, he refused to address the charges against him but instead tried to use his trial as a forum for attacking the doctrinal soundness of the signers of the Auburn Affirmation, the PBFM, and Princeton Seminary. He also denied the constitutionality of the General Assembly directive and the jurisdiction of New Brunswick Presbytery to try him.

The court answered these attacks by ruling out of order any argument on the doctrine of the other groups (such as the PBFM) and by citing the Presbyterian rule that a lower judicatory (a presbytery) cannot judge the actions of a higher (the General Assembly).[17] A long argument took place concerning the jurisdiction question, because Machen had transferred to Philadelphia Presbytery the previous year. However, since some of the ministers of Philadelphia Presbytery had protested to the Synod of Pennsylvania about the way in which Machen had been accepted, the status of the transfer was unclear. The prosecution argued that New Brunswick Presbytery should go ahead with the trial, since the General Assembly had ordered that IBPFM members be tried and since New Brunswick was responsible for carrying out such directives for Machen until he clearly had transferred elsewhere. On a technical ruling, the court judged that New Brunswick Presbytery did have jurisdiction and should proceed.

During the trial, Machen went to the secular newspapers, claiming that his trial was biased and a farce. This, not surprisingly, enraged the moderator of the court, who asked Machen to explain himself. Machen's lawyer refused to let Machen answer or even to acknowledge that he had been quoted properly by the newspaper.[18]

The court heard the prosecution. The defense had planned then to make its case by showing Machen to be justified in his course, due to the doctrinal unsoundness of other people in the church. When the court ruled that other people's doctrine was not relevant to the defense of Machen's own actions, Machen's counsel refused to offer any answer to the charges. The Presbytery of New Brunswick found Machen guilty and suspended him from the ministry, with the recommendation that the sentence not take effect until his expected appeals had been exhausted.[19]

Machen, along with the other IBPFM members, did appeal to the General Assembly in 1936, and they all lost.[20] In his 1936 appeal, Machen was given full opportunity to contest the constitutionality of the General Assembly's "Deliverance" of 1934 before the Permanent Judicial Commission. That body, by nearly a thousand votes, ruled against him.[21] Without fanfare, the General Assembly upheld the convictions rendered by all the lower courts.

The exclusivists had, of course, expected this. They were already organized for schism.

The Orthodox Presbyterian Church and the Aftermath of the Split

In 1935, while the first trials were going on, a group of conservatives had formed the Presbyterian Constitutional Covenant Union in Philadelphia, to fight what they called modernism, "Indifferentism," and majority tyranny in the Presbyterian Church.[22] In 1936, knowing that the General Assembly would rule against all the IBPFM defendants, the Covenant Union held its own meeting in Philadelphia. At this meeting, it created the Presbyterian Church in America, with J. Gresham Machen as the first moderator. By the end of 1936, this new denomination had seventy-five ministers and about as many congregations in nine presbyteries across the country, almost all of which had come out of the Presbyterian Church in the USA[23]

It soon became clear, however, that Machen would not carry even the most conservative group with him into his new church. A number of the faculty and students of Westminster Seminary, as well as several of his most prominent conservative allies within the Presbyterian Church in the U.S.A., declined to follow Machen into what they considered to be schism. Most notably, Clarence Macartney, perhaps the leading conservative in the church and a son of the strongly antischismatic Reformed Presbyterian Church, declined to join the southerner Machen in his secession.[24]

The movement for a purely conservative Presbyterian church did not stop with the creation of the new denomination. Immediately after its separation from the Presbyterian Church in the U.S.A., Machen was challenged within his new denomination by an even more conservative group. The Rev. Carl McIntire led the premillenial dispensationalist fundamentalists against Machen. They believed that God had ordained a set number of ages, or dispensations, each with a different character, and by a careful correlation of biblical prophecy with contemporary events, they judged that the last dispensation was near, when Jesus will usher in his thousand-year reign (the millennium). Machen did not agree with this view, but he was willing to tolerate it in the church.[25] He also disagreed with McIntire's claim that the Bible required the legal prohibition of all alcohol. The McIntire faction, which was strongly represented on the IBPFM, were not tolerant of disagreement, and they wrested control of the board from Machen in 1936. Soon thereafter, McIntire led a schism that split Westminster Seminary and Machen's church.[26]

The year 1936 was extremely busy and probably stressful for Machen. In addition to his trials and suspension, his role in the formation of the new denomination, and his regular duties at Westminster Seminary, he was very active as moderator and leading figure in the still-growing new church. In this capacity, and against the advice of his friends, the fifty-four-year-old Machen accepted a request to preach at the end of the year in a small congregation in North Dakota that had just joined the new church. After several days of sermons and speeches, Machen became ill. On New Year's Day, 1937, J. Gresham Machen collapsed and died in North Dakota.

The Presbyterian Church in the U.S.A. later brought, and won, what amounted to a trademark suit against the name of the new church. As a result, the new body was forced to change its name to the Orthodox Presbyterian Church in 1939, the name by which it is known today.[27] The Orthodox Presbyterian Church did not become a sizable challenge to the "big church," but it has remained a small traditionalist body maintained mostly by Westminster Seminary graduates.[28] When another conservative group split off from the major Presbyterian churches in a later generation, that body took the name "Presbyterian Church in America," this time without challenge from the parent bodies. And Machen himself, who said he was defending "no new 'ism'" but orthodox Christianity, today is remembered as the "Intellectual Fundamentalist."[29]

The struggles of the 1930s might have turned out quite differently. Foreign missions were an area of traditional conservative strength, and the loyalists, such as Robert Speer, who controlled the church's missions seem genuinely to have been concerned about exclusivist charges of apostasy in the mission field. It is likely that they would have worked with the critics to end specific abuses. The conservatives therefore had an opportunity to establish a respected place for themselves within the denomination by cooperating with the mission agencies in discovering specific cases of unsound missionaries. The loyalists were surprised, therefore, when Machen and his associates instead persisted in making wholesale attacks on the church's missions. The conservatives relied on sensational charges to win sympathy for their cause, rather than on disciplinary action to actually reform Presbyterian missions. This approach was in keeping with their doctrinal, rather than constitutional, conception of the church. With that strategy, however, the conservatives forfeited their last best chance to find a place of authority for themselves within the Presbyterian Church in the U.S.A.

Part II

The Structure of Competition

Chapter 8

THE LIBERAL:
CHARLES A. BRIGGS

BRIGGS BEFORE THE "BRIGGS CASE"

*C*harles Augustus Briggs was born in 1841 in New York City. His family was of colonial New England stock, and his father was a substantial merchant, the "Barrel King" of New York. Alanson Briggs did not consider himself fully a Christian, apparently because he had not been, as we would say now, "born again." Though not connected with them himself, he favored the Methodists and recommended them to his son. His mother, Sarah Briggs, had the preponderant influence on young Charles, raising him in the "Old School" Rutgers Street Presbyterian Church. The Briggs household was evangelical, socially conservative, and strict in its ethics.[1]

Briggs seems to have had a conventionally Christian youth, with no particular religious fervor or strong denominational attachment, and he considered careers in the ministry or law as equally interesting and respectable alternatives to a career in the family business. For college, he thought first of Yale but eventually chose the University of Virginia because his young Uncle Marvin, a favorite, was a student there. Charles was a good student from his entry in 1857, concentrating on the Greek classics. Along with Marvin, he became involved in an evangelical student group and in founding the college chapter of the Young Men's Christian Association. In November 1858, Briggs experienced a conversion at a revival at the university, and thereafter he urged the other members of his family to experience conversion as well.[2]

The impending Civil War prevented Briggs from returning to Virginia in 1860 for his final year of college. He worked in the family barrel business and kept up his studies until the outbreak of war, when he volunteered for the Union Army. Stationed in a fort guarding Washington, D.C., during 1861, his unit saw no action, and at the end of the year he was discharged. Having settled on the ministry in college, after his military service Briggs enrolled in Union Theological Seminary in New York, selecting it because intellectually it was the toughest of the evangelical seminaries. Just as he had been in college, at Union Briggs was a good student. His father's illness interrupted Briggs's final year at the seminary (1863–64), and he was obliged to help in the family business. For the remainder of the war, which was very profitable for the company, he worked in the firm.[3]

To further his studies in theology and Biblical criticism, Briggs's professors urged him to go to Germany, as several of them had done. Germany then was the center of the historical criticism of the Bible, which treated Scripture as the product of many literary traditions which had been combined during a long historical process. It was common for Protestant theological students to come to Germany from all over the world. Accordingly, in 1866, Briggs and his bride, the former Julia Valentine Dobbs, went to Germany. He did not take a degree, but spent several years attending lectures and study groups in several German universities. There he became convinced by the "Higher Criticism" and made it his mission to bring it to the United States. He also became disenchanted with "scholastic" systems in theology, especially the Old School Presbyterianism that he had encountered in church and which had driven his Uncle Marvin from Princeton Theological Seminary after two years of study there.[4]

After his return to the United States in 1870, Briggs was ordained as the pastor of the former "Old School" Presbyterian Church of Roselle, New Jersey. There he remained for four years, until he was called to join the faculty of Union Theological Seminary. He was the first alumnus of the school to join the faculty, where he taught Hebrew and the Hebrew Scriptures. His inaugural address in the Davenport Professorship of Hebrew and Cognate Languages in 1876 clearly articulated his Higher Critical views.[5]

The details of Briggs's public career and the controversy that drove him from the Presbyterian Church have been detailed above.

BRIGGS'S VISION OF THE CHURCH

Charles Briggs was an "inclusive" liberal in his conception of the church. He insisted on the orthodoxy of the Bible and the Westminster Confession, but also insisted that these historical standards allowed latitude for disagreement in interpretation. Briggs treated doctrine as the outcome of historical development, and his piety was of an evangelical type that emphasized Christian life over doctrine. Briggs took a Christian progressive view of history, arguing that Christianity and the Church—of which the Presbyterian Church was only one passing form—would advance to ultimate triumph. Briggs's watchword for the church was "unity in diversity."

On January 1, 1891, a few weeks before he delivered the address at Union Seminary for which he was tried, Briggs published a clear statement of his vision of the church in "The Advance Toward Church Unity":

> [I]t is only within recent years that liberty and variety have been won within denominational lines. This victory results in the decay of denominationalism; for in most, if not all, of the denominations there are those who break over the lines to the right and the left and clasp hands with kindred spirits in other denominations. The conservatives are, for the most part, denominationalists, but the progressives are indifferent to denominational difference, and are most interested in the progress of the Church of Christ as a whole. The progressives [in each denomination] . . . are now the most powerful parties. The only hope of conservatism is to unite the conservatives of all denominations against the progressives of all denominations. But so soon as this is accomplished the denominations will pass out of existence, and two great parties will divide Christianity between them. The old controversies are dead and buried; it is impossible to revive them. Those differences that gave the denominations their existence have lost their importance. . . . The signs of the times indicate that we are rapidly approaching . . . a crisis that will destroy denominationalism and make the Church of Christ one.[6]

Briggs was committed to the Church, but not necessarily to the Presbyterian Church. Although Briggs had been raised a Presbyterian, he deliberately considered other denominations before choosing the Presbyterian Church. In 1885, he wrote that "Presbyterianism . . . is more in accordance with all [orthodox] . . . doctrines than is any other section of Christendom," and that "moderate Presbyterianism . . . is alone worthy to prevail over the world." Yet, even then he was looking beyond his own church, contending that "Presbyterianism is not a finality . . . [but] is the stepping stone to something higher and grander yet to come."[7]

After his suspension from the Presbyterian ministry, and even after he joined the Episcopal Church, Briggs still argued for Presbyterian principles. These, however, he put in a larger context, in order to give each form of the church its due. This reinforced his tendency to see Presbyterianism—and the other Christian "isms"—as a certain *idea* about the church, rather than as a particular human *organization* with organizational, as well as religious, imperatives. Toward the end of his life, he had lost almost entirely a "denominational consciousness," and he summed up his appreciation of the church in this way:

> Early life among the Methodists gave me a sympathy with Arminianism, although I deliberately followed Calvinism. Four years of study in Germany enabled me to sympathize with Lutheranism. Many years of labour as a Presbyterian minister and Professor of Theology enabled me to understand . . . the Presbyterian and other Reformed Churches. Many vacations in England enabled me to overcome early prejudices against liturgy and ceremony in public worship. Several residences in Rome gave me the opportunity to enter into sympathy with Roman Catholic doctrine and worship. And so God's Holy Spirit had guided me through sympathetic study of all these divisions of Christendom to lose hostility to them, . . . and to labour for the reunion of them all in one organic whole.[8]

Charles Briggs thought that the Church should be a "broad church," an institution in which a wide agreement on a small body of essential teachings would allow the acceptance of a great variety of views on other matters. He argued for this conception as both an ideal for the universal Church and as a true description of the American Presbyterian Church, at least at certain points in its history. He described the original American Presbytery as having a "broad, generous, and tolerant spirit," and he used this and other broad church phrases—such as "comprehensive," "catholic," and "progressive"— to describe later developments in the Presbyterian Church.[9]

In the introduction to *Whither?* (1889), his most polemical and personal book, Briggs wrote: "It is necessary for all parties in the Presbyterian Churches to be generous, tolerant, and broad-minded. The author does not wish to exclude from the Church those theologians whom he attacks for their errors. He is a broadchurchman and all his sympathies are with a comprehensive Church, in which . . . all other true Christian scholars shall be recognized . . . He rejoices in all earnest efforts for Christian Unity . . . in the entire Christian world."[10] Briggs argued that the Westminster divines had a similarly broad view of the church, which had been corrupted in later Puritanism and Presbyterianism. Briggs's broad church views led him to a "high church" Episcopalianism, in sharp contrast to McGiffert's move from Presbyterianism to "low church" Congregationalism.[11]

Briggs appears to have written *American Presbyterianism* (1885) in order to show that this broad view of the church was the original condition of American Presbyterianism. He argued that those espousing the broad view repeatedly in Presbyterian history have had to fight to avoid having the church transformed into a rigid and "scholastic" form of Calvinism. In this work, and more especially in *Whither?* (1889), Briggs makes clear that, in his view, Princeton Seminary Presbyterianism was a form of Protestant scholasticism and the enemy of true broad church Presbyterianism. Incidentally, *Whither?* became quite the rage among Princeton Seminary students, even while it enraged their professors.[12]

Briggs was willing to fight for toleration, especially toleration of free inquiry, in the church. Free inquiry was an issue dear to his heart even before his suspension from the ministry, and he was willing to defend the rights of those whose views he disagreed with, such as the then-embattled scholars of Andover Seminary.[13] Though an ardent proponent of church reunion, he was willing to delay the reunion of the northern and southern Presbyterian churches if this development would threaten the "tolerant and generous spirit" which the northern church had learned "in its treatment of error in useful evangelical ministers."[14] Note that Briggs is proposing not simply tolerance of *difference,* but tolerance of *error.*

Briggs insisted that the church must be *catholic,* teaching what is universal and essential to the church, and *orthodox,* teaching only what is true.[15] A church that contains the universal essentials is catholic, even if it contains other things. An orthodox church is not only catholic, but also adds nothing untrue to the catholic essentials. Briggs judged that Presbyterianism was fully catholic and truly orthodox.[16] Notice, however, that this measure applies only to the official or constitutional position of the church. "There are," he contended, "many questions in religion, doctrine, and morals which the Church has not defined and where the guidance of Holy Scripture is as yet not altogether clear, about which men of our time differ widely."[17] Views not specifically covered in the constitution, though unorthodox, are not heterodox, and therefore are permitted within the church until the church amends the constitution. This is because "[a]ll human orthodoxy is partial and incomplete. No one can be entirely orthodox, as no one can be altogether good, save God only."[18]

Briggs did not think that orthodoxy was simply whatever the church officially taught. Rather, orthodoxy was Truth, God's truth, as nearly as it could be approximated in a human institution. In its search for truth, the church had the guidance of reason, tradition, the Holy Spirit, and especially the Bible. The Bible was an official part of the constitution of the Presbyterian Church, the other documents deriving their authority from it.

"Biblical Theology," in Briggs's hands, was used as a corrective to the Protestant scholasticism of "Princeton Theology," which was becoming the standard theology of the Presbyterian Church. The Princeton theologians, of course, contended that their theology *was* biblical theology, that it was the "faith once delivered to the saints," without innovation or development. The difficulty with this conception, as Briggs (and other proponents of the historicist view) pointed out, was that the theology taught by the church, including that of the Princeton men, *had* changed, partly through the reinterpretation of Scripture. Briggs used as an example the claim that "tolerating a false religion" was a sin, which the Westminster Larger Catechism asserts on the strength of the Second Commandment. Yet "this statement was stricken out [of the church constitution] by the men of the American revolution as unscriptural,"[19] a change that Princeton accepted.

Briggs's modest view of what constituted the essential doctrines served to restrain dogmatizing. It allowed all manner of sinners to come into the church so that they might pursue sanctification there, rather than having to meet a high standard of perfection before they could be admitted. By treating most church practices as conventional rather than essential, Briggs's view allowed the church more readily to adapt to new circumstances. Briggs could sustain a modest view of the doctrines essential to the church because he believed that "Holy Scripture is for all alike . . . that all may maintain such sufficient understanding of it as is necessary unto salvation. Therefore a dogmatic faith is unnecessary unto salvation."[20]

Briggs took an activist view of Christianity, arguing that "[d]oing the teachings of Jesus is an ethical norm, corresponding with that of following him. This is not satisfied by merely recognizing him as sovereign Lord. Doing is the determinative factor and not merely professing."[21] This emphasis on work rather than doctrine is characteristic of liberal thought in the church. The program of peace and work put forth by the liberals gave them common ground with the loyalists. Agreeing on work took the pressure off agreeing on doctrine, buttressing the argument that diversity of doctrine could be legitimate.

Briggs was a pioneer in proposing the idea that the church and its doctrine are best understood as undergoing historical development, clearly stated in his *Biblical Study* (1883):

> Experience shows us that no body of divinity can answer more than its generation. Every catechism and confession of faith will in time become obsolete and powerless, remaining as historical monuments and symbols . . . Each age has its own peculiar work and needs, and . . . not even the Bible could devote itself to the entire satisfaction of the wants of any particular age, without thereby sacrificing its value as the book for all ages. It is sufficient that the Bible gives us the *material* for all ages, and leaves to man the noble task of shaping the material so as to suit the wants of his own time.[22]

Briggs's conception of the development—the progress—of the church had a sweep greater than that imagined even by other ecumenical thinkers of his day: "Through all the ages of Church History there has been a progressive appropriation of the Word of God. . . . Can we suppose that our Teutonic type of Christianity will be imposed upon the Oriental and African races? . . . Let us not deceive ourselves. . . . The ultimate Christianity that will suit our race will be as much higher than Protestantism as Protestantism is higher than Romanism."[23] This progressive vision brought Briggs into direct conflict with his "scholastic" co-religionists, who sought—and claimed to have found—a theology that was the same in all ages and places, who saw the culmination of biblical theology in Calvinism and the Presbyterian Church. To such thinkers, Briggs said, "Presbyterianism is not the last word of God to man. God has something vastly better for us than Calvinism."[24]

Briggs argued that the developmental view of the church was a necessary consequence of God's free grace. He claimed that developmentalism was an orthodox Presbyterian doctrine found in the Westminster Confession itself: "The Westminster divines did not themselves go any further than elect infants and elect incapables, but the heirs of Puritanism have with unanimity extended their doctrine [of salvation]. . . to *all* infants and *all* incapables; and have also added the class of elect heathen . . . The Westminster Confession . . . opens the gate into this territory. . . ; who then shall venture to close it?"[25] This freedom to develop is, in Presbyterian thought, not only a possibility but a hard-won heritage. "Let us never forget," Briggs wrote, "the principle of liberty of conscience for which the Puritan fathers fought and died . . . They [themselves] do not propose to speak the final word in theology."[26]

Briggs favored the "comprehension" (inclusion) of diversity in the church, a dynamic view that became the standard for the ecumenical program of the liberal party in the church. Briggs held that "[T]here can be no true unity that does not spring from . . . diversity. . . . If the visible Church is to be one, the pathway to unity is in the recognition of the necessity and the great advantage of comprehending the types in one broad, catholic Church of Christ."[27] To see the advantages of diversity, though, the Presbyterian Church had to have freedom thrust upon it. In fact, Briggs wrote,

> Presbyterianism had to . . . forfeit the religious supremacy in America, in order that there might be a Free Church in a Free State; in order to the establishment of the principles of Religious Toleration, Fraternal Recognition of different Denominations, and Ecclesiastical Comprehension . . . All of these principles are wrapt up in the essential principles of . . . Presbyterianism, but they . . . would not have manifested themselves in a dominant Presbyterianism in America. It was the external struggle against civil injustice and tyranny, and the internal struggle with narrowness, intolerance, and bigotry that made Presbyterianism in America the champion of civil and religious liberty.[28]

Comprehension was the central vision of the liberal party, which envisioned that

> About this banner of a broad, generous, and tolerant Presbyterianism, all the Presbyterian bodies of the land will eventually rally. When they have learned to value less the national peculiarities which they have inherited from their foreign ancestors, and to insist less upon the minor matters and circumstantials of religion which they have received by tradition of the elders, they will see that the essential and prudential American Presbyterianism which combines the conservative and progressive forces of the age, and comprehends all legitimate types of Presbyterianism, is vastly higher than any of the elements of which it is composed.[29]

Charles Briggs's own inclusive vision went far beyond the Presbyterian Church, and beyond what loyalist Presbyterians could accept for their church. "Denominationalism," he wrote, "is the great sin and curse of the modern Church."[30] The reach of Briggs's inclusivist conception is nothing less than the whole world: "[In] the Coming Catholicism, . . . not only Protestant and Roman Catholic, but also Greek and Syrian, Armenian and Copt—yes, the Jew, the Mohammedan, and even India, China, and Japan—will share; for in a world-wide religion, embracing all the races of mankind, every nation and every race will have something to say and something to do."[31]

Briggs thought it important for a church to have the courage of its convictions in order to maintain its integrity.[32] Religious struggle, in Briggs's view, should be tempered by liberty, civility, and constitutional order, but in the final analysis,

> Progress is possible only by research, discussion, and conflict. The more conflict the better. Battle for the truth is infinitely better than stagnation in error. Every error should be slain as soon as possible. If it be our error we should be the most anxious to get rid of it . . . Let us unite in the truth already gained and agree to contend in Christian love and chivalry for the truth that has not yet been sufficiently determined, having faith that in due time the Divine Spirit will make all things clear to us.[33]

Charles Briggs had a vision of the church that was broad, inclusive, constitutional, and conflictual. Something of the breadth and openness of his vision can be seen in this revealing and poignant statement from his last important work, *Church Unity* (1909):

> It is necessary for us to enter into the very heart of the statements of others in order to truly know them. This may be done by the power of human sympathy. Some men are incapable of this. They cannot truly state the views of an opponent . . . Others are so sympathetic that if they provisionally put aside their own convictions they are in peril of assuming the convictions of those with whom they come into sympathy . . . No one should attempt it who has not so mastered the position of his own Church that it possesses him, and has become a part of his very nature . . . Approaching the opponents with such open-mindedness . . . he will thus in a measure think and feel with them, and the truth that they have will be recognized and eliminated from the error which envelopes it. He will soon learn

that there is more truth in common in the opposing statements than anyone supposed; that there is truth in the possession of the opponent which he is glad to learn, and add to the truth which he had in possession before. He will learn with sadness that there is error and inadequacy enough, . . . on both sides. Such has been my experience.[34]

The Chastening of the Briggs Liberals

By portraying the "advance toward church unity" as a vast struggle between progressives and conservatives throughout Christendom, Briggs failed to do justice to the claims of the loyalist center within each denomination. By treating the distinctive features of the denominations, which had been created through considerable struggle and sacrifice, as mere obstacles to be swept away, Briggs alienated the party that he most needed to win over in order to fend off the conservatives in the battle for the future of the church. Briggs appears to have been chastened by this failure, and in later years he was more attentive to building concrete institutional and historical connections between denominations. Such connections would be essential prerequisites for making actual organic union possible.

Chapter 9

THE CONSERVATIVE:
J. GRESHAM MACHEN

MACHEN BEFORE THE "MACHEN CASES"

*J*ohn Gresham Machen was born in Baltimore in 1881. Throughout his life, he remained close to his father Arthur, a prominent lawyer and Presbyterian elder, and his two brothers. The deepest influence on Machen, though, was his mother, Mary Gresham Machen, a literate and very religious woman to whom he turned for guidance until her death in 1931. "Minnie" Gresham was a member of a prominent family in Macon, Georgia, and was well connected among southern Presbyterians. She set the tone in the Machen home, teaching her son the Bible and the Westminster Shorter Catechism thoroughly. Minnie Machen was close to the pastor of the southern Presbyterian congregation to which the family belonged. She also imparted to her son Gresham a love of art, poetry, the theater, and nature. For Machen, a bachelor, his mother was "the one very close tie in his life." To her he dedicated both his most famous work, *Christianity and Liberalism* (1923), and his *magnum opus, The Virgin Birth of Christ* (1930). As a result of his upbringing, Machen's conservatism always had a southern cast, so he opposed not only women's suffrage and racial integration, but also centralized government of any kind.[1]

Machen attended good private schools in Baltimore, then entered Johns Hopkins University, where he excelled in the study of classics. He graduated in 1901 as valedictorian and was elected to Phi Beta Kappa. He remained at Johns Hopkins for a further year of study in Greek antiquities.[2] In the fall of 1902, Machen entered Princeton Theological Seminary, an institution to which he became devoted. His principal mentor over the years was B. B.

Warfield, who had, a generation earlier, coedited the *Presbyterian Review* with Charles Briggs. Warfield later became one of Briggs's main academic opponents. Machen called Warfield "the greatest man I have known."[3] While in Princeton, Machen also studied philosophy at Princeton University, from which he received an M.A. degree in 1904. At the seminary, Machen built upon his classical studies to specialize in the Greek New Testament. He graduated from Princeton Seminary in 1905.[4]

In 1905, Machen, like Briggs a generation before, was sent by his professors to Germany to complete his education. Whereas Briggs had studied with the whole spectrum of German scholars of religion in his day, however, Machen studied only with the naturalistic liberals. Machen arrived predisposed to reject this naturalistic view of Christianity, and in the end he did reject it.

While in Germany, however, he was unexpectedly impressed with the "deep religious feeling" of Wilhelm Herrmann, who represented the liberal "Ritschlianism at its best." The radical tendency in German and American Protestant theology, which Machen came to call "modernism," promoted a naturalistic (as opposed to supernatural) view of Jesus as only a man, though a great ethical teacher. On this view, Christianity consisted of living like Jesus the man; Machen contended, in contrast, that Christianity meant being saved by Jesus the God Incarnate. There were also less radical forms of German theology which did consider Jesus to be divine but which placed greater reliance upon human action and reason, and less on divine action and Scripture, than did traditional, Machen-style Protestantism. The thoroughgoing naturalism of the German radicals made some small impact upon American Protestantism, but the greater influence came from the latter, liberal form of Christianity. Machen later hinted that in this period he had profound doubts about traditional Presbyterian teachings, but eventually he rejected liberal and naturalistic Christianity on the grounds that it failed to understand sin.[5]

In the fall of 1906, Machen returned to Princeton Seminary as an instructor in New Testament. He remained happily in that position for two decades, during the course of which he rose (in 1914) to the post of assistant professor. In that same year, he was ordained into the Presbyterian ministry. In 1918 and 1919, Machen served with the YMCA in Belgium and France, ministering to the Allied armies, after which he returned to Princeton Seminary.[6]

After World War I, Machen became a prominent figure in the debate in the Protestant churches between the Fundamentalists and the Modernists. Although he disliked the term, asserting that he taught "no new 'ism'," Machen weighed in with the fundamentalists. He was an odd sort of fundamentalist, though, and, as an educated, rich urbanite, had some disdain for fundamentalists of William Jennings Bryan's type.[7] His most important contribution to this debate was his book *Christianity and Liberalism* (1923). In it he stated the argument that would become the basis of his position in the Presbyterian struggles for the next decade and a half. Liberalism, he stated, was not a variant, or even a heresy, of Christianity, but a completely different religion. What he meant by liberalism was a completely naturalistic doctrine that emphasized social progress through the scientific perfectibility of human beings. Insofar as such liberals, or modernists, called themselves Christians, they would speak of Jesus and his divinity, but in doing so, they would mean only that an actual historical figure, Jesus, had existed, who, though only a man, was a great ethical teacher and the "fairest flower" of humanity.[8]

Machen was at pains to show in most of his works that such a faith was contrary to the historical understanding of Christianity and could in no way be considered orthodox. He was exasperated and offended to think that such views might be propounded by ministers and officials of the Presbyterian Church. Two events in particular drew his ire: the preaching of the Baptist Harry Emerson Fosdick from a Presbyterian pulpit, and the issuing of the Auburn Affirmation. The controversy surrounding these events served to form Machen and others holding similar convictions into a self-consciously conservative party in the Presbyterian Church in the U.S.A. To religious conservatives of Machen's bent, the phrase "signer of the Auburn Affirmation" came to carry as much opprobrium as the phrase "card-carrying Communist" would hold for political conservatives of another generation.[9]

A description of Machen's role in the Auburn Affirmation fight, the struggle for Princeton Seminary, and the battle over foreign missions is woven through the narrative in part I. The culmination of this long war was his trial and subsequent suspension from the Presbyterian ministry. The trial, and his death soon after, put a seal on an era. Machen's fall meant the end of the conservative vision of the church that had been institutionalized in the Presbyterian Church in the Briggs case, and its replacement by a loyalist and liberal pluralism in the church.

MACHEN'S "MARTYRDOM"

For two generations of conservative Presbyterians, Machen has been a symbol of resistance to the doctrinal diversity that they believe has undermined the larger Presbyterian denominations. Part of the passion for this mythic symbol has come from the belief that liberals in the church railroaded Machen in his trial, in order to get rid of him.[10] The strongest evidence of the plot against Machen has been the claim that hostile prosecutors forced his trial to be held in a presbytery dominated by his Princeton enemies, even though Machen had moved to the more conservative Philadelphia Presbytery years before and had transferred his membership there. That the church allowed his old opponents to try Machen, even though they had no jurisdiction, the argument runs, shows that they were out to get him from the beginning and that the trial was, as Machen claimed, a farce.

Let us, therefore, examine the much-debated issue of jurisdiction at Machen's trial. Machen had been living in the bounds of Philadelphia Presbytery since 1929 but only tried to transfer his membership in 1934. In the Presbyterian system, the presbytery is the most important agency for safeguarding the church, and its members traditionally are allowed broad latitude in examining prospective officers of the church. At the 1934 meeting of Philadelphia Presbytery, in which Machen's transfer was being considered, several members tried to question him about his loyalty to the boards and agencies of the church. During the controversy over the Independent Board for Presbyterian Foreign Missions, this question often was asked of those associated with Westminster Seminary or the board, when one sought to join a presbytery.

The conservative moderator of the Presbytery of Philadelphia, however, ruled these questions out of order, and the majority voted to receive Machen without further discussion. A protest was sent to the Synod of Pennsylvania, challenging the ruling of the moderator and asking for a stay of the reception of Machen until the question could be settled. The protest was signed by a third of the members of the presbytery, the amount required by the church's rules to stay an action. Machen's counsel contended that the proper number had not signed, because one signer later changed his mind, but the court later ruled that the requisite number of signatures were on the petition when it was received by the synod and therefore it was, indeed, in order. The synod had the matter in its hands when Machen was being tried in New Brunswick Presbytery.[11]

The defense argued that Machen had been received in Philadelphia, and that New Brunswick had no jurisdiction. The prosecution argued that, because of the stay, Machen had not been "actually received," according to the exact wording of the rule, and therefore New Brunswick had not yet relinquished its jurisdiction. In support of this contention, the prosecution noted that the clerk of Philadelphia Presbytery had not followed the usual custom of mailing back to the sending presbytery a "coupon" from the transfer document, indicating that the sent minister actually had been received. The prosecution noted that this was only a custom and not a rule, but it was inferred from this that there had been some doubt in the minds of Philadelphia Presbytery about whether Machen's reception was complete.[12]

The General Assembly had ordered that Machen be tried by his presbytery, and the prosecution feared that, if New Brunswick Presbytery did not act, it could be held in contempt by the assembly. Therefore, they argued, as the presbytery with the clearest claim to jurisdiction, New Brunswick ought to proceed. Events proved the prosecution's fears justified: when Chester Presbytery, a conservative stronghold adjacent to Philadelphia, failed to try one of its number, Wilbur Smith, who was a member of the Independent Board, the General Assembly sent a special commission to treat with them. If Smith had not resigned from the church, legally it would have been possible for the whole presbytery to be held in contempt. Such an action was unlikely, since neither loyalists nor liberals in the assembly wanted conflict and division, but they would have been within their rights to move in this fashion. This right was known to the prosecution in the Machen case.

Despite their fears of being in contempt of the assembly, the prosecution might have let the whole matter wait until the jurisdiction question before the Synod of Pennsylvania had been decided. The General Assembly did, in fact, rule that the stay on Machen's reception in Philadelphia Presbytery was in order, and therefore Machen was still subject to the jurisdiction of New Brunswick Presbytery.[13] If the prosecution had waited for this ruling, the question of jurisdiction could have been cleared up, and Machen could have been given an undisputed trial.

The practical consequence of such a move would have been to delay Machen's trial until after the other Independent Board cases had been decided. Every appeal to the 1936 General Assembly in these cases was decided against the Independent Board members. Machen had anticipated this result, even before his own trial began. If his case had been delayed, he would have seen the outcome of the other cases in fact, and thus foreseen the certain outcome of his own case. Even if he had won in the conservative Presbytery of Philadelphia, he almost certainly would have lost in the General Assembly.

At that point, three courses of action would have been open to him. He could have resigned from the Independent Board, which, given all that had occurred, was highly unlikely. He could have gone through with his trial, though the outcome was almost predetermined, and then decide what to do, which would probably have been to leave the denomination. Finally, Machen could have quit the Presbyterian Church then and there.

What Machen hoped for, it appears, was a such an intense confrontation with the loyalists who ran the church that he would be expelled and, as a martyr to the pure gospel, lead the largest possible number of conservatives out of the Presbyterian Church in the U.S.A. Machen had been contemplating schism for years, and by 1936 he regarded it as highly desirable. When, in 1936, the members of the Independent Board as a group were suspended from the ministry, the moment was right for organizing a new denomination. Machen even may have hoped to win in Philadelphia Presbytery, so that, if and when he lost in the higher judicatories, those who had voted for him in the presbytery might feel disgruntled enough to withdraw, too. If Machen, the natural leader of the schism, waited a year for his trial to be played out, the moment might have passed; on the other hand, if he had withdrawn voluntarily when the others were suspended, he would not have gone out a martyr.

In any case, the outcome would not have been much different from what did happen.

THE DOCTRINAL CHURCH OF J. GRESHAM MACHEN

The recurrent theme in all Machen's conflicts was that Machen thought of the Presbyterian Church as representing a specific doctrine, and he did not see how he could remain in the same body with people who did not agree with all of that doctrine. Machen's long struggle, in other words, was against pluralism in the church.

Machen conceived of the church as an association for the teaching of Christian doctrine. This pure doctrine had its source in the Bible and its highest embodiment in the Westminster Confession, and it is not subject to change or development.[14] To maintain the purity of that doctrine, the church must be intolerant, exclusive, and free from the state. Therefore, when Machen spoke of *the church*, he normally meant only the content of its teachings and not all the phenomena one might encounter in the empirical Presbyterian Church in the U.S.A. Machen considered his group to be the truly constitutional party in the church, but by the term *constitution* he meant only the sections dealing with doctrine, not the larger body of material on order, government, and discipline.[15]

Machen clearly stated this doctrinal view of the church to the Thompson Committee when it investigated Princeton Seminary: "The thing for which the Presbyterian Church exists, I hold, is the propagation of a certain doctrine that we call the gospel of the Lord Jesus Christ. . . . The Church might do many other things—it might tinker with social conditions, it might use all sorts of palliative measures with men who have not been born again—but only by persuading men to accept the blessed 'doctrine' or gospel can it save human souls."[16] The Presbyterian Church, on this view, is not defined by what it does in the world, nor by the religious experience of those within it, nor even by the form of government which gives the "presbyterian" church its name.

Machen explicitly rejected pluralism, both within the church and among religions. He claimed that:

A true Christian Church is radically intolerant. . . . The Church must maintain the high exclusiveness and universality of its message. It presents the gospel of Jesus Christ not merely as one way of salvation, but as the only way. It cannot make common cause with other faiths. It cannot agree not to proselytize. Its appeal is universal, and admits of no exceptions. . . . Therein lies the offense of the Christian religion, but therein also lies its glory and its power. A Christianity tolerant of other religions is just no Christianity at all.[17]

The church could be pure only if it were freely chosen; therefore Machen insisted upon freedom in society, to the point of being a civil libertarian. He argued that

One of the most important elements of civil and religious liberty is the right of voluntary association—the right of citizens to band themselves together for any lawful purposes whatever, whether that purpose does or does not commend itself to the generality of their fellow men. Now, a church is a voluntary association. . . . It would, indeed, be an interference with liberty for a church . . . to use the power of the state to compel men to assent to the church's creed or conform to the church's program. To that kind of intolerance I am opposed with all my might and main.[18]

Machen argued that a church, unlike the state, had a right to insist that those within it agree with all of its standards, and to remove any who did not. "Involuntary organizations," he wrote, "ought to be tolerant, but voluntary organizations, so far as the fundamental purpose of their existence is concerned, must be intolerant or else cease to exist."[19] He tolerated diversity of religions in civil society, but he did not go on to say that this was a religious good; that is, he did not go on to accept religious pluralism among denominations.

Machen defended propaganda and proselytizing of doctrines as a role—indeed, an essential duty—of any self-respecting church. In an address on "Relations Between Christians and Jews," he said, "The plain fact is that we Christians regard all of you who are not Christians as lost under the guilt of sin. . . . Do you not see that, holding the view that we hold, we should, if we ceased to proselytize among you, be not kind and considerate but guilty of the most heartless neglect that could possibly be conceived[?]"[20] This duty, Machen argued, has since apostolic times taken Christianity into direct conflict with faiths that it regarded as false. In those days, "instead of withdrawing into remote districts where purity might have been more easily maintained, the Christians fought their battles in the very strongholds of Satan's realm."[21]

Machen had a conception of the church that was doctrinal, exclusive, intolerant, free—but not institutional. In his writings, doctrines were the actors, not institutions. Machen did not, of course, deny the existence or even the importance of the institutional aspects of the church; they simply did not figure importantly in his portrayal of Christian life. It was due, perhaps, to this view that Machen had relatively little experience with, or responsibility for, the institutional aspects of the Presbyterian Church. He had very limited pastoral experience and gave little service to the committees and boards that constituted the nuts and bolts of denominational life. As a Christian, his loyalty was to the gospel rather than to the denomination; therefore, exit from the denomination was relatively easy. When Machen began losing his battles in the church, he began to speak openly of schism.

MACHEN'S CRITIQUE OF THE PRESBYTERIAN CHURCH

Machen criticized the Presbyterian Church on the grounds that it was liberal and "non-doctrinal."[22] Liberals, in Machen's view, held that "creeds are merely the changing expression of a unitary Christian experience, and provided only they express that experience they are equally good." This made liberalism not a variant or even a heresy of Christianity, but a non-Christian religion that was attempting to take over the Christian churches. This argument is the whole point of the book that made him well known, *Christianity and Liberalism* (1923).[23] In contrast with religious liberals, Machen opposed all attempts to reinterpret what he thought was orthodox Christian doctrine, or to unite denominations without full agreement on that doctrine. Machen's battles in the church were as much over *whether* doctrine legitimately could be reinterpreted as over precisely *how* it should be interpreted.

Liberalism or modernism, in Machen's view, opposed Christian doctrine with a "polite paganism,"[24] and in "the modern vituperation of 'doctrine,' . . . The liberal preacher is really rejecting the whole basis of Christianity."[25] Machen thought doctrine was both unchanging and necessary for Christian faith. He was thus out of sympathy with the liberal view, which he summarizes thus: "The knowledge of God, it is often said, is unnecessary to our contact with Him, or at least it occupies a secondary place, as the symbolic and necessarily changing expression of an experience which is itself ineffable. . . . [I]t underlies the popular exaltation of 'abiding experiences' at the expense of the mental categories in which they are supposed to be expressed."[26] This historicist view of doctrine, he thought, was subjective and unscientific: "If a man were truly scientific," he wrote, "he would be convinced of the truth of Christianity whether he were a saint or a demon; since the truth of Christianity does not depend upon the state of the soul of the investigator, but is objectively fixed."[27] Machen, and Princeton Seminary, characteristically saw theology as the "classification of facts," as opposed to the interpretation of experience.[28] On Machen's account, to reinterpret doctrine is to reject it, and to reject doctrine is to reject the church.[29]

Having concluded that the Presbyterian Church contained two distinct religions, Machen naturally began to think about a division of the church. He began publicly promoting schism in the church at least as early as 1923,[30] and in 1926 he told the *Boston Evening Transcript* that "[t]he Presbyterian Church will reach the non-Christian stage . . . in a period of from three to ten years."[31] By 1936, he was ready to say that "the Presbyterian Church in the U.S.A. is an apostate Church at its very heart."[32]

Toward the end of the 1920s, Machen began to think that it would be the conservatives who would pull out of the church first, and by 1933 was avowing: "Certainly I do long for . . . a division in the present church. . . . The only question is whether that is to be done by withdrawal of the Christian element . . . or elimination of the Modernist element."[33] Wayne Headman, though generally supportive of Machen, concluded after a careful reading of Machen's correspondence that, while "[i]t is difficult to tell exactly when Machen gave up on the Church, for his comments on the subject differ according to the person to whom he was writing . . . [i]t appears that he had [by 1931] personally arrived at a decision but was not yet willing to publicly tip his hand."[34]

Machen's conduct after that date seems designed to provoke his expulsion from the church, so that, as a "martyr," he might more effectively lead his party out of the old church. The Independent Board was created specifically to provoke disciplining, because he thought that "if we simply talk against the Modernizing agencies and do nothing about it, we face no ecclesiastical penalties."[35] While publicly complaining about his trial, privately Machen's only worry was that he would *not* be convicted: "Naturally," he wrote, "if anybody is to be a 'martyr' I should feel rather disgruntled if I were not the one."[36] When Clarence Macartney offered to represent Machen in his appeal before the Court of the General Assembly, "He [Machen] replied with a kind letter, but declined my offer, saying that if I defended him, he might be acquitted, and that was not what he wanted." Machen said he feared that Macartney, a former moderator and respected conservative, might get him off with a light sentence, and the issue would thereby be "evaded." Machen did not want that, because, he wrote, "I am longing for a division, and hoping and praying with all my soul that the division may come soon."[37] Some of Machen's statements from this period do not reflect his general reputation for scrupulosity, as, for example, his admission that, "if I were suddenly asked to prove my assertion that Dr. [Kenneth] Latourette is a Modernist, I might have difficulty in doing so."[38]

MACHEN'S IRONIC REVERSALS

Neither Machen's intellectual position on the doctrinal character of the Church, nor his sociological position as a seminary scholar, made it necessary for him to have a strong tie to the normal institutional life of the Presbyterian Church. Consequently, the diversity that actually existed in the church did not lead him to a pluralistic theory to justify it, as it had the liberals and the loyalists since the Briggs case. Machen defended a pluralist position just twice, once when trying to legitimize conservative control of Princeton against the loyalist leadership of the denomination, and again at the end of his life, when he was trying to preserve unity in his fledgling denomination. Both were instances—perhaps the only instances—in which Machen had a personal stake in the institutional, as distinct from the doctrinal, conditions of the church.

Given his claim that the unity of the church depends upon its intolerance and exclusivity, it is startling to find Machen defending tolerance and diversity in the church, as when he contended that "Princeton has the right and indeed the very solemn obligation of maintaining a *distinctive* position within the larger unity of the Church." In fact, Machen held that there was a general "right of various theological seminaries to maintain distinctive views within the larger communion of the Church."[39] He went so far as to defend this position on the very liberal principles of tolerance that previously he had disparaged: "If," he wrote, President Stevenson's inclusive "policy becomes dominant . . . by ecclesiastical action, then all the high-sounding words . . . about peace and tolerance will be mocked."[40] In his statement to the Thompson Committee when it investigated Princeton Seminary, Machen asked the classic "inclusivist" question: "Is the Presbyterian Church large enough to include one seminary that assumes a position like ours? Perhaps it may be objected that if we continue to be tolerated we shall harm the Church by an insistence upon the maintenance of a strict view of its doctrinal standards. I think that just from the 'Liberal' point of view there ought not to be any such fear. The truth after all will prevail. If we are wrong we shall come to naught."[41] No Auburn Affirmationist could have said it more clearly.

Machen often defended the well-established Presbyterian principle of majority rule, especially when defending the rights of the faculty "majority" at Princeton Seminary.[42] Yet the seminary "majority" had come to be a minority in the church, and its rights were coming into conflict with the rights of the majority in the church. According to the Princeton "Plan and Charter," the church majority had a right to full control of the seminary, a point that Machen repeatedly refused to concede.[43] Machen did not try to square this principle of diversity in the church with his earlier positions against it. With his usual forthrightness, Machen simply demanded control of Princeton Seminary and backed this demand with a threat of schism: "The truth is that unless the disruption of the Presbyterian Church is to take place at once, the conservatives in the Church, no matter how extreme their attitude may be thought by others to be, must be allowed to have at least one seminary that clearly and unequivocally represents their view."[44] With this threat, Machen gambled, but he lost. It was after that loss that he began planning the schism.

Machen, at times, granted legitimacy to some doctrinal differences in the same society, but not in the same church. Even in *Christianity and Liberalism* (1923), he held that there were some doctrines over which reasonable Christians might reasonably differ, but these were differences between, rather than within, denominations. They included the mode of the efficacy of the sacraments (Lutherans versus Calvinists); the apostolic succession (episcopal churches versus others); and free will as against predestination (Arminians versus Calvinists). Machen argued that these differences between denominations were not bars to Christian fellowship. Machen also allowed for Christian disagreement on premillenialism, but, perhaps because at that time there were few strictly premillenial denominations, it is not clear in this work whether he thought such differences were permissible within the same church.[45]

None of these accommodations, however, constituted a legitimation of diversity in the church like that of his 1936 proposal for "eschatological liberty." After the split from the Presbyterian Church in the U.S.A. in 1936, Machen almost immediately was faced with a revolt in his new denomination. The faction led by Carl McIntire insisted that dispensational premillenialism was true, and therefore the only possible doctrine for the church. Machen, trying to keep the peace, supported a plan of "eschatological liberty" within the church, insisting that "[p]remillenialists as well as those who hold the opposing view may become ministers or elders or deacons in the Presbyterian Church of America."[46] However, this plan of tolerance failed to satisfy the more insistent premillenialists, and they withdrew.

This led to a further, and particularly rich, irony. The Orthodox Presbyterian Church concluded that independent mission agencies were unreliable for planting the denomination's own churches. Therefore, the new church canceled support for the Independent Board and set up a denominationally-controlled mission agency. It did this, moreover, almost on the anniversary of the 1837 schism by the original Old School Presbyterians, who split, in part, to repudiate independent mission agencies.[47]

In the light of his oft-stated commitment to exclusivity and intolerance in the church, Machen's pleas for a right of diversity in the case of his own institutions—seminary, then denomination—are surprising, and raise the possibility that these experiences might have led him to reconsider his "exclusivism" when faced with the possibility of being excluded himself. That he did not reconsider his position on pluralism is due, I believe, to his doctrinal conception of the Church. A doctrinal church can be pure in its beliefs—indeed, it must be, because the uniformity of its beliefs is what gives it identity. Such a church could not tolerate diversity and still exist.

Chapter 10

THE LOYALISTS: THE SPECIAL COMMISSION OF 1925

*I*n contrast to the two strong individuals, Charles Briggs and J. Gresham Machen, who represent the liberal and conservative parties in this story, the loyalists are represented, fittingly, by a committee. Briggs and Machen both were accomplished biblical scholars in a church that made scriptural study central, and they were effective polemical combatants who rose to leadership in their parties through personal initiative. The Special Commission of 1925, on the other hand, was composed of ministers and elders who had distinguished themselves by their devotion to the specific institutions of the Presbyterian Church in the United States of America. They did not put themselves forward for their roles as judges in the conflicts of the church, but had the task thrust upon them. What follows, then, is a collective portrait of that commission and an analysis of what its work contributed to the story of pluralism in the church.

THE MEMBERS OF THE SPECIAL COMMISSION

The Special Commission, appointed in 1925 by Moderator Charles Erdman, consisted of eight ministers: Henry Swearingen (chairman), Alfred Barr, Hugh Kerr, Mark Matthews, Lapsley McAfee, Harry Rogers, William Thompson, and Edgar Work; and seven ruling elders: John M. T. Finney (vice-chairman), John DeWitt, Edward Duffield, Cheesman Herrick, Nelson Loomis, Nathan Moore, and Robert Speer. The denomination's principal administrative officer, Stated Clerk Lewis Mudge, was appointed secretary to the commission. Erdman himself was invited to sit in on the group's opening meetings, but he did not participate in its final deliberations.[1]

The commission was decidedly moderate to conservative theologically; and one member, Mark Matthews was a strong fundamentalist. In fact, Erdman later credited Matthews with first proposing the commission at the 1925 General Assembly.[2] The weight of the commission lay with men who, like Chairman Henry Swearingen of St. Paul, were successful in the pastorate; or who, like Vice-Chairman John Finney, an eminent surgeon at Johns Hopkins University Hospital, had stature in the secular professions. Few were academics, few were known for their religious polemics, and none was of the liberal party in the church.

The most striking indication of the central importance of this group to the Presbyterian Church is the number of moderators of the General Assembly it contained. The moderator position is the highest honor and the most powerful office in the church, and moderatorial elections were heavily contested between conservatives and loyalists from the teens through the thirties. Mark Matthews, the most conservative member of the commission, was elected moderator in 1912, and Chairman Henry Swearingen won in 1921. Charles Erdman, who appointed the commission, was defeated in 1924 by the conservative Clarence Macartney but came back to win with loyalist and liberal votes in 1925. He was succeeded by William O. Thompson in 1926, the year in which the commission made its initial report, and by Robert Speer in 1927, the year of the group's final report. Cleland McAfee, brother of commission member Lapsley McAfee, was elected in 1929, Hugh Kerr in 1930, Lewis Mudge in 1931 (concurrent with his re-election to a third five-year term as stated clerk), and Harry Clayton Rogers was a candidate for moderator in 1932. In addition, John Finney and Cheesman Herrick each served as vice-moderators.[3] The result of the fundamentalist-modernist battle in the Presbyterian Church was a clear triumph not for one of these parties, but rather for the loyalists.

Of the eight ministers, seven were successful pastors, and the eighth was an active preacher in addition to being a college president. Let us describe each of these men briefly.

Henry Swearingen, the committee chair, was fifty-six years old when the Special Commission was formed. At that time, he had been pastor of the House of Hope Presbyterian Church in St. Paul, Minnesota, for eighteen years. A Pennsylvanian, he had graduated from Westminster College and Allegheny Theological Seminary, both institutions of the United Presbyterian Church in his native state. For many years he served as a trustee of Macalester College and of McCormick Theological Seminary (then called the Presbyterian Theological Seminary of Chicago), both PCUSA schools. He was deeply involved in the Presbyterian Church in the U.S.A., serving as moderator of the Synod of Minnesota, as president of the Presbyterian Home Mission Council, and as a member of the executive committee of the Presbyterian Alliance. Swearingen also was involved in Presbyterian cooperation with other churches, serving in the denomination's Department of Church Cooperation and Union, as a delegate to the Pan-Presbyterian Council and to the Universal Conference on Life and Work, and on the Executive Committee of the Federal Council of Churches. Loyalists in many denominations often were involved in this sort of "life and work" ecumenism, which was organized through a federation of distinct denominations rather than through the transdenominational parachurch organizations created by both liberals and conservatives.[4]

Mark A. Matthews, age fifty-eight, was pastor of the largest church in the denomination, First Presbyterian of Seattle, which had some eight thousand members. Born into an active Presbyterian family in Georgia just after the Civil War, Matthews had no schooling beyond the middle of high school. He read heavily, especially in the theology of Princeton Seminary's Professor Charles Hodge, and as a teenager was licensed to preach. He threw himself into reform work, especially against alcohol, and, while serving as a pastor in Tennessee, taught himself law and passed the bar to help the reform cause. From Tennessee, he was called to Seattle, where he was a combative reformer and a very successful—and decidedly fundamentalist—church builder. Although he often attacked "modernism" in the Presbyterian Church, he also was committed to the church's institutions, serving as a trustee of Whitworth and Whitman colleges and of San Francisco Theological Seminary.

Hugh T. Kerr, fifty-four years of age, had been pastor of Shadyside Presbyterian Church in Pittsburgh for twelve years. A Canadian, he had studied at the University of Toronto before enrolling in Western Theological Seminary, a PCUSA school in Pennsylvania. Before accepting his pastorate, he taught at McCormick Seminary. His son and namesake later would become a well-known Princeton Seminary professor, and another son would be a Presbyterian minister. Kerr was president of the denomination's Board of Christian Education at the time of the Special Commission, and later he headed the Western Hemisphere section of the (World) Alliance of Presbyterian and Reformed Churches.

Lapsley McAfee, at sixty-one, was in the middle of a twenty-five-year pastorate at First Presbyterian Church in Berkeley, California. Son of the founder of (Presbyterian) Park College in Missouri, McAfee was of a family well connected in the Presbyterian Church for generations. A strong supporter of Asian missions, he died in 1935 in the Philippines, while inspecting institutions formed by missionaries sent by his congregation.

Harry Clayton Rogers, forty-eight years old, had been the very successful pastor of Linwood Boulevard Presbyterian Church in Kansas City for seventeen years. Raised in a strong Presbyterian family in Kentucky, he attended the church's Centre College; later he was offered its presidency. Rogers also studied at McCormick Seminary, of which he became a trustee. He was a trustee of Park and Lindenwood Colleges. For many years he served on the General Council of the PCUSA, including thirty years on its evangelism committee.

Two other loyalist pastors, less prominent than those above, were members of the commission. *Alfred H. Barr*, age fifty-seven, moved to Chicago after long pastorates in Detroit and Baltimore. *Edgar W. Work*, sixty-four years old, once had been pastor of what became Lapsley McAfee's congregation in Berkeley and later moved to New York City.

A strong figure on the Special Commission, and chair of the 1926 General Assembly commission that investigated Princeton Seminary, was *William Oxley Thompson*, seventy years of age and just completing twenty-six years as president of Ohio State University. A graduate of Muskingum College and Western Theological Seminary, Thompson regarded himself as a preacher who happened to be a college president. He chaired the board of trustees of the (Presbyterian) College of Wooster, served as trustee president of the Westminster Foundation, and for forty years was a trustee of Lane Theological Seminary. He was president of the International Sunday School Union in 1918, moderator of the Synod of Ohio in 1925, and a member of the General Council, budget committee, and Department of Church Cooperation and Union of the PCUSA. At the time of his death in 1934, he was a member of the Joint Committee on Organic Union with the United Presbyterian Church of North America.

Of the seven lay ruling elders, six were eminent men in secular institutions, and the seventh was a prominent bureaucrat of the Presbyterian Church. They were:

John M. T. Finney, a sixty-two-year-old surgeon at Johns Hopkins Hospital in Baltimore, served as vice-chairman. The grandson, son, and brother of Presbyterian ministers in Maryland (his father was a graduate of Princeton Seminary), Finney graduated from Princeton University and Harvard Medical School. He was an elder of the Brown Memorial Church in Baltimore, where J. Ross Stevenson had been pastor before assuming the presidency of Princeton Seminary. One of the nation's most eminent physicians, Finney had been president of the American Surgical Association, the American College of Surgeons, and of the Southern Surgical and Gynecological Association. He had been offered the presidency of Princeton University after Woodrow Wilson's resignation. Finney was a trustee of Princeton Seminary during the conflict later in the 1920s and served as vice-moderator of the General Assembly under his college classmate, Charles Erdman.

At age fifty-three, *John H. DeWitt* had just been appointed a judge on the Tennessee Court of Appeals in 1925. The son of a prominent Presbyterian minister, he attended Vanderbilt University and Columbia College of Law in Washington, D.C., and was an elder of Hillsboro Presbyterian Church in Nashville for thirty years. DeWitt was president of the Tennessee Historical Association and chaired the Judicial Commission of the Presbyterian Church in 1923.

Cheesman A. Herrick, fifty-seven years old in 1925, had been president of Girard College in Philadelphia for fifteen years. A graduate of the Wharton School of the University of Pennsylvania, from which he received a Ph.D. degree, Herrick had served the Presbyterian Church as an elder of Arch Street Presbyterian Church in Philadelphia, as a member of the Board of Foreign Missions, and as vice-moderator of the General Assembly.

The other three secular professionals played less prominent roles in the church, if not in the world. *Nelson Loomis,* the general solicitor (that is, chief attorney) of the Union Pacific Railroad in Omaha, Nebraska, had served on the church's Layman's Council and had supported the New Era Movement. *Edward Duffield* was the president of the Prudential Insurance Company. *Nathan Moore,* who had descended from a long line of Presbyterian ministers in Pennsylvania and served as elder and organist in his own church, was a prominent Chicago attorney.[5]

Robert Speer was the most eminent churchman among the ruling elders on the Special Commission. At fifty-seven, Speer was in the middle of a forty-year term as the senior secretary of the church's Board of Foreign Missions. The son of a Pennsylvania congressman, Speer was raised in a deeply Presbyterian home. After graduating from Andover, he went to Princeton University, where he was a leader of the Young Men's Christian Association and the missionary Student Volunteer Movement, as well as a varsity athlete, editor of the college newspaper, and valedictorian. He attended Princeton Seminary but left before graduation to work for the Board of Foreign Missions. Years later, he returned as president of the board of trustees of Princeton Seminary, where the library is named for him.[6] Speer also was president of the Federal Council of Churches.

The final participant in the work of the Special Commission of 1925 was its secretary, Stated Clerk *Lewis Mudge*. At age sixty, Mudge was completing the first of three five-year terms as the elected administrator of the denomination. Descended from a long line of ministers, he attended Princeton University, and at Princeton Seminary he roomed with Robert Speer. He was pastor of Pine Street Presbyterian Church in Harrisburg, Pennsylvania, when first elected Stated Clerk in 1921. A trustee of (Presbyterian) Wilson College and Princeton Seminary, he was elected moderator in 1931.

THE WORK OF THE SPECIAL COMMISSION

The Special Commission was created at the General Assembly in June 1925 and was to bring in its report at the next General Assembly in June 1926. The members met four times in the intervening year: in September to organize committees; in December to consider the reports of these subgroups; in March to consider a draft report; and in late May, just before the assembly, to consider the final report. The body submitted its unanimous report to the General Assembly of 1926 and asked to be continued for a second year to present final recommendations to the General Assembly of 1927.

Of the five committees, the two most important for subsequent events would deal with the "causes of unrest and the possibilities of relief" and with "constitutional procedures." The causes committee, assisted by another on "historical background," had the crucial task of defining what the problem was that the commission was trying to solve. It consisted of Robert Speer,

William O. Thompson, and Edgar Work. The constitution committee had the complementary task of deciding how the problem could be dealt with *within* the order of the Presbyterian Church, a central value to denominationally-oriented loyalists. This committee was composed of lawyer Nelson Loomis, Judge John DeWitt, and Mark Matthews, who was a lawyer as well as a pastor.

The placement of Speer and Matthews is most important. While there were no liberals on the commission, Speer was probably its broadest, most ecumenically minded, and least denominational member.[7] As the undisputed leader of Presbyterian foreign missions, Speer would become the target of conservative attacks in the 1930s over "modernism" in the mission field. Matthews, on the other hand, was the commission's most conservative member, an avowed and militant fundamentalist who was sent by his presbytery to the General Assembly a record twenty times in thirty-eight years, to "save the Church from the Modernists."[8] Whether he came down on the side of the ideologically-oriented conservatives or the institutionally-oriented loyalists would shape the conservatives' course in the church. Matthews was placed (in his absence) on the committee that would face the issue raised in the "Auburn Affirmation": whether the five points had been promulgated in a constitutional manner.[9]

At its second meeting, in December, the commission invited conservative leaders Clarence Macartney and J. Gresham Machen and liberal leaders Henry Sloane Coffin and William Adams Brown to address the group in individual sessions. The commission received several other testimonials and petitions, both written and oral, including a presentation by the "Committee on Protestant Liberties in the Presbyterian Church," composed by the authors of the Auburn Affirmation and some of their supporters.

The causes committee faced two clearly different conceptions of the nature of the problem in the church. The conservatives maintained that the cause of unrest was that there was a naturalistic liberal party in the church that was not Christian, which was being tolerated by the sleeping majority of the church. The conservative solution was to make the Presbyterian Church take a stand on the essentials of Christian doctrine, thereby driving the liberals out. This was the strategy behind the "five points."[10] The liberals, on the other hand, maintained that there always had been tolerance of diversity of opinion in the Presbyterian Church, and that the problem was the result of unconstitutional efforts by dogmatic conservatives to make everyone toe their line. This was the rationale behind the "Auburn Affirmation."

The "causes of unrest" committee agreed partially with each side. It held, with the conservatives, that the real issues in the conflict concerned different views of the Bible and the Virgin Birth of Christ. With the liberals, though, the committee agreed that another real issue concerned the authority of the General Assembly to issue doctrinal deliverances, especially as they affected the ordination of ministers.[11] Against the conservative vision, the report stated flatly that no naturalistic, Jesus-is-merely-a-good-man party existed in the Presbyterian Church.[12]

The causes committee took a distinctly centrist approach to what it viewed as the real issues. Whereas the liberals and conservatives thought the fight in the church was a substantive disagreement between two sides, the loyalist causes committee thought the problems arose because some were certain about the church's traditional doctrines while others were unsure, and they urged that those "whose minds are clear and definite may well exercise for-bearance and charity toward those who are less able to affirm their faith in specific doctrines."[13] On the Virgin Birth issue, the committee claimed to speak for "a third party of large force in the church" which believed in the doctrine and would not debate it further, but which thought that, if "there be rever-ent men among us, whose response is not clear on this point, let the church resolve that it will not harry them."[14] This is the kind of view that would lead Machen, whose particular specialty was the Virgin Birth, to become furiously exasperated over loyalist "indifferentism."

Robert Speer summed up the loyalist view of the Presbyterian church in the concluding section of the report. He wrote: "[T]he history of our church . . . has been a history of union, then division, then reunion. And unless we now face a new and different type of divergence we can only escape the principle of constitutional comprehension and of the union of hearts, in spite of divergence, by escaping from our whole history as a church."[15] As the preceding section of the report had made clear, the committee did not think, as the conservatives did, that a "new and different type of divergence" existed in the church. The loyal-ist position was that the church could solve its problems in the traditional way, by "constitutional comprehension" and the "union of hearts."

The constitutional procedures committee also took a loyalist, denominational view. Addressing the central issue in the five points/Auburn Affirmation dispute, the committee held: "[I]t seems like trifling with sacred things to chance the fate of fundamental religious beliefs upon a mere vote of the General Assembly. An open and avowed change in the Constitution cannot be brought about without following a procedure which insures most careful consideration and action by the Presbyteries."[16] The committee affirmed the authority of presbyteries, not the General Assembly, in deciding the qualifications of ministerial candidates. Most remarkable, from a committee of which Mark Matthews was a member, was the claim that "[i]n every presbytery there must be ministers who represent both schools of thought—the strict constructionist and the liberal constructionist." Modernists and fundamentalists were urged to try to agree on accepting ministerial candidates.[17]

At the third meeting, in March, a draft of the whole report was considered. The draft was divided into three sections: "Causes of Unrest"; "On Tolerance"; and "On Constitutional Questions." The critical "causes of unrest" section was given to Robert Speer and Mark Matthews to review. By the end of that meeting, the commission had agreed on its report.[18]

The "Report of the Special Commission of 1925" to the General Assembly of 1926 clearly articulated the loyalist, denominationally-oriented position that "constitutional comprehension" and "union of hearts" always had been and ought to continue being the Presbyterian way of settling disputes. The members wrote:

> The principle of toleration when rightly conceived and frankly and fairly applied is as truly a part of our constitution as are any of the doctrines stated in that instrument. . . . Toleration as a principle applicable within the Presbyterian Church refers to an attitude and a practice according to which the status of a minister or other ordained officer, is acknowledged and fellowship is extended to him, even though he may hold some views that are individual on points not regarded as essential to the system of faith which the Church professes. Presbyterianism is a great body of belief, but it is more than a belief; it is also a tradition, a controlling sentiment. The ties which bind us to it are not of the mind only; they are ties of the heart as well. There are people who, despite variant opinions, can never be at home in any other communion. They were born into the Presbyterian Church. They love its name, its order and its great distinctive teachings. In its fellowship they have a precious inheritance from their forebears. Their hearts bow at its altars and cherish a just pride in its noble his-

tory. Attitudes and sentiments like these are treasures which should not be undervalued hastily nor cast aside lightly. A sound policy of constitutional toleration is designed to conserve such assets whenever it is possible to do so without endangering the basic positions of the Church.[19]

The commission proclaimed toleration in the church in a way that keeps the authority of the constitution foremost. More than defending toleration, though, the Special Commission report eloquently expressed the loyalists' devotion to the Presbyterian Church itself.

When the General Assembly of 1926 embraced this tolerant and constitutional understanding of the Presbyterian Church, the tide turned in favor of pluralism in the church.

The General Assembly's adoption of the Special Commission report is still being misinterpreted. The assembly's conclusion that it could not change the constitution of the church to define "essential and necessary articles" without the concurrence of the presbyteries is taken by some to mean that the church thinks it cannot change its constitution *at all*. This is like saying that, since Congress cannot amend the United States Constitution without the concurrence of the states, the Constitution cannot be amended at all. This similarity is not at all coincidental, as the constitutions of both the Presbyterian Church and the United States were created at the same time.[20]

The General Assembly of 1927 unequivocally demonstrated its enthusiasm for moderation when by acclamation it elected as its moderator Robert Speer. Speer's vision shines through the commission report. When the assembly accepted the extended commission's final report, which sorted out some organizational matters left undecided the previous year, the loyalist triumph was sealed.

Chapter 11

PRINCETON AND UNION:
THE DIALOGUE OF PLURALISM

*T*he Theological Seminary of the Presbyterian Church in the U.S.A. at Princeton, New Jersey, and the Union Theological Seminary in New York are institutions at the center of this story of pluralism in the Presbyterian Church. In part, this is so because the events that frame the tale were the trial of a Union professor and the trial of a Princeton professor. In a more important sense, however, the struggle in the Presbyterian Church from the 1890s to the 1930s was a dialogue between ideas represented by Princeton and Union. The Presbyterian Church is not only a faith or a body of individuals, but also an organization in which specific institutions play central roles. In the Presbyterian Church in the U.S.A. in this period, these central institutional roles were played mainly by Princeton Seminary and Union Seminary.

The parallel and intertwined histories of Princeton Seminary and Union Seminary represent a dialogue between two contrasting positions on pluralism within the Church at large and, more specifically, within the Presbyterian Church. At issue is not simply whether there exists diversity within the Church, but whether this diversity is legitimate or even beneficial. In other words, the dialogue of pluralism is not about the *fact* of diversity but is, rather, about an *ideology justifying diversity*. The dialogue between Princeton and Union began early in the nineteenth century and climaxed in the early decades of the twentieth century. Then, by quite different paths, Princeton and Union converged, at least temporarily, upon a common pluralist position.

Princeton was Presbyterian and intellectual from the beginning, while Union was Puritan and practical from the beginning. In the late nineteenth century, Princeton placed increasing emphasis upon orderly religious belief, based on the Bible and Common Sense philosophy. From this stance emerged the "right wing" of the Presbyterian Church, which pointed toward a non-denominational fundamentalism. In the late nineteenth century, Union placed increasing emphasis upon vital religious experience, based on Christian tradition and historicist philosophy. From this stance emerged the "left wing" of the Presbyterian Church, which pointed toward a non-Christian humanism. These two conceptions of Christianity competed with one another in the Presbyterian Church and in much of American religion. In the 1930s, after decades of struggle, both Princeton and Union made important openings toward a "neo-orthodox" theology that attempted to transcend this conflict.[1]

PRINCETON THEOLOGICAL SEMINARY

Princeton Seminary was founded in 1812 by the General Assembly of the Presbyterian Church; Archibald Alexander was its first professor.[2] The seminary was independent of the College of New Jersey (the future Princeton University) but had close relations with it. Alexander taught a "rational theology": a *theology* to answer the naturalistic use of reason by Enlightenment thinkers, but *rational* to balance the emphasis upon subjective experience in the pietistic revivals. The curriculum rested upon Scottish Common Sense philosophy, which answered the skepticism of Hume by championing the reliability of the "common sense" of humanity in knowing "self-evident truths."[3] By 1836, the year of the Old School–New School split in the Presbyterian Church, Alexander had been joined on the faculty by Samuel Miller and Charles Hodge. Hodge was to become the dominant figure in the "Princeton Theology," but the influence of Alexander, Hodge's teacher, pervaded the institution for more than a century.[4]

In order for the Princetonians to appeal to common sense—common across all ages and cultures—they had to insist on definite and unchanging standards of the truths established by this common sense. The pillars of Princeton Theology, therefore, were an unchanging history, an inerrant Bible, and strict adherence to ecclesiastical distinctives. With this theological position, it is not surprising that Princeton Seminary not only resisted diversity and change in the Church, but also made intransigence a point of honor.[5]

Alexander viewed America's religious diversity as so many deviations from the true Church. Even worse than a diversity of denominations in society, in

Alexander's view, was theological diversity *within* the Church, within his own denomination. When, in 1801, the General Assembly sent Alexander to bear a "Plan of Union" to the New England Congregationalists, he was shocked by the Congregationalists' acceptance of what he saw as heretics within the fold. Alexander's Princeton successors shared his exclusive ecclesiology and skepticism of church union.[6]

The first three professors of Princeton Seminary—Archibald Alexander, Samuel Miller, and Charles Hodge—were very involved in the life of the denomination. Each had been a pastor and had served Presbyterian Church committees and agencies. Alexander himself had been the moderator of the General Assembly of 1807. In the "schools" split in 1836, Alexander voted with the Old School to abrogate the Plan of Union, which he had carried to the Congregationalists three decades before. By then, however, he had retired, and he took little part in the controversy.

Charles Hodge became the leading intellectual light of the Old School and made Princeton the standard Old School institution. He was one of the few die-hards opposing the 1869 reunion of the northern schools.[7] According to his son and Princeton successor Archibald Alexander Hodge, Charles Hodge

> never believed or said that his New School brethren were the holders or teachers of heresy. He did not pretend to judge or mistrust their orthodoxy. He simply maintained that as a historical fact those brethren had always, and did [at the reunion], maintain and practice a principle and latitude of toleration different from that of the Old School. He held that if not for themselves, yet for others they interpreted the formula of subscription to our doctrinal standards in a different sense, or at least a different spirit; that even if hereafter the Old School should produce all the heretics, the New School division of the New Church would provide all their principal and most influential defenders, or excusers.[8]

Intolerance of tolerance was a characteristic Princeton position.

In 1872, Charles Hodge made the notorious statement, "I am not afraid to say that a new idea never originated in this Seminary."[9] Princeton saw its mission as giving technical training in the "faith once delivered to the saints," as embodied in the Westminster Confession and Catechisms. Princeton theology became increasingly dry, theoretical, and "rationalistic." This was not a secular or Enlightenment kind of rationalism, but a "science of the Bible," which, citing Francis Bacon as its philosophical authority, was empirical without being historical.[10]

At Princeton, the standard text for many years was not Calvin's *Institutes* but the work of a second-generation "scholastic" Calvinist: *Institutio Theologiae Elencticae,* by Francis Turretine. It was partly from Turretine that Princeton scholars developed their distinctive doctrine of the inspiration of the Bible. The Princeton theory was that the Bible was "verbally inspired," that is, that every word was inspired by God.

There is an important dispute about terminology. Christian critics of the Princeton position, such as Charles Briggs, maintain that, while the Bible has been preserved from error in essential matters of faith and practice, it is not inerrant in all matters. Such critics call their own theory "plenary inspiration" (that the Bible is generally inspired in concepts), as distinguished from the fundamentalist Princeton theory of "verbal inspiration" (inspired in every word). Princeton apologists, on the other hand, reject this distinction, maintaining that there can be no inspiration in concepts if there is error in words. They often use "plenary" and "verbal" interchangeably.

While not claiming that Scripture was mechanically dictated, the Princetonians did think that the human authors had been guided directly by God and kept free from any error. Since critics of this theory (such as Charles Briggs) were quick to point out that today's Scriptural text contains inconsistencies and apparent errors, the Princeton apologists relied on the idea that the "original autographs" of Scripture, the actual manuscripts written by their human authors, were inerrant, so that errors now apparent must have appeared in copying. Since the original autographs presumably are lost forever, the theory is not falsifiable. This claim, according to critics of the Princeton position, undermines the authority of the Bible that we have today.[11]

While Charles Hodge had a "high" view of Biblical inspiration, the full "inerrantist" position was developed by his successors, A. A. Hodge and Benjamin Breckenridge Warfield. Warfield, an eminent scholar who became the leader of the faculty in the 1880s and 1890s, insisted that rigorous intellectual training was more important for a Presbyterian minister than "practical" courses. Warfield was not active in the denomination and rarely left Princeton, in part due to his wife's long-standing poor health.[12] After the turn of the century, there was an increased demand, especially from the students, that Princeton offer more practical training. Warfield thought that the curriculum was "scientifically complete" and fought any changes.[13] The directors overruled Warfield and the faculty majority and in 1905 hired pastor Charles Erdman for a new chair in English Bible.[14]

When the directors sought a new seminary president in 1913, the faculty supported Warfield.[15] Instead, however, the board called one of its own members, J. Ross Stevenson, a pastor with broad Presbyterian experience. Sylvester Beach, secretary of the board of directors, wrote to Stevenson: "But my chief joy in your coming is the assurance that it means a new and great epoch in our Seminary's history. . . . The first prerequisite is a headship in the Seminary who knows and understands the practical problems of our day not less than the theological issues."[16] The Princeton faculty had become very ingrown; at the turn of the century, all but one of the professors were Princeton graduates. Stevenson not only was a graduate of the denomination's McCormick Seminary in Chicago, but also he had taught there before returning to the pastorate. His first initiative as president was to strengthen the practical part of the curriculum, at the expense of the theoretical, and allow students some electives. Such changes were antithetical to Warfield's conception of ministerial training as complete intellectual armor. Warfield refused to give academic credit for these new courses and stopped attending faculty meetings.[17]

By this time, J. Gresham Machen had joined the faculty. Machen eventually would become the leader of the conservatives who opposed modernism and "indifferentism" in the seminary and in Christianity at large. Machen saw himself as Warfield's successor as the defender of "Old Princeton." In a rare compromise, however, Machen voted against Warfield in this early curriculum fight, in order to save the Greek requirement.[18]

In the struggle for Princeton Seminary in the 1920s, the practical and denominational group allied with President Stevenson defeated the intellectual and ideological group allied with Machen. After the reorganization of the seminary in 1929, Machen led an exodus to create Westminster Theological Seminary in Philadelphia; in 1936 the Westminster group formed the nucleus of a Machen-led schism that created today's Orthodox Presbyterian Church. While these events to some extent constituted a defeat for the Common Sense philosophy and the theological tradition associated with it, it was not a victory for historicism or any other competing philosophy at Princeton. Stevenson insisted that there was and would be no change in the doctrinal foundation of Princeton Seminary, and this generally proved to be the case during his term.[19]

In 1936, Stevenson retired and was succeeded by John Mackay. With the withdrawal of the young conservatives, such as Machen, in 1929 and the retirement of the old ones, such as C. W. Hodge, in 1934, there was an opening for a new direction for Princeton. Mackay brought in representatives of the European "crisis theology" or "neo-orthodoxy" of Karl Barth, which attempted to transcend the old battle between liberals and conservatives. Barth's early associate, Emil Brunner, began teaching at Princeton on a regular basis, and Elmer Homrighausen joined the faculty. Although Barthians were as critical of liberal theology as the Machen-type conservatives were, the latter group blasted the new movement, especially because it accepted the historical-critical approach to the Bible.[20]

It is tempting to think that "Princeton Theology" ended at Princeton in 1929 or perhaps 1936. This is the view of the seminary Machen founded in 1929, Westminster of Philadelphia, which views itself as the true successor of "old" Princeton.[21] It is also tempting to see strong continuity in Princeton's thought, from its founding until then. One student of the "Princeton apologetic" wrote: "From the day in 1812 when Archibald Alexander became the first and only professor of the Seminary to the decease of Caspar Wistar Hodge, Jr., in 1934, there was the greatest unanimity of thought as regards the fundamental theological tenets."[22]

Neither of these views, however, is correct. In spite of itself, the thought of Princeton Seminary *did* develop and change, did have a history of its own. The theology that Machen carried to Westminster represented only certain aspects of the Princeton tradition, while those who remained at Princeton after 1929 retained other strands of that tradition.[23] Later events showed that the loyalists had underestimated the threat of liberalism; and, to be sure, Princeton changed more than President Stevenson thought it would. Yet Princeton Seminary no more became a liberal institution after Machen left than it had been a fundamentalist institution before.

The struggle in Princeton Seminary had not made it liberal, but it had broken the "ideal of intransigence" that had grown up there. The new majority of the faculty now became free to represent the whole church, becoming leaders of the denomination as they had not been during the years of Princeton's "opposition." In particular, the presidents of Princeton Seminary after the 1930s emerged as leaders of the ecumenical movement—as the presidents of Union Seminary already had been.[24]

There is one respect in which the self-conscious conservatism of the Princeton Theology, from Charles Hodge to J. Gresham Machen, was an ironic failure. The Princetonians' steadfast resistance to acknowledging any historical development and cultural influence in Scripture and Calvinist theology blinded them to the way in which they *themselves* constituted a developing historical tradition which was influenced by the surrounding culture. Union professor Charles Briggs subjected the "Princeton Theology" to a scathing attack on just this point in *Whither?*[25] In the decades after the 1869 reunion, this critique grew more pointed; despite sixty years of united development in the church and (unacknowledged) doctrinal innovation in the seminary, J. Gresham Machen still thought that Princeton was fighting for an Old School that before his birth had ceased to exist.

UNION THEOLOGICAL SEMINARY

In the movement toward pluralism in the church—that is, toward an *ideology* justifying theological diversity—Union Theological Seminary was a pioneer. The thought of Union Seminary developed from the 1890s to the 1930s, as had that of Princeton Seminary; unlike Princeton, however, Union made a virtue of this development. Under the banner of "progress," Union developed a line of Christian thought that emphasized the experience and practice of religion. The optimism that fueled this activist Christianity was undermined by World War I, creating an opening in the 1930s for a new turn in Union's thought. Therefore, like Princeton but for opposite reasons, Union explored a "neo-orthodox" theology that attempted to transcend—and criticize—the conservatism and liberalism which had gone before.

The founders of Union Seminary in 1836 were "all Presbyterians, . . . but 'ecumenical' Presbyterians, foremost in interdenominational organizations and eager for the co-operation of all Christians in the work of the kingdom of God." The Union charter required that "equal privileges of admission and instruction, . . . shall be allowed to students of every denomination of Christians."[26] Founded just before the New School–Old School schism, Union celebrated the Plan of Union between the Presbyterians and Congregationalists. When the Old School branch repudiated that merger, Union stood off from formal denominational connections, although it was, in effect, the leading New School Presbyterian seminary. Union enthusiastically supported the

Presbyterian reunion of 1869 and at that time established a partial connection with the Presbyterian General Assembly.

Union was not merely a liberal seminary in which a variety of views were tolerated and given free rein, but a pluralist seminary in which diversity was actively sought. Almost all the first directors and professors, for example, were New School Presbyterians, but they elected Henry White, an Old School man, professor of systematic theology. The "seminary's liberalism," Henry Sloane Coffin argued, "involved unity in loyalty to truth, and to Jesus Christ as the Truth, while expecting wide diversities in theological interpretation, in social outlook and in ecclesiastical opinions." To this end, Union deliberately filled vacancies with those who did not "duplicate" the views of others.[27]

When Union Seminary's Professor Charles A. Briggs was suspended from the ministry of the Presbyterian Church in 1893, Union cut its formal ties to the Presbyterian Church, becoming nondenominational in control. There was, however, some sentiment that Briggs should leave the seminary, but President Thomas Hastings insisted that he stay, contending, presciently, that Briggs would be needed to moderate the *really* radical men on the faculty.[28] In 1907, only the personal plea of his friend President Francis Brown kept Briggs from bringing his colleague and former student, Arthur McGiffert, before the board for attacking the historical credibility of the virgin birth of Christ.[29] Briggs, in the developing Union tradition, devoted the end of his career to concrete plans for church union.[30]

In the decade after the separation of the seminary from the Presbyterian General Assembly, Union broadened its constituency and outlook. An attempted boycott of the seminary by certain presbyteries meant a small reduction in the number of Presbyterian students, but these were more than made up for by more liberal denominations, especially the Congregationalists, strengthening the already strong ties between Union and the New England churches. In 1904, after Briggs had joined the Episcopal Church (1898) and McGiffert, the Congregationalist (1900), faculty members no longer were required to subscribe to the Westminster Confession, but only to the preamble to the seminary charter. This allowed non-Presbyterians to join the faculty, and in 1909 George Coe, a Methodist, came as professor of Christian Education. Other non-Presbyterians followed, and the faculty soon represented most of mainline Protestantism.[31] The student body likewise diversified, until about twenty denominations (including Unitarians) were represented. In

1906, then, any "accredited" student could be admitted, with or without church membership. Union became a model of liberal thought and academic freedom among seminaries.[32]

The hallmark of liberal theology was the emphasis on religious experience, on religion as lived. This stance suggested that there was a generic "experience" common to all religions—an idea that undermined devotion to any particular denomination and, in its stead, inspired interest in religious unity. This common religious experience was approached at Union in the 1890s (following James Fraser's *The Golden Bough*) through the study of primitive cultures, and in the 1900s (from William James's *Varieties of Religious Experience*) through psychology. "Then, like a gust of fresh air blowing into a stuffy room, came Walter Rauschenbusch's *Christianity and the Social Crisis*," the manifesto of the pandenominational Social Gospel, which became the hot topic in the decade before World War I. These interests diminished commitment to worship and service to the church. This made Union's board uneasy, and when President Francis Brown died, they sought a pastor to replace him. After several unsuccessful attempts, however, they agreed to the faculty's wishes for a scholar, naming Arthur McGiffert president in 1917.[33]

McGiffert, like Briggs, had been charged with heresy and forced out of the Presbyterian Church in the 1890s. He was a radical, but Christian, scholar, devoted to the intellectual development of students but little interested in making pastors or church leaders. The seminary had reached its scholarly pinnacle at the time of McGiffert's retirement in 1925.[34] Simultaneously, however, in the "religious depression" after World War I, chapel services were poorly attended, and McGiffert himself, according to a student, had "little sense for worship." Religious education and philosophy of religion were the dominant interests of students. For this reason, upon McGiffert's retirement, the board was determined to have a pastor as president and selected Henry Sloane Coffin.[35]

Coffin was a 1900 graduate of Union and had been teaching there since 1904, while simultaneously serving as pastor of the Madison Avenue Presbyterian Church. President of Union from 1926 until 1945, Coffin called himself a "liberal evangelical" and introduced a new evangelical emphasis into the seminary.[36] As a teenager he had observed the Briggs trial (his father was legal counsel to Union Seminary), an event that indelibly impressed upon Coffin the necessity of freedom and tolerance in the church.[37] Coffin was co-author of the "Auburn Affirmation," and when Auburn Seminary merged with Union in 1939, Coffin welcomed the affirmation's co-author, Robert Hastings Nichols, to the Union faculty. Coffin was an acknowledged leader of the liberal party and an active Presbyterian, answering conservative attacks and moderating liberal reaction.[38] For a time during the fundamentalist-modernist controversy in the Presbyterian Church, it appeared that the liberals, rather than Machen and the conservatives, might be the ones to withdraw; but Coffin remained accommodating—and remained in the church. Crowning this success, in 1943 Henry Sloane Coffin was elected moderator of the General Assembly of the Presbyterian Church.[39]

One other member of the Union faculty who deserves special mention is William Adams Brown. Brown was descended from two long-time Union families and graduated from the seminary in 1890, having studied under Briggs. In 1892 he joined the faculty, eventually succeeding the conservative W. G. T. Shedd in the theology chair.[40] His *Christian Theology in Outline* (1906) was one of the most widely used textbooks of liberal theology. He was active in the faculty until 1936, and in the Presbyterian Church until his death in 1943. Brown was an "evangelical liberal"—in contrast to the "liberal evangelical" Coffin—and was "one of the most influential and widely read American theologians of his time."[41]

Union Seminary became a leading center of liberal Protestant theology. In 1936, an eminent Union graduate and Coffin's successor as president, Henry Pitney Van Dusen, summarized "the spirit of the new theology and its governing principles" as "continuity with the past, the reinterpretation of old doctrines in new language, the absolute authority and sufficiency of Christian experience, loyalty to the Bible, uncertainty of the final results of biblical criticism, the centrality of the living Christ, the Christologizing of all other doctrines, the obligation to renovate society, insistence upon the supernatural character of Christian redemption, expectant optimism toward the immediate future."[42] This dense statement summarizes the distinctive teachings of Union in this period. The doctrine of continuity and the practice of reinterpretation were the most powerful aspects of the new theology—and the most troublesome.

"Continuity" of past and present, of natural and supernatural, of Christian and non-Christian, was the foundation of that tolerance, freedom of inquiry, and ecumenical spirit in which Union took the lead. The theories of "evolution" and "immanence" so important in the nineteenth century clearly lie behind the notion of continuity, and the latter "bred a new and more sympathetic *tolerance toward other religions, and toward no religion.*"[43] The danger of continuity for the Church is that such tolerance could undermine the belief in the truth and value of the distinctive features of Christianity. This was the conclusion drawn by Harvard's William Hocking and his committee in *Re-Thinking Missions,* which was the catalyst for the Presbyterian missions crisis that led to Machen's schism.

"Reinterpretation" was the basis for Union's attempted reconciliation between Christianity and modern culture; the danger was of reinterpreting away that which gave Christianity its unique power. Reinterpretation was the way in which liberal evangelicalism, unlike other kinds of liberalism, stayed within the church, because it allowed liberal Christians to preserve the "truths of the ancient faith" by translating them into modern language. In a widely-used formula, Union's famous preacher Harry Emerson Fosdick described this as proclaiming "abiding experiences in changing categories."[44]

For those who came to Union thinking that one had to choose between Christianity and free, modern culture, reinterpretation was a liberation. A student of William Adams Brown expresses the sense that the reinterpreters had of saving Christianity for the modern age: "In the first decade of the twentieth century we theological students were seeking a new language for our preaching so that we could translate the doctrinal expressions of the past for the benefit of thinking people inside the Church and those who had been estranged from it. This was a permanent gain, for after one had learned to separate the truth from a particular expression of it, he could ever after adapt himself to changing needs."[45] By reinterpreting Christian faith in this way, the liberal evangelicalism of Union did remain within the church, even if it stretched doctrinal boundaries. Even "evangelical liberals," such as William Adams Brown, Harry Emerson Fosdick, and Eugene Lyman (another influential Union professor) did not become full-blown modernists, as did, for example, William E. Hocking of Harvard, D. C. Macintosh of Yale, or Shailer Matthews of the University of Chicago.[46]

As a consequence of its Broad Church pluralism, every prominent member of the Union faculty (except McGiffert) was an ecumenical leader. Henry Boynton Smith, the eminent New School theologian of the mid-nineteenth century, was the "hero of the reunion" between the New and Old schools.

Philip Schaff was very active in the international cooperative work of the Reformed Churches.[47] Charles Briggs devoted the last decades of his life to church union. William Adams Brown was a "foremost leader in the Ecumenical Movement."[48] Harry Emerson Fosdick, as pastor of the Park Avenue Baptist Church, insisted that his congregation give up all sectarian restrictions on membership and serve an inclusive constituency.[49] Henry Sloane Coffin was a passionate ecumenist who summed up the whole Union attitude this way: "Deep in the hearts of the founders of Union Seminary and of those who have led and taught in it throughout the years was the passionate desire for the ending of denominational divisions in the Church of Christ and the unifying of all her people for the achievement of the ends set before her by her divine Head."[50]

By the time Henry Pitney Van Dusen wrote "The Liberal Movement in Theology" in 1936, the weakness of the liberal theology on certain points had created an opening for a new start, a "neo-orthodoxy."[51] The center of this new development at Union was Reinhold Niebuhr. Niebuhr came to the seminary in 1928 to teach Christian ethics. He ran for city office on the Socialist ticket, annoying the board. Even more difficult, however, was that

> Shortly his views changed and he became profoundly interested in theology, and developed his own variety of Neo-Orthodoxy. This was a test of the genuineness and extent of the Seminary's liberalism, for his views contravened those taught at the time by Professors W. A. Brown and E. W. Lyman, and were antagonistic to those of former President McGiffert in which many of the alumni and Faculty had been trained. Happily the liberalism of the Seminary was so stalwart that Niebuhr was listened to and after a short while became a most influential factor.[52]

The distinctive emphasis of this American neo-orthodoxy, or "Christian realism," was a renewed appreciation of the problem of sin in human affairs, and of the unique role of the Church in bringing the unwelcome news of sin and the good news of the gospel. These same ideas were being considered in Princeton Seminary at the same time, and, in fact, Emil Brunner, who brought European "neo-orthodoxy" to Princeton, had studied at Union.[53]

The pluralism of Union Seminary depended on the liberal view of theology. The historicist, critical study of the Bible, the Church, and the Christian tradition undermined any sense that the received tradition was absolute. To see developing religious experience as what was truly valuable in Christianity undermined the sense of the permanence of any previous stage. The diversity of expressions of religious experience is transformed from a scandal to a treasure for the Church. Liberal theology thus made pluralism plausible.

PLURALISM AT PRINCETON AND UNION

Pluralism is a challenging doctrine for any corporate body which values orthodoxy. In order to fit into any church, pluralism would need to be domesticated, connected with traditional doctrines and practices. At Union Seminary, this domestication was aided by several factors, factors absent from Princeton Seminary. Union developed a liberalism which owed much to the traditions of the New England churches and the American universities, at the same time that Princeton was moving away from these influences. In contrast, the kind of liberalism that Princeton fought against—and imagined that Union represented—was based on the radical traditions of European political parties and continental universities.

One way in which Union's pluralism was legitimated was through a closer tie between the seminary and the university. Union originally was located downtown in New York City, and at that time it had close relations with New York University and Columbia University. Charles Briggs in his later years often proposed the idea of making Union into a "theological university," and for a time the seminary ran a graduate department, consisting mostly of Briggs himself. A more satisfactory—and permanent—solution to the problem of advanced scholarship in the seminary was provided in 1910, when Union Seminary moved to its present location on Broadway across from Columbia University. The two institutions, though formally independent, developed close ties and a joint graduate program.[54]

Princeton Seminary, on the other hand, always has been next door to Princeton University, but it long had kept its distance intellectually. The seminary was founded because of dissatisfaction in the Presbyterian Church with the teaching of the university.[55] Although many ties bound the two institutions together, the strain increased in the twentieth century between the exclusivist conservatism of the seminary and the "rationalism" of the university. In line with its self-conception as the keeper of the "faith once delivered to the saints,"

Princeton Seminary did not early embrace the idea of academic freedom that Union Seminary pioneered.

A more important way in which Union justified its doctrine of pluralism to the Presbyterian Church was by asserting that it was rooted in the New England theological tradition.[56] Since colonial times, New York Presbyterianism had been closer to New England thought than southern and western Presbyterianism had been; the latest developments in Congregationalist theology usually had their first Presbyterian hearing in New York.[57] When Union Seminary was a New School institution in the mid-nineteenth century, it staked out a position for itself between the liberal Calvinism of New England and the conservative Calvinism of Princeton.[58] Many on the faculty then were former Congregationalists, as many on the later faculty would join or remain in the Congregational Church. Union understood its liberalism to be in this tradition.

Philip Schaff, for example, stated the Union position: "Our theological systems are but dim rays of the sun of truth which illuminates the universe. . . . Truth first, doctrine next, dogma last. . . . The Church must keep pace with civilization, adjust herself to the modern conditions of religious and political freedom, and accept established results of biblical and historical criticism, and natural science."[59]

Princeton, in the mid-nineteenth century, also saw the liberalism of Union as part of the liberal New England theology, the part it thought too liberal to be Calvinist.[60] By the end of the nineteenth century, however, some Princetonians began to see Union's liberalism not as the extension of an American tradition, but as the importation of a foreign, German radicalism. J. Gresham Machen represents the extreme of this view, and a good case can be made that his passionate attacks on "liberalism" in America really were fired by his fear of the radicalism that he saw in German religious thought.[61] He expressed his suspicions thus:

> But I fear the Union Seminary men with their deceitful phrases, and their contempt for the Christian faith, will go quite unmolested. . . . The mass of the Church here is still conservative—but conservative in an ignorant, non-polemic, sweetness-and-light kind of way which is just meat for the wolves. . . . [M]en like McGiffert and William Adams Brown at Union Seminary are perfectly clear about the enormous gulf that separates their

religion from orthodox Protestantism. . . . Why do they try to deceive simple-minded people in the Church? There is the real ground for my quarrel with them.[62]

The scholars of Union Seminary had been deeply influenced by their training in Germany—but so had the scholars of Princeton Seminary. In the nineteenth and early twentieth centuries, American religious scholars, liberal and conservative alike, were drawn to the German universities. Henry Boynton Smith, Union's theological luminary of the nineteenth century, studied in Germany, but so did Charles Hodge, his counterpart at Princeton. "Henry Smith was one of the first American theologians to venture deeply into the supposed dark forests of German philosophy and to return to his native country with his Reformed faith intact,"[63] whereas Charles Hodge's studies with the Schleiermacherians "awakened in him only a determined opposition."[64]

Many of the Princeton professors, both "majority" and "minority," had studied in Germany, and, as with Hodge, their experiences had inspired only opposition. B. B. Warfield had been sent by Charles Hodge to study in Germany in 1876, and afterwards often attacked "Ritschl-ite Rationalism," by which he meant principally the thought of Arthur McGiffert.[65] William Park Armstrong, Machen's best friend on the Princeton faculty, had studied in Germany with pleasure and had sent Machen there. Of the "minority," President J. Ross Stevenson also had studied in Berlin and had rejected the radicalism of what he heard there. He did not, however, join Machen in attributing German attitudes to American liberals.[66]

Of the Union professors who studied in Germany, a few may have been won over without reservation to a radical position. This most clearly was true for Arthur McGiffert, but a case could be made for including Eugene Lyman as well. McGiffert was a student of Harnack, "whom he resembled . . . in theological outlook."[67] Lyman had studied with Herrmann and Harnack at the end of the 1890s; he returned to Europe before World War I to study with Henri Bergson and Ernst Troeltsch.[68] Others at Union, however, while impressed by some of the extreme liberal scholars with whom they studied in Germany, were determined to remain evangelical Christians. Henry Boynton Smith was the pioneer in this "mediating" position, followed by his student Briggs. William Adams Brown also was in this camp; he studied in Berlin with Harnack and therefore was suspect to some conservatives, but when he was treated for heresy in 1911 for *The Old Theology and the New*, he was not found guilty.[69] This group saw itself as constructing a mediating position between the radicalism of German scholarship and the rigidity of American conservatism.

One particularly important strand of German thought was the spiritual but unorthodox Christianity of Albrecht Ritschl and, in the later generation, of the dominant representative of his tradition, Wilhelm Herrmann. Briggs, though a liberal on Biblical criticism, was opposed to the heterodoxies of Ritschlianism. On the later Union faculty, the quite liberal Eugene Lyman had studied with Herrmann, as had Henry Sloane Coffin, the leader of "liberal evangelicalism."[70] On the other hand, Machen also studied with Herrmann, who had a great effect on the American. Equally interesting, given the neo-orthodox turn at both Princeton and Union at the end of this tale, Karl Barth studied with Herrmann at about the same time that Machen did, calling him "*the* theological teacher of my student years." In fact, Marsden notes a number of strong parallels between Barth and Machen, as well as between Machen and those other outsider critics of northern liberal Protestantism in America, Reinhold Niebuhr and H. Richard Niebuhr.[71]

A third way in which Union domesticated its idea of pluralism was by sticking close to the mainstream in practical action. This may seem a peculiar contention to those who today picture Union as a "radical institution." It would be closer to the mark, however, to say, following a suggestion of long-time Union professor Robert Handy, that Union Seminary is an institution that contains radicals, among other types. This, of course, is what "pluralism" requires. The radicalism of the radicals gets attention, as in the celebrated 1940 case in which a dozen Union students refused to register for the draft. It should be remembered, however, that the vast majority of Union students *did* register for the draft. Reinhold Niebuhr, President Henry Sloane Coffin, and future President Henry Pitney Van Dusen were not isolationists in World War II, and it was they, not the Soviet apologist Harry Ward, who led the institution.[72]

Since the 1870s, most seminaries nationwide had been developing a more practical and pastoral curriculum. Union's curriculum in 1910 was in line with this development, while Princeton was still struggling with the issue. Robert L. Kelly's *Theological Education in America* shows that the Princeton curriculum in 1872 was like that of other seminaries; by 1895, those others were moving toward historical and practical studies; and by 1921, there had been big changes just about everywhere except at Princeton Seminary.[73] At Union, "the practical use of the English Bible ha[d] been recognized as a distinct branch of instruction . . . [since] 1894," whereas at Princeton it was not so recognized for another decade, and was still being fought over a decade after that.[74]

The histories of the two seminaries provides us with an unusual "natural experiment" that compares their different conceptions of practical and pastoral development. In both institutions, in the years around 1915 the governing board wanted to bring in a pastor as president to take the seminary in a new, more churchly direction. In both cases the faculty favored a scholar, while the board favored a pastor. At Union the faculty won (elevating McGiffert), whereas at Princeton it lost (Warfield losing to Stevenson), with acrimonious results.

However, Union later called a pastor as president without major trauma for the seminary. The difference is not due simply to the personalities of the two presidents, nor of the two faculties. Rather, the different results are due, at least in part, to basic differences in philosophy and even theology. The exclusivist majority on the Princeton faculty aimed to produce a church unified in an unchanging theology. Its members did not concern themselves deeply with the practical consequences at the congregation level that resulted from their intellectual work.[75] Union, on the other hand, even when it was most scholarly, accepted the historical development of Christianity and did not support an insistence on unchanging—or unified—thought. Moreover, no matter how intellectual it might be, Union was very concerned with its activities' practical consequences for the churches; under McGiffert, Union's homiletics department was unrivaled. It was from this homiletics department that Henry Sloane Coffin was called to the presidency in 1926.[76]

Finally, Union domesticated its conception of pluralism by enforcing, in effect, a practical and political unity as a counterweight to the seminary's deliberate intellectual diversity. Princeton, in contrast, insisted upon intellectual unity; but, as a counterweight, it allowed practical and political diversity. Each seminary—indeed, any institution—needs some area of agreement to hold the institution together, and an area of liberty to enable it to accommodate individual differences.

Princeton insisted upon intellectual unity among the faculty. Even the "minority" insisted upon unity in orthodoxy. The seminary further insisted that each member of the faculty have an official relationship with the Presbyterian Church in the U.S.A. What it did not insist upon was political unity, in either ecclesiastical or civil politics. When Machen and the majority broke with Princeton tradition and attempted to force a united position on church policy, the seminary split, and the Machen group withdrew.

Even Machen, however, did not attempt to enforce unity in civil politics; indeed, the subject seems not to have been spoken of in Princeton Seminary. Yet on this point Machen himself was at odds with most of the Presbyterian Church: he was a Democrat in a generally Republican church, a "wet" opponent of Prohibition in an ardently dry denomination, and an active libertarian, often involved in public opposition to reform movements in which other Presbyterians took leading roles.[77] Political unity was not sought at Princeton, and the attempt to impose it would have caused the carefully cultivated theological unity to crumble.

Union Seminary sought intellectual and ecclesiastical diversity. On that level, it was pluralist. Yet there was a liberal consensus in other spheres that seems to have allowed the institution to hold together. There were, to be sure, conservatives on the faculty, for these, like the radicals, were sought under the doctrine of pluralism. In addition to Henry White, the Old School man referred to above, there was W. G. T. Shedd, who opposed Briggs on the criticism of Scripture, and Ernest F. Scott, who ridiculed the Social Gospel and social science, favored by many at the seminary. There also were many liberals who found Niebuhr too conservative.[78] Yet there was a strong current in the seminary throughout this period that was liberal, ecumenical, and internationalist in civil and ecclesiastical politics.

The limits of Union's tolerance for diversity became obvious when, in an episode thoroughly uncharacteristic of Union Seminary, Thomas C. Hall was fired for his views on World War I. Hall was a tenured professor, who had studied in Germany (like several other members of the faculty) and had married a German woman. With the outbreak of the war in Europe, Hall publicly took the German side, even defending the sinking of the *Lusitania*—a stance which was extremely unpopular in the seminary and which brought criticism upon the institution from outside. In 1916, Hall took a leave of absence from the seminary to work with prisoners of war in Switzerland. After America's entry into the war, Hall asked for another leave to remain in Europe. In May 1917, the Union board refused to give him another leave, voting that, because in the judgment of the directors, Dr. Hall's attitude towards and his public expressions upon the moral issues in the war disqualify him from the occupation of the chair of Christian Ethics in the Seminary, therefore be it Resolved that in view of the fact that we believe that the usefulness of the Rev. Thomas C. Hall, D.D., as a teacher in this Seminary has been destroyed, we hereby terminate the relation heretofore existing between Dr. Hall and the Seminary.[79]

The liberal political consensus that operated at Union had been broken.

The man hired by the seminary to replace Thomas Hall was Harry Ward. There is some irony in this, because Ward became an ardent proponent of the Soviet Union, even in the Stalin era, and his "attitude towards and his public expressions upon the moral issues" of the 1920s and 1930s brought Union more grief than Thomas Hall's positions ever had. Yet it was not Ward who set the political consensus at the seminary; while Ward "became increasingly isolated from most of his Union colleagues," his realist opponent Reinhold Niebuhr "became the increasingly magnetic figure."[80]

Union Seminary developed a doctrine of pluralism, of the active search for diversity, and put this doctrine into practice in the seminary itself. In 1936, in the Centennial Sermon at Union, Henry Sloane Coffin said that one of the main outcomes of the Briggs affair was that "the Seminary was assisted by hostile brethren to a larger service—a mission under God to champion the freedom of Christian scholars, loyal to Christ, the one Head of the Church, to explore truth unafraid and to teach it frankly. This is the position of liberal evangelicalism—liberty in loyalty to the gospel of Christ."[81] In these same decades after the Briggs trial, Princeton Seminary pursued an opposite idea, that of increasing the unity and clarity of the theological teaching of the institution.

Union developed a self-consciously inclusive liberalism, while Princeton developed a self-consciously exclusive conservatism. After decades of tension between these two conceptions in the Presbyterian Church and in other American denominations, the struggle came to a head in the 1920s. Neither side won. In the Presbyterian Church, the liberal advocates of an inclusive church had learned enough from the *practice* of pluralism not to insist on the *ideology* of pluralism in reaching a practical accommodation with the center of the church. The conservative exclusivists pursued their vision of unity so zealously that they ended up in smaller institutions and eventually in a smaller church.

In the aftermath of this struggle, both Princeton and Union pursued a new theological direction that promised to remove the sources of conflict. The theologies of Union and of Princeton changed. The doctrine of pluralism that had developed at Union did not change. If anything, as a practical matter it was deepened and strengthened there. Furthermore, this same practice and idea of pluralism began to appear, in a limited way, within Princeton Seminary, in the form of ecumenism and academic freedom. The struggles in Union and Princeton seminaries, then, were not about pluralism as such; but pluralism was the outcome.

Chapter 12

PARTIES IN THE
PRESBYTERIAN CHURCH

*T*he three great parties of this conflict—liberals, loyalists, and conservatives—provided the structure of the church and shaped the conflict over pluralism that took place within it. This structure existed in the church before, during, and after the story told here. In fact, a structure like this is found in nearly every organization, giving shape to its culture and constraining its conflicts. The struggle over pluralism in the Presbyterian Church did not, however, leave this deep structure unchanged. In the short run, one wing or another was weakened—first the liberals, then the conservatives—but in time both grew back. The more enduring effect on the church's structure of creating a pluralist culture was to render the tripartite structure of the church legitimate.

THE STRUCTURE OF PARTIES IN THE CHURCH

The existence of three principal parties is attested to by a strong consensus among students of the Presbyterian Church. Lefferts Loetscher, in his liberal-leaning account of American Presbyterianism (titled, significantly, *The Broadening Church*), clearly discerns these three parties at the beginning of the conflict:

> A third party was emerging [during the Briggs case] between the party demanding theological innovation and the party resisting all theological innovation—a third party composed of those who might or might not incline personally to one or the other of these more extreme positions, but who were resolved to

transcend ideological differences in united action. To this party the Church's future, for more than half a century at least, was to belong. In an increasingly confusing, pluralistic culture such a program held promise of maintaining outward unity and efficiently conducting large enterprises.[1]

George Marsden, in his conservative and highly regarded study of fundamentalism, discerns the same parties just as clearly at the end of the pluralist conflict:

> By 1924 it was becoming evident that there were at least three major parties in the Presbyterian controversy. . . . The theological progressives . . . were clearly a minority party, but with strength in many seminaries and the church hierarchy. They, of course, took an inclusive view of the denomination. Joining them was a . . . group who were conservative theologically, . . . [but who] did not wish theological issues to destroy the peace, unity, and evangelical outreach of the church. Opposing them were the conservative exclusivists . . . , now generally known as fundamentalists.[2]

Rather than emerging in each of these conflicts, though, the three parties had been there all along. The conflicts only served to make the lines of cleavage more visible.

The conservative party was strong in the Presbytery of Philadelphia and in Princeton Theological Seminary, and their principal leaders were Machen, *Presbyterian* editor David Kennedy, Clarence Macartney, Mark Matthews, and Maitland Alexander. The last three, at one time or another, served as moderators. The liberal party was strongest in the Synod of New York and Union Theological Seminary, and its principal leaders included Union Seminary President Henry Sloane Coffin, Princeton University Professor Henry van Dyke, and Auburn Seminary Professor Robert Hastings Nichols. In the center of the church were the loyalists, who were undoubtedly the largest, most powerful, and least organized party. McCormick was the most important loyalist seminary, and the leaders of the party included Foreign Missions Secretary Robert Speer, Princeton Seminary President J. Ross Stevenson, and Princeton Professor Charles Erdman.[3]

Loyalists tend to have a conception of the church that is historical and institutional, and they are loyal to their *particular* denomination. Liberals also tend to have a grasp of the church as an institution; however, their loyalty to the "church in general" allows them to exit one denomination in favor of another. Conservatives tend to focus not on the institutional church but on its distinctive doctrines, and their loyalty to doctrine sometimes leads them to exit one denomination in favor of a new, pure one.[4]

MISREADING THE MAP MEANS LOSING THE BATTLE: BRIGGS AND MACHEN

Charles A. Briggs and J. Gresham Machen lost their battles because neither had a clear conception of the actual structure of the parties within the Presbyterian Church. Briggs and Machen illustrate how a liberal and a conservative view of the church, respectively, can endanger the liberal and conservative parties within the church. Briggs plunged the liberal party into a chasm that could not be scaled for a generation; Machen broke the conservative party in a schism from which it has not yet entirely recovered.

The crucial error that both men made was in seeing the conflict in the church as between two parties, "us" and "them," rather than as a competition among the three groups that always exist there. This procrustean sociology of the church forced the loyalist party to give up its mediating position in the center. When forced to choose a side, the majority chose against the leaders who forced it to choose. With the majority mobilized against it, the losing party found itself transformed from one wing of a differentiated whole into a marginal group being pressed to conform—or leave. At that point, it became the losing party's turn to make a forced choice, which in either case would damage the integrity of the party as a party. A few liberals joined Briggs in exile, but most conformed; a larger number of conservatives followed Machen out of the mother church, while those who conformed to the majority felt deeply compromised because Machen had raised the stakes of the battle so high.

Why did Briggs and Machen fail to understand the structure of their church? Why did they fail to accommodate the loyalist majority which held the future of the church in its hands? The answer is *not* that Briggs was simply too radical to find common ground with the loyalists. Though Charles Briggs was prosecuted as a "radical," in truth he was a fairly conservative liberal. Doctrinally he was not very far from the loyalists, a fact that became more apparent in the years after his suspension from the ministry. Even in his lifetime, Briggs came to be seen as a conservative—a judgment shared by all of his biographers.[5]

It is clear that Briggs thought that he represented the majority in the church, which he saw as united against a single conservative opposition party. At the time of his suspension from the ministry, Briggs described the church as consisting of a progressive, evangelical majority being dominated by an aggressive, rigid, and reactionary minority.[6] The fact that the overwhelming majority in the General Assembly that year voted against Briggs, though, casts some doubt upon his description. He probably was correct that the "aggressive, rigid, reactionary" group which spearheaded his prosecution was a minority in the church, but it is equally probable that "progressives" of the Charles Briggs stripe comprised a minority, too.

Had Briggs pursued a more accommodating policy, he indeed might have avoided suspension from the ministry and even won some of his points. Even without offering any accommodation, he had several victories in his own presbytery; his seminary was behind him; and he was defended by leaders of the church, some of whom were respected loyalists who disagreed with him on his views. For example, Dr. Israel J. Hathaway, though a "loyal Princetonian," rose at the 1891 General Assembly to say, "I plead not for Dr. Briggs; . . . I plead for the broadest liberty of investigation in the scholarship of our Church."[7] Simon J. McPherson preached in 1893 against the way in which Briggs and Henry Preserved Smith were being prosecuted, saying, "I may be a conservative in my doctrinal views, but I want a church as comprehensive as Jesus Christ requires."[8] A similar sentiment was voiced in a sermon by James S. Ramsay, despite the fact that he was a "rigid anti-revisionist, and one who had favored the calling of Dr. Briggs to trial."[9]

J. Gresham Machen's picture of the church was equally polarized and unaccommodating. If one were to take at face value his oft-repeated argument about the opposition of "Christianity" and "modernism," one would think that Machen fought a decades-long battle with modernists and naturalists for control of the Presbyterian Church, and that in the end "the Christians were driven out of the church." In fact, however, for all his talk about modernism in the church, Machen's real opponents in all the church struggles of the 1920s and 1930s were not the modernists but the loyalists. For all his talk of defending Christian doctrine against the naturalists, he reserved his bitterest attacks for those who *agreed* with him on doctrine. If Machen had fought actual modernists in the church, he probably would have kept the allegiance of the center and won the struggle.

Machen failed to grasp his true position in the party structure of the Presbyterian Church because of his doctrinal conception of the church. This conception had two consequences which served him poorly. First, as has been noted in the examination of Machen's conception of the church, it obscured the institutional nature of the denomination. In other words, Machen was not looking at the empirical organization of the church and so was not attending to the actual groupings of idea and interest—the social structure—of the church. He did not know that there was a loyalist party, because he did not know that there were any parties.

Machen's inattention to the sociological character of the church could make it difficult for him even to understand what his opponents were talking about when they spoke of the Presbyterian Church. For example, in his impassioned "plea for fair play" for Princeton Seminary, Machen wrote: "We cannot agree with those who say that although they are members of the Presbyterian Church, they 'have not the slightest zeal to have the Presbyterian Church extended through the length and breadth of the world.' As for us, we hold the faith of the Presbyterian Church, the great Reformed Faith that is set forth in the Westminster Confession, to be true; and holding it to be true we hold that it is intended for the whole world."[10] Notice that the unnamed opponent was speaking of spreading the *Presbyterian Church* throughout the world, while Machen, without noticing it, speaks of spreading the *faith* of the Presbyterian Church.

Second, and related, Machen's doctrinal conception led him to see the people who disagreed with him on doctrine—the modernists—but not the people who agreed with him on doctrine but disagreed with him on church policy—the loyalists. Given his doctrinal conception of the church, those who agreed with him on doctrine but nonetheless opposed his actions he could only view as misguided and perverse.

Machen also had difficulty enlisting the loyalists in a fight against the liberals because his strict definition of "liberalism" made it difficult to find any actual liberals in the Presbyterian Church. Machen defined liberals as those who accepted a "thorough-going naturalism" about Christian origins; he was similarly strict about a "doctrinally true" Presbyterian Church, defining it as one in which all the officers gave full subscription to the Westminster Confession. By such standards, very few actual liberals *or* "true" Presbyterians existed in the Presbyterian Church.[11]

This may explain why Machen, despite his talk of a liberal and modernist threat in the church, was so reluctant to bring charges against any specific Presbyterians; he could not actually find anyone to charge. Although he said that the Auburn Affirmation was a modernist document, he never initiated discipline against any of the thirteen hundred Presbyterian ministers who signed it. Some Presbyterians whom Machen had suggested were modernists challenged him to bring specific charges against them, but he never responded. Most pointedly, he repeatedly was asked by Robert Speer and the committees responsible for foreign missions to substantiate his charges of modernism among the missions, which he was unable or unwilling to do.[12]

Machen often was called a conservative. He sometimes used that term himself. In more reflective moments, however, he admitted that he and his group should not be classed among the conservatives in the church. In 1925 he noted, "In one sense, . . . we are traditionalists: we do maintain that any institution that is really great has its roots in the past; we do not therefore desire to substitute modern sects for the historic Christian Church. But on the whole . . . it would be more correct to call us 'radicals' than to call us 'conservatives'."[13] This radical party put itself at odds with the genuinely conservative center of the church. Not surprisingly, the centrist group usually was not agreeable to uncompromising radicalism, whether of the left or the right. If such a radical party then attacked the loyalist conception of the church and turned on the loyalists themselves, as Machen did, the loyalists joined the battle to defend themselves—and the church.

In the battle for Princeton Seminary, there really were only two parties: the loyalists and the conservatives.[14] The liberals did not even take the field. President Stevenson was a man of decidedly conservative theological views, a "conservative Presbyterian Christian"[15] whose theological position was not questioned, even though an "underlying hostility" toward him could be felt within the seminary.[16] Charles Erdman, Stevenson's faculty ally against Machen, was even more conservative theologically than Stevenson and, unlike Machen and the faculty "majority," actually was an author of *The Fundamentals,* the tracts that gave fundamentalism its name. In the foreign missions fight, Machen attacked Robert Speer, who, theologically and institutionally, was well respected. By that time, Machen had gone to extremes, calling anyone who disagreed with him a "modernist" or an "indifferentist."[17]

Machen wanted a showdown over doctrine, but what he got was a fight over order. When Machen realized, with some exasperation, that the loyalists would not support him in his doctrinal battle if he did not follow normal procedures, he tried to force them to take sides on doctrinal lines. In 1924 he wrote: "You may stand for Christ. That is best. . . . You may stand for anti-Christian Modernism. That is next best. . . . [Or] you may be neutral. That is perhaps worst of all."[18] He criticized the "indifferentism," with respect to doctrine, of Stevenson and his supporters, and he asserted that indifferentism inevitably leads to modernism.[19]

As this struggle grew more intense, so did Machen's attack upon "indifferentism," moderation, or any accommodation by any party with those whom Machen regarded as doctrinally unsound. There could be no reconciliation in the struggle, because, Machen asserted, it "is quite impossible for a man to be in favor with the Auburn Affirmationists and at the same time have the confidence of the evangelical party in the Church."[20] By "evangelical party" Machen meant, of course, his own party. Notice that here he does not speak of a man who "favors the Affirmation," but rather of one who is, for whatever reason, *in favor with* the affirmationists.

Eventually, Machen made an all-out attack on the center party in the church, leveling the most powerful charge that a doctrinal churchman could make against fellow clergy: "The 'heretics' . . . are, with their helpers, the indifferentists, in control of the . . . Presbyterian Church in the United States of America, as they are in control of nearly all the larger Protestant Churches in the world."[21] This seems a clear indication that Machen had given up all thought of trying to accommodate the center party, if he had ever had such a thought. He probably also had given up on remaining in the Presbyterian Church in the U.S.A.

Until the end, Machen continued to reduce all disagreements to "us versus them" fights. His inability to acknowledge that there were several parties to these disputes within the church cost him most of his allies. After he lost the fight with the loyalists over Princeton Seminary in the late 1920s, he started attacking conservatives whose views were even closer to his own. In 1930, after Machen's ally Samuel Craig was forced out as the editor of *The Presbyterian,* the pair founded *Christianity Today,* with Craig as editor. The new editor of *The Presbyterian*, Stewart Robinson, was known as a conservative, but Machen insisted that anyone associated with an organization that would remove Craig must be a modernist or an indifferentist.[22] Yet, just a few years later, when Samuel Craig himself wrote an editorial in *Christianity Today* critical of the Constitutional Covenant Union (the predecessor to the Orthodox Presbyterian Church), Machen wrote to the supporters of Westminster Seminary that "Dr. Samuel Craig has declared war upon us," describing Craig, Clarence Macartney, and other former Machen sympathizers as "middle-of-the-road."[23]

Briggs and Machen alike misunderstood the tripartite structure of the Presbyterian Church, seeing it instead in bipolar terms. Although they differed in many respects, their similar misunderstanding had roots in similar structural positions and experiences within the church. Moreover, from these analogous positions they acted according to similar theories of religious struggle, theories of conflict without compromise. As a result, the two ended up in similar positions—namely, out of the ministry of the denomination and ultimately out of the denomination altogether.

There are, in fact, a number of similarities between Briggs and Machen. Both were influenced by strongly Presbyterian mothers with sympathies for the Old School. The fathers of both men were very successful in business. Both Briggs and Machen attended southern universities and were excellent students. Both were ambivalent about entering the ministry. They were outstanding students in leading seminaries of the northern Presbyterian Church, where they established close ties with their professors. Both were marked by their professors for special scholarly achievement and sent to Germany to study with the leading liberal scholars of the day. Both came back to their seminaries at a young age and established themselves as stalwarts of their institutions.

Briggs and Machen were professors of Bible in a denomination that gave preeminence to mastery of Scripture. Both wrote works on biblical languages which became the standard texts of those fields, being the most enduring work of each author.[24] Both Briggs and Machen became party leaders in the denomination and urged alliances with similar parties in other denominations. Each man tied his scholarly work to his partisan position, as well as contending in the popular press, both religious and secular. Most importantly, each man saw a duty to press his position in the church without compromise, sacrificing himself for the cause. Both Briggs and Machen refused to accept the existing diversity in the church as a permanent condition. As a result, each man forced an important struggle in the church, a struggle which permanently changed the character of his seminary—and the Presbyterian Church in the U.S.A.

Charles A. Briggs and J. Gresham Machen had a poor sociological grasp of the church because they were scholars and intellectuals, very involved in theological arguments affecting the church but not experienced in the actual running of the denomination. Briggs had held a pastorate briefly and was involved in Presbyterian and international ecumenical organizations, but he was not a regular on denominational boards and committees. Machen was not even that involved in the affairs of the church. It would be fair to say that both Briggs and Machen knew more about the teaching of the Bible in German universities than they did about the preaching of the Bible in Germantown Presbyterian Church.

THE LOYALIST MAJORITY TAKES COMMAND

A crisis in the church only can be settled when the loyalist majority asserts itself. The majority, however, is difficult to mobilize. It is hard to create a collective consciousness among a group whose principal commonality lies more in what they *do* alike than in what they *believe* alike. The loyalist party becomes a party when it is attacked, when it has a common enemy to mobilize against. The loyalist Presbyterians rose against Briggs when he threatened their beloved church by calling for the dissolution of all existing denominations and the formation of a union of all progressive Christians; in response, they put him out. In the struggles of the 1920s and 1930s, when Machen went to further and further extremes in attacking the "indifferentists," the loyalists became even more unified and self-conscious as a party, and they put him and his works out of the church.

The crux of what the loyalists mobilized to defend was the constitution of the Presbyterian Church. This vision was ably expressed by Charles Erdman in his successful campaign for moderator in 1925: "I belong to no particular clique or group, but stand for the constitution of the Church. That means loyalty to our Church doctrine as well as to our form of government. . . . We must guard the doctrine of the Church, but we must do so by constitutional methods and by the law of the Church."[25] The constitution is more than the expression of an experience or a doctrine, though it contains those things, too. The constitution is the foundation of the church as a particular living organization, its frame as a social body. The Briggs liberals, and to a greater extent the Machen conservatives, had a faulty sociology of the Presbyterian Church, because they failed to appreciate the meaning of the church's constitution in the hearts and minds of the loyalist majority.

The loyalists, when effectively mobilized, created a distinctive position based on denominational loyalty. Most accounts of the Presbyterian conflict (and perhaps of any institutional struggle) treat the extreme parties as the active agents and the loyalist center as an inert mass to be swayed in one direction or another. Marsden, for example, relates:

> In 1924 and 1925 . . . [in] the large Baptist and Presbyterian denominations of the Northern United States . . . liberalism was under such heavy assault that it could not win . . . by direct frontal attack [on fundamentalism]. . . . A far more effective . . . counterattack . . . was the appeal to the strong American tradition of tolerance. . . . Liberals could cite this tradition as they attempted to gain support . . . from the large middle parties not firmly committed. Thus began to break up the fundamentalist coalitions. Under strong pressure to disown the fundamentalist's avowed position of intolerance, many conservatives fell back.[26]

The loyalists are portrayed here as uncommitted, rather than as committed to a different position than either the liberals or the conservatives. In this view, they do not step forward to take charge of the church and settle the conflict— as the Special Commission of 1925 actually was doing at that moment—but instead they "fall back."

At critical moments in the pluralist conflict, the loyalists shaped the church according to their distinctive vision. Briggs claimed that the true objective of his trial was to defeat the revision of the creed—that is, the constitution—that he championed, and this was true; the majority of the church rejected a revision that was designed to merge the Presbyterian Church into a grand union of many different kinds of churches. A decade later, when creed revision and another grand church union scheme were pursued separately, the majority accepted revision while rejecting the denomination-destroying merger plan.

In the Machen struggles, as we have seen, the loyalist party was mobilized more fully, and in the same degree its distinctive position was developed more fully. Three moments in this development merit special note: the work of the Special Commission of 1925, the General Assembly's "Studies in the Constitution of the Presbyterian Church in the U.S.A." of 1934, and the playing out of the final conflict in Machen's trial in 1936.

The distinctively loyalist position forged by the Special Commission of 1925 has been detailed above. What is important to note in the context of the party structure of the church is that the commission was responding to competition by the conservatives and the liberals for the loyalty of the loyalist majority. The conservatives competed by voting in the "five points," the liberals by the plea for tolerance and constitutional procedure in the "Auburn Affirmation."

The liberals, having been (as they saw it) burned by constitutional irregularities since the Briggs trials, had learned to make a firm alliance with the loyalists in defense of the constitutional order. This alliance lay behind the Auburn Affirmation, which was principally a protest against what the affirmationists considered to be the unconstitutional way in which the "five points" had been established. For both parties, the empirical and visible church was as important as the transcendental and invisible church: to the liberals, the Presbyterian Church was an agency for the reconstruction of society; to the loyalists, the Presbyterian Church was home.

The liberals did not win everything they wanted from the Special Commission. They did, though, ultimately get more of what they wanted because they gave more to the loyalists—namely, more recognition of the authority of the church's constitution—than conservative pugnacity did.

In contrast, the Machen group's failure to grasp the legal and emotional significance of constitutional procedure in the church led it to pursue a losing strategy in its battles within that church. For Machen, the constitution guaranteed only his liberty against the church, not his responsibility to it. When he thought that his liberties had been violated, he resorted to the southern constitutional theory of secession, neglecting the Presbyterian constitutional ban on schism.[27] The Machenites failed to bring a case against the Auburn Affirmationists in the church courts, but instead resorted to denunciation of the Auburn Affirmation, liberalism, and "indifferentism." This strategy, not surprisingly, failed to produce constitutional changes in the church.

Perhaps the most important extension of the loyalist position occurred in 1934, when the General Council, the executive body of the General Assembly, responded to several overtures about the Independent Board of Presbyterian Foreign Missions with "Studies in the Constitution of the Presbyterian Church in the U.S.A." This remarkable document formed the basis of the council's recommendation, subsequently adopted by the full General Assembly, that all officers of the Presbyterian Church resign from the IBPFM.

After detailing the history of its efforts to deal with Machen's charges, the "Studies" offered a careful, and in places ingenious, argument about how an agency like the IBPFM should be treated under the constitution of the Presbyterian Church. The church (as, ironically, Machen himself had argued) is a strictly voluntary body, the argument went, but when one volunteers to join it, one accepts certain rules and principles given by its constitution. All officers of the church are required to promote the peace and unity of the body defined by that constitution.[28]

The constitution had explicit protections for the expression of conscience or private judgment, which were acknowledged and asserted in the "Studies." This question of "private judgment," however, had been something of a problem, as some minorities in the church had tried to use this protection to justify ignoring the judgments of the church courts and circumventing the agencies of the church. The argument advanced in the "Studies" to solve this problem broke new ground in Presbyterian constitutional theory, securing the authority of the loyalists' constitutional and institutional conception of the church, over against a strictly doctrinal conception.

According to the constitution of the Presbyterian Church, the "right of private judgment has always been 'unalienable.'" However, "an individual cannot claim the right to two opposite private judgments at one and the same time. In the Presbyterian Church, the assumption of office is an exercise of private judgment." This concept of "two opposite private judgments" then was developed in this way:

> If, however, during the course of his tenure of office the time comes when he insists that according to his present private judgment he no longer approves the government and discipline of the Presbyterian Church, . . . then he is exercising an entirely different private judgment from that which he originally exercised when inducted into office. . . . No constitutional Church could exist by allowing one private judgment which professed approval to the government and discipline of the Church, and at the same time admitted another contrary pri-

vate judgment which renounced the rule and authority of the Church. A Presbyterian office holder, therefore, . . . must either submit to the provisions as established in the Constitution in the Church, or declaring that his conscience no longer will allow him to submit himself to the Church which has the rule over him, renounce the advantages which the Presbyterian Church bestows upon all who sincerely receive and adopt her distinctive principles, and withdraw from his office. God is a God of order, not confusion, in the Presbyterian Church in the United States of America.[29]

This argument reasserted the traditional policy of the Presbyterian Church on questions of conscience. This policy was generous in comparison with the absolute claims of some churches in the past, for it struck a balance between the integrity of the individual conscience and the need for order and unity in the organized church. A particular advance was the provision that one could in conscience withdraw from the church without being considered a schismatic, *if* one did not try to make a schism.

Concerning the constitutional status of independent agencies for church work, the "Studies" cited precedents from Presbyterian history to show that such agencies may be supported by parts of the church if, and only if, they have been specifically approved by the General Assembly.[30] Presbyterian individuals were free, of course, to support any agencies they chose; this requirement of General Assembly approval applied only to the subordinate bodies of the church. Machen's Independent Board for Presbyterian Foreign Missions did not have such approval because it was seen by the General Assembly as having been set up in opposition to the church's own mission agency, and in 1934 the General Assembly made its disapproval official.

This argument answered those critics of the General Assembly's "Deliverance of 1934," such as Machen, who charged that the IBPFM had a right to be supported by parts of the church because other non-Presbyterian agencies had received such support in the past.[31] Here the assembly made clear that, as the authorized representative body of the whole church, it would judge which outside bodies were genuinely friendly to the advance of the church. The assembly based its argument on the assumption that anyone who opposed the General Assembly and its judgments would not wish to be in the Presbyterian Church.

When the General Assembly adopted this argument in 1934, it mandated that officers of the church resign from the IBPFM or face discipline. Such discipline was for a violation of the constitutional order of the church, which its officers were as much obligated to uphold as they were its doctrine. Machen had been heard repeatedly on the doctrinal issues in the foreign missions case, and repeatedly he had lost. According to his own conception of the church, Machen could do nothing but maintain his protest until he was satisfied on the doctrinal point. Given the loyalist standard articulated by the "Studies," however, when Machen took an action judged by the General Assembly to be contrary to the good order of the church, it was no defense to claim that, despite the judgments of the church, he truly was protecting its doctrine.

This clash between the conservative doctrinal conception of the church and the loyalist constitutional conception was at the heart of Machen's trial. In his trial before New Brunswick Presbytery, Machen was charged with: (1) "disapproval, defiance and acts in contravention of the government and discipline" of the Presbyterian Church in the U.S.A., "contrary to the word of God and to the rules and regulations of this Church, founded thereupon"; (2) "not being zealous and faithful in maintaining the peace of the Church"; (3) "refusing subjection to your brethren in the Lord"; (4) "violating your ordination vows"; (5) "contempt of and rebellion against your superiors in the Church in their lawful counsels, commands and corrections"; and (6) "breach of your lawful promises."[32] Machen's lawyer, reflecting Machen's view of the church, responded that the real issues in the case were matters of doctrine and that none of these charges, even if true, would be offenses.[33]

Here we see the constitutional and the doctrinal conceptions of the church face to face. The court recognized that there was a proper place for doctrinal dispute as well as for administrative order in the church, while Machen insisted on doctrinal dispute but did not, at his trial, acknowledge any place for administrative order. Machen maintained that the denomination was suppressing the doctrinal issue by not letting him make his charges against others at his trial. In reply, the court maintained that there was a doctrinal phase of the controversy but that it already had been settled.

The court's position was established early in the trial, when Machen's counsel challenged one of the members of the judicial commission on the grounds that he had signed the Auburn Affirmation, a document the defense regarded as heretical. The prosecutor questioned the relevance of this challenge, to which the defense replied that it was relevant because "this case is

bound to involve great doctrinal questions." A member of the court inter-
jected on a point of order, saying, "I think that this court is competent to
decide that this is not a doctrinal controversy nor a doctrinal question, and
. . . therefore . . . I move you that it be the judgment of this court any argument or challenge based on the Auburn Affirmation . . . be declared out of
order." The motion carried unanimously. Shortly thereafter, the court clari-
fied this ruling to judge out of order "anything that goes back to the . . .
doctrinal phase of this case." This, too, carried unanimously.[34]

Machen's side expressed surprise over this ruling but at the time did not
lodge a protest. At a later session of the trial, when the court announced that
attacks upon the doctrinal integrity of other people who were not parties to
this case—the signers of the Auburn Affirmation, the Board of Foreign Missions, the officers of Princeton Seminary—would be considered out of order,
the defense expressed shock and amazement, asked for several postponements,
and eventually gave up all attempt at a defense.[35] When Machen was suspended from the ministry for procedural violations, the loyalist constitutional
and institutional conception of the church triumphed over the exclusively
doctrinal view.

THE ONGOING DEBATE ABOUT THE CLASH OF PARTIES

Misreading the party structure of the Presbyterian conflict affects the debate
about those events even today. Gary Scott Smith, in his *Seeds of Secularization: Calvinism, Culture, and Pluralism in America, 1870–1915*, argues that
the religious struggles at the turn of the century pitted Calvinists against "non-
Christian worldviews," in arguments both between Protestant denominations
and within them.[36] While there is, I believe, some truth to this thesis, it is
seriously misleading to understand the fight within the Presbyterian Church
in these terms. To see the struggle as between "Calvinism" and a "non-Christian" ideology is to take at face value Machen's account of the central issue.
In fact, however, attending to the party structure of the Presbyterian Church
reveals that the real battles were *between* Calvinist groups fighting over the
procedures of an essentially Calvinist organization.

The debate concerning the strategies of the parties is articulated clearly in
a pair of 1979 articles in the *Westminster Theological Journal,* celebrating
the fiftieth anniversary of the founding of Machen's Westminster Theologi-

cal Seminary. These papers address the question of struggle within the structure of the Presbyterian Church. Richard Lovelace, a well-known evangelical in the Presbyterian Church (U.S.A.), who teaches at conservative Gordon-Conwell Seminary, contends:

> If these varying currents of doctrine had simply been allowed to make their case before the church in an open market of ideas, in dialogue and even in polemic, the churches . . . might have been spared a great deal of trauma. . . . However, the Fundamentalists and Old Princeton leaders chose instead to try to evict those who disagreed with them through the use of the Presbyterian system of graded courts. In this use of the disciplinary machinery to gun down theological opponents, the conservatives for decades won most of the battles, from the Briggs case on, but the more liberal martyrs they made, the more they seemed to be losing the war. In the late 1920s, the center of the Presbyterian Church turned from this conflict with immense relief to renounce the effort to enforce the Fundamentals from the center of the church, while its seminaries were embracing the continental neo-Reformation theology which was equally critical of Liberalism and Fundamentalism. . . . When J. Gresham Machen attempted to promote Westminster Calvinism through the establishment of an independent board for foreign missions, the center and left of the church turned its disciplinary apparatus against him. From this point onward the Westminster leaders turned their main attention away from the theological dialogue in the mainline church, and adopted as their goal the building of doctrinally pure churches, conceived of as voluntary societies for the propagation of pure Westminster Calvinism.[37]

D. Clair Davis, a member of the conservative Presbyterian Church of America and a professor at Westminster Seminary, responds to Lovelace thus:

> [Lovelace believes that] the evangelical party lost the middle of the church in the first place . . . because of their successful disciplinary process against liberals. . . . To me, it looks rather that . . . there were not too many trials, but rather too few. It is when the evangelical party lost its nerve and changed its strategy from trials to lay rallies and adoption of General Assembly resolutions that the game was over. Not only was the latter of questionable constitutionality, as the Auburn Affirmation pointed out, but the whole effort was diffused and muddied. Instead of concentrating on clear heresy of particular individuals, the evangelicals were content with drawing up definitions. I believe that [Henry

Sloane] Coffin's autobiography makes clear that the liberals were almost convinced in the 20s that *they* would have to leave—but the evangelicals blinked first.[38]

I agree with both of these analyses, but on the critical point of difference, I think Davis is correct. In Lovelace's assertion that "in the late 1920s, the center of the Presbyterian Church turned from this conflict with immense relief to renounce the effort to enforce the Fundamentals for the center of the church," what is obscured is the nature of the parties acting in the church. It was not that the center "turned from" or even "renounced" this strategy of disciplinary procedure, but rather, as Davis contends, that the "evangelical party lost its nerve and changed its strategy from trials to lay rallies and adoption of General Assembly resolutions"—perhaps because the conservatives could not find any actual liberals to charge.

The center party in 1924, contrary to Lovelace's claim, *was* willing to take up disciplinary actions, as long as these followed constitutional procedures. Even in 1934 they would have been thus willing, and indeed they bent over backwards to get Machen and the conservative party to bring charges. Neglect of these constitutional procedures, and the attacks on those who insisted upon them, pushed the center away from the right-wing party, while insistence upon toleration and constitutional procedure by the left-wing party pulled the center into a new alliance.

Who won the Presbyterian struggle of the 1920s and 1930s? In the short run, the liberal party won toleration in the church. In the longer term, however, "the outcome of the protracted controversy was a victory for *moderates* [or, rather, loyalists] *willing to tolerate* theological liberalism in the Church, and the eventual exclusion of Machen and a few of his followers."[39]

There were some who saw the conclusion of the Machen case as a victory for modernism in the Presbyterian Church, but by the end of the fight, modernism had almost nothing to do with it. An editorial in the liberal *Christian Century* summed up the results after the IBPFM appeals were lost:

> It will be a mistake of the public to assume from the outcome of this long-standing controversy that the Presbyterian Church has become 'modernist' in its doctrine. It is true that the origin of the dispute was doctrinal, but it has long passed that stage. The real issue in the minds of the rank and file of the church

has been the question of respect for the official decisions of the church court. If these were not respected, then obviously there would be no longer a constitutional court. Men of the most conservative doctrinal view joined with those who were liberal in insisting that no group within the church be permitted to defy its official mandates.[40]

By resolving the conservative challenge in this way, the loyalists did strengthen the position of the liberals and of the program that they represented. Accordingly, a foundation was laid for an increasingly confident pluralism in the Presbyterian Church. By this resolution, however, the loyalists, as the party identified with the constitution, also strengthened their own controlling position in the church.

The lasting effects of the Presbyterian struggle were to break the alliance between the church's center and its right, an alliance which had been based on a common conception of church doctrine; and to forge a new alliance between the center and the left, based on a common conception of church work. Three further consequences followed: (1) the conservatives were fragmented, and some left the Presbyterian Church altogether; (2) Princeton Seminary returned to a leading and loyalist position in the denomination; and (3) the liberals built upon their toleration to create, in some places, genuine pluralism. The fragmentation of the conservatives has been detailed above. The subsequent course of Princeton Seminary was recounted in the preceding chapter. Still, the kind of pluralism created in the Presbyterian Church as a result of this struggle needs a further word here.

The position that was established in the PCUSA as a result of the protracted struggle from the Briggs trial to the Machen trial was what might be called "constitutional inclusivism." The church is a doctrinal association, and must defend what it considers to be essential teachings. The church also, however, is a human institution, with a form of order—a constitution—that must be defended. This was the point that Machen—and many conservatives today—did not see; that the defense of the constitutional order of the church is not unprincipled turf-guarding, but rather is a principle as important to the church as the rest of its theological doctrine.[41] An institutional church has to have some way of justifying diversity, or it could not contain a variety of individuals who differ in their experience, interests, understanding, and wisdom, as well as in their beliefs.

The long-term effect of the Presbyterian struggle from Briggs to Machen, then, was to legitimize the party structure itself in the understanding of the church. The Special Commission successfully asserted that toleration of differing views was a tradition of the church that was protected by the constitution. That is, the loyalist party successfully asserted its prerogative to tolerate the liberal party *and* the conservative party. Party pluralism—a diversity of parties in the church—was rendered legitimate.

Machen thought that it was possible to sort out the true from the false amid this diversity. One who shared this belief was Edwin Rian, and his career parallels the Presbyterian conflict in miniature, providing a fitting close. Rian had joined with Machen in the schism in 1936, had chaired the board of Westminster Seminary, and had written a pro-Machen history of the "Presbyterian Conflict." In 1947, however, Rian reread Calvin's *Institutes* on the nature of the Church and concluded that Machen's vision, as embodied in the Orthodox Presbyterian Church, was sectarian and not truly Calvinist or biblical. In explaining his dramatic return to the Presbyterian Church in the U.S.A., Rian argued that the truly Calvinist conception, one that had been supported by Charles Hodge and A. A. Hodge, was of a "mixed church." Sorting out the true and the false completely is beyond human capacities, and such a church cannot hope to be pure and uniform until the end of the world. The church must be a mixed institution, both doctrinally and institutionally, and the wheat inevitably will be mixed with the tares.[42]

Part III

The Theory of Pluralism and the End of the Tale

Chapter 13

COMPETITIVE PLURALISM

*M*any religions and religious institutions coexist in America. This situation often is called "pluralism" and is thought to provide a reason for tolerance on religious matters. But what *is* the relation between the existence of many religions in one nation and their mutual toleration? Likewise, what is the relation between the existence of many religious positions within an organization and their mutual accommodation? What kind of social dynamic does the system created by such religious bodies have? What, after all, *is* pluralism?

The argument of this book runs as follows. Religious diversity is a fact and a problem. Pluralism is an idea that justifies diversity. Competitive pluralism is the best solution to the problem of diversity.

RELIGIOUS DIVERSITY IS A FACT AND A PROBLEM

Religious diversity in the United States is an empirical fact. *Diversity* names an actual situation, a description independent of what people think of that situation. The term *religious diversity* can be used to denote a situation in which there are several religions, such as Christianity and Hinduism; several denominations of the same religion, such as Presbyterian Christians and Methodist Christians; or even several religious views within the same denomination, such as "predestinarian" Presbyterians and "free will" Presbyterians.[1]

Diversity in religious understanding is an empirical and a theoretical problem. Historically, religious diversity has led to conflict; conceptually, it has led to incoherence. Insofar as religions deal with the most fundamental questions concerning the nature of existence and the meaning of life, religious differences can mean radical divisions, divisions which are among the most difficult to overcome. Such barriers to unity, agreement, or even mutual intelligibility can be a problem for society as a whole, as well as for the institutions within society. As Jay Newman, one of the most thorough students of religious tolerance, put it, "Any ideological pluralism, and especially a religious one, does take its toll on the laws of society, which usually come to reflect the 'lowest common denominator' of ethical principles accepted by members of *all* the major groups making up the society. . . . [W]e and our children and our grandchildren do pay a price for today's tolerance."[2] Religious diversity contains a threat of incoherence that can undermine the legitimacy of society and the motivation of individuals.[3]

Of all the kinds of religious diversity, differences within religious institutions can pose the most difficult problems, because religious institutions commonly profess the ideal of "orthodoxy," the ideal of one true system of doctrine or understanding. Indeed, it is often agreement on doctrine which defines the religious denomination, which gives it its distinctive identity and its special reason for existing. An institution that holds an ideal of one right doctrine will find it extremely difficult to justify allowing several different doctrines to exist within it. As Dean Hoge contends, "Some persons have argued that theological pluralism is not troublesome, since a denomination still has the institutional church as its central identity. This argument is wrong. The theological pluralism will cause troublesome conflict over the priorities and mission of the church . . . [and] pressures toward institutional pluralism."[4] Religious differences within a church tend to undermine the authority that makes it possible for a church to settle religious differences.[5]

Some religious institutions, to be sure, seek their unity not in orthodoxy (common understanding) but in orthopraxy (common practice). This does not eliminate the problem of pluralism, however; it only displaces it to a different arena. An orthoprax religious institution has as much of a problem deciding how much diversity of "right ritual" to accept as an orthodox institution has with diversity of "right doctrine." Moreover, the *idea* that an institution can accept a variety of beliefs so long as it is unified in its practices is itself a doctrine, which is subject to all the difficulties of orthodoxy.[6]

Diversity appears at every social level. The positions held by individuals, such as Briggs, Machen, and the Special Commission of 1925, can differ from one another. The institutions within a culture, such as Princeton and Union Seminaries, can represent distinctive conceptions. The whole itself—whether it is a whole church or a whole society—can be composed of parties, as the Presbyterian Church is made up of recognizable liberal, loyalist, and conservative groups. Since diversity appears at every level, the solutions to the problems of diversity may be attempted at every level.

PLURALISM IS AN IDEA THAT JUSTIFIES DIVERSITY

The ideal of one right doctrine brings us to the theoretical problem posed by diversity. A premise of nearly every religious tradition is that Truth ultimately is one. Two genuinely contradictory contentions cannot both be true, though both may be false. This does not settle the question of how one may know what is true, but it does mean that one cannot be content to settle for diversity as truth. The ideal of "orthodoxy," which is normal in religious organizations as well as in other bodies, is an attempt to realize this unified truth. Diversity, in and of itself, poses a *potential* threat to orthodoxy, because, given the premise of noncontradiction, it introduces an element of incoherence. Pluralism, on the other hand, is a *realized* threat to orthodoxy. Pluralism justifies diversity; it legitimates the incoherence of diversity.

THREE THEORETICAL APPROACHES TO DIVERSITY

Pluralism is one of three theories, conceptions, or ideas responding to the fact of diversity. Pluralism is an "ism," an argument about how diversity should be treated.[7] As an argument, pluralism is the middle position on a spectrum running from *triumphalism,* the belief that only one way of thinking is true, to *relativism,* the belief that all ways of thinking may be true.[8] The idea of pluralism is a historical invention that finds its greatest appeal in situations in which triumphalism and relativism are locked in mortal combat. Pluralism appeals to those who want to "take their own side in an argument," avoiding both coercive dogmatism and utter relativism.

Theoretically these three positions are equally valid; in practice, however, only pluralism is truly viable. Relativism functions more as a hypothetical position or a logical inference, the end point of the slippery slope leading away from strict triumphalism. Relativism is a difficult position actually to believe in, because it dissolves into paradox: if all ideas are equally true, then the idea of relativism is as true (and as false) as its opposite.[9]

Triumphalism is a more serious contender against pluralism, both theoretically and historically. Each of these two theoretical stances has an exhaustive set of categories with which it tries to grasp the world. Triumphalism sees reality through the categories of "truth" and "falsehood." Pluralism also believes in truth and falsehood, to which it adds a critical third category that might be called the "realm of legitimate diversity." In this realm lie matters about which reasonable people may reasonably differ.

Both triumphalism and pluralism speak also of *adiaphora*, matters about which we may be indifferent. These are things which it may be possible to discover the truth of, but which are not important enough to be worth the effort. This category is a residual one, applied in a casual and somewhat haphazard way. We may contrast the category of adiaphora with the pluralists' realm of legitimate difference, a category that exists precisely for matters which *are* important, matters which can be assigned to it only as the result of a deliberate struggle.

The battle between triumphalism and pluralism has been bitter, because it is a conflict between whole ways of understanding the world. Insofar as these positions produce ingrained habits of thought, they shape the way the world is perceived. The struggle between triumphalism and pluralism is not over whether a particular conception is a matter of legitimate diversity or not, but over whether there is such a thing as "a matter of legitimate diversity." Within the framework of triumphalism, such a claim by the pluralist must appear not simply as wrong, but as nonsense, as a meaningless utterance.

The triumphalist ideal rests upon the straightforward notion that reality exists, that it is what it is and is not anything else. Truth, therefore, is the expression of reality as it actually exists, and any other expression must be false.

The problem that has made the theory of triumphalism so difficult to realize in practice is that it is very difficult to know the truth about some important matters. The recognition of adiaphora already is a concession to the "problem of knowing" that is built into the theory of triumphalism. Moreover, acknowledgment of the intractable epistemological problems posed by *essential* matters has been won only through protracted and repeated conflict. The historical struggle for religious freedom has been driven by the problem of knowing.[10]

The strength of triumphalism is its grasp of the ideal of true understanding; its characteristic danger is a coercive dogmatism. The strength of relativism is that it is *not* coercive; its danger is an inability to distinguish truth from falsehood. The relativist position would include those who say that "all religions are equally valid" (universalism) as well as those who hold that all human understanding is inadequate or irrelevant.[11] "Pluralism" stakes out a practical position between these theoretical poles, between the vices of intolerance and excessive tolerance.[12] Its strength is that it preserves the distinction between truth and falsehood; its danger is that it simply preserves the status quo.

The practical solution to the problem of diversity requires that the differing parties within a social whole be able to recognize and deal with one another according to rules—that is, some form of "constitution." When differing groups deal with one another through a constitution, they render their diversity legitimate. In other words, they establish pluralism.

There are three kinds of constitutional pluralisms: conflict, dialogue, and competition. Conflict and dialogue work best when there are just two disputing parties. Competitive pluralism works best when there are three (or more) parties.

TWO-PARTY PLURALISM: CONFLICT AND DIALOGUE

Civil conflict is one kind of two-party pluralism; dialogue is another.[13] Both are head-to-head relations. Civil conflict is the old desire to annihilate the opposition, but rendered civil by ruling out physical coercion so that it may be carried on within the confines of civil (constitutional) society. Such conflict aims at the direct conversion of one's opponents to one's own position. Conflict appeals to the militant.

In dialogue, by contrast, the two parties consider their differences together in order to reason their way to agreement. The aim of dialogue is not necessarily to convert "them" to "our" position: in principle, "we" must be open to being converted to "their" position, or both of us to a third position. Dialogue appeals to the peacemaker.

While civil conflict and dialogue both have their proponents in the church today, dialogue is by far the more favored idea.[14] Today, a pluralism of dialogue is practically an essential doctrine in the Presbyterian Church (U.S.A.).[15]

Some proponents of pluralism go on to argue that diversity can be a positive good, in that it stimulates creativity.[16]

As means of resolving the problem of diversity, both conflict and dialogue leave something to be desired. Often it is the case that conflict is quite bitter and dialogue laborious, yet neither results in a changed position. This is especially true of religious differences, as people adhere to religious groups for a host a reasons—tradition, sentiment, and inexpressible personal experience, for example—that are not touched directly by argument.[17] Furthermore, in the United States, there are few social incentives to convince religious groups that it is urgent that they settle their differences. Conflict may end in the hegemonic assimilation of one side by the other, obviating a potential culture war—or it may not.[18] Dialogue is used principally as a strategy in the "politics of accommodation" common to voluntary associations which are trying to prevent high rates of exit.[19] The status quo tends to survive, even the status quo of conflict or dialogue.[20]

THREE-PARTY PLURALISM: COMPETITION

The theory of competitive pluralism introduces a third term that converts two-party conflict into three-party competition. The opposing parties compete for the allegiance of an uncommitted third party, rather than squaring off directly against one another. Each body offers to the world its distinctive features, making its case that these are good. Each contestant then actively may advance its cause, without waiting on the will of the other side. Competition appeals to the practical.

The seminal sociological work on this conception of competition was done by Georg Simmel. In his essay on conflict, Simmel wrote: "The foremost sociological characteristic of competition is the fact that conflict in it is indirect. In so far as one gets rid of an adversary or damages him directly, one does not compete with him. In general, linguistic usage reserves the term only for conflicts which consist in parallel efforts by both parties concerning the same prize."[21] Competition can be of benefit not only to the winner, but also to the loser. The competitors are induced to give their best efforts in order to achieve their own ends, while society as a whole benefits from the sum of these best efforts.[22]

Simmel saw this process of competition as increasingly important in determining the shape of all areas of modern society. Moreover, he said, "The result of these competitions will in turn depend in most cases upon the interest, love, hope which the competitors know to arouse in different degrees in these or those third parties, the centers of the competitive movements."[23]

The claim that third parties are the centers of the competitive movements is central to the whole notion of competitive pluralism. Concerning this, Simmel wrote: "The typical difference in sociological constellation . . . always remains that of two, as over against three, chief parties. A number of parties can share in different degrees in the function of the third, which is to mediate between the two extremes."[24] The third party mediates between the extremes, and the extremes compete for the central third party.

Having said so much about competition throughout society, it is somewhat surprising that Simmel specifically denies that competition is appropriate within a church.

> The second sociological type [besides the family] which excludes competition is exemplified in the religious community. Here the parallel efforts of all are directed toward a goal which is the same for all. But there is not competition because the attainment of the goal by one member does not exclude the others. At least according to the Christian conception, the house of God has room for all. And if the grace of God does not reserve it for some while it gives it to others, it thereby proves the uselessness of competition.[25]

What is curious is that, for a sociologist, Simmel here displays a remarkably individualistic conception of religion. While it is true that there cannot be a true competition within the church for salvation, there are a great many other aspects of the church *as an institution* which indeed may be competed for. The "third party" in this kind of church competition is not God, but the membership of the church.

Religious competition means that people are being offered a religious choice. Some find "choice" in itself a virtue, and a justification for competition.[26] There is, however, no necessary connection between accepting competitive pluralism and making a virtue of choice. The latter view is, as it were, arrived at from outside any particular religious institution or tradition. From the perspective of those inside a specific religious institution or tradition, on the other hand, what is good is not making a choice, but making the *right* choice, or even *being* right without ever having made a choice.[27] From its own perspective, the virtue of a faith is that it is true, not that it may be a choice. From this position, competition is accepted because it is a practical compromise by which several opposing groups may get the most out of a situation of diversity. Choice is only an end in itself from the perspective of the system; from the perspective of any group within the system, choice (or competition) is a means to a higher end.[28]

In the short run, winning over this third party would bolster either of the principal parties. Over time, however, an even more powerful possibility emerges: the complete disappearance of one principal party or the other, by a process of attrition. This is because, in the long run, the children of any group appear as an uncommitted third party, who must be won over. While the parents may have an advantage in this competition, the very fact that new generations succeed old ones means that diversities (and pluralism) based on solidarity at one time will not automatically be maintained. Each generation must be convinced anew; those groups which fail to convince the new generation will die out. This is true no matter how generous and tolerant the pluralism is; no matter how free people are to hold a position, it will not exist if no one wills to maintain it.

COMPETITIVE PLURALISM IS THE BEST SOLUTION TO THE PROBLEM OF DIVERSITY

Competition is a more realistic way to deal with pluralism than either conflict or dialogue, because organizations rarely have only two parties. In fact, organizations normally divide into three parties—two extremes and a middle. This is the ideal arrangement for a competition.

In principle, there could be as many diverse positions as there are people; in practice, though, normally only three parties exist. There are good structural reasons for this. Some people, in any organization, are committed to novel ideas, while others are committed to traditional ideas. By itself, this fact would not create parties, if for no other reason than that members of the first group do not all believe the *same* new ideas, and members of the second group do not all agree on the identical set of old ones. What forms each group into a party is its opposition to the other party. The "liberals" band together for mutual defense against the "conservatives," and vice versa. By being forced to come together, the liberals discover a common commitment to the *idea* of new ideas, and the conservatives discover a common commitment to the *idea* of old ideas. These commitments to opposing ideas—which might be called "progressive" versus "orthodox" as easily as "liberal" and "conservative"— are central to the meaning that each party finds in living, and in the organization.[29]

Between these two parties exists a vast central group whose members derive their meaning in life not so much from which ideas they believe as from what they practice, from what they *do*. They tend to be loyal to what the institution is because what they do *constitutes* what the institution is. These are the people who say "we should do it this way because we always have done it this way." The liberals, with their new ideas, have difficulty changing the thinking of these loyalists, but the conservatives, with their old ideas, have equal difficulty changing the practice of the loyalists.

The loyalist party is the one most difficult to mobilize, but this party is not inert. There is a loyalist position in the argument of diversity, just as there are liberal and conservative positions. For the extreme parties to win the support of the loyalists—and thereby to control the center of gravity in the organization—they must tailor their positions to the concerns of the group most loyal to the organization as it actually is.

COMPETITION IN THE SPHERES OF SOCIETY

Pluralism—the idea that diversity is legitimate—is well established in the economic, political, and cultural spheres of Western society.[30] The idea that competition is the most viable way to organize society is well established in the economic and political spheres. Yet, to many, it seems distasteful, even wrong, to settle any cultural differences competitively—most especially religious disagreements. This is a serious problem and will get a serious answer. First, though, it is helpful to see that nine-tenths of the argument for competitive religious pluralism already is well accepted.

In the economic sphere, the idea of competition is commonplace. When economists discuss the principles of competition, they assume the three-part relation—among two sellers and a buyer—which constitutes the basic structure of a market.[31] This idea is so well established that it does not even need the special name "pluralism" to be recognized as legitimate; on the contrary, in economics it is the "monopolist" who is marked by a special term.

Competition is established in the political sphere as well, forming the basis of modern democratic politics, in which parties compete for voters.[32] Pluralism in this sphere was won with more difficulty than in the economic arena, and the legitimacy of a diversity of parties still is contested even in Western political theory.[33] It is clear, however, that competitive democracy is the dominant political ideal (if not the dominant reality) in the world today.

The principle of pluralism in the cultural sphere is well established in the United States, as a fundamental characteristic of a free society. Cultural diversity—in art, music, literature, design, and so forth—is not merely legitimate; indeed, it is thought to be a positive good for society and essential to the health of the culture. The same arguments are made about diversity of religions. Yet serious consideration of the practice of pluralism in the cultural sphere is only just beginning. Moreover, even the few attempts made thus far view competition as a kind of conflict, rather than as an alternative to conflict, and treat both conflict and competition as much inferior to dialogue.[34]

There is one respect, though, in which religious competition already is well institutionalized: in the idea of a "denomination." The traditional sociological understanding of religious institutions drew a distinction between "sect" and "church." As an ideal type, a *sect* is a body of the spiritually or doctrinally pure, in which all the members are expected to maintain the distinctive beliefs and practices that clearly separate the sect from "the world"—that is, from everyone else. A *church*, as a type, is characterized by "catholicity," an internal breadth that embraces all kinds of people and an internal complexity that provides many layers of roles, rules, and practices within the institution and the religious life. Both sect and church tend to view their organization as the "only true" embodiment of the faith, although the former does so more by excluding alternatives and the latter more by assimilating them.[35]

The denomination, in contrast to both sect and church, does not view itself as the only true embodiment of the faith, but rather as one of several forms of that institution, which are distinguished from one another by the way they are named—that is, "denominated." The differences between denominations are real and important, but they are not equivalent to the distinction between "true" and "false." In the United States, all religious bodies tend to take the form of denominations, even those which in other societies were sects or churches.[36]

Denominations are essentially pluralistic.[37] This characteristic is implicit in the very idea that multiple forms of a religious institution may legitimately coexist. Denominations also are competitive. Whereas sects deal with diversity by separating from it and churches deal with diversity by including it, denominations embrace diversity. Unlike the sect, denominations accept free movement from one institution to another; unlike the church, denominations accept the free creation of new institutions. They may not like these freedoms, but they accept them as fully legitimate. Free "exit" and free creation of new opportunities for "voice" in one's own religious institution mean that all denominations are forced to compete with one another for the loyalty of their members.[38]

Recently, a group of sociologists and economists has begun to embrace the idea that denominational competition is essential to the American form of religion. R. Stephen Warner contrasts this new competitive paradigm with the old European paradigm of secularization. When religion is divorced from the state, it does not, as Enlightenment thought long hoped, dissolve into irrelevance; rather, it is spread deeper and wider in the population through denominational competition. This point has been developed most thoroughly for American religious history by Roger Finke and Rodney Stark, who discovered that denominations offering a genuinely supernatural religion, coupled with a high degree of tension with the world, win a higher religious market share. Laurence Iannaccone has shown that Protestant denominations prosper most in nations with the greatest degree of religious competition, while Mark Chaves and David Cann have shown that this success is due principally to the freedom of these competitors from the state.[39] This developing body of work is very promising. With regard to the problem we are considering here, its only limitation is that it has been confined, thus far, to interdenominational pluralism and has not addressed the intradenominational variety.

COMPETITION WITHIN AN INSTITUTION

The question of pluralism within institutions is not the same as the question of pluralism within the spheres of society, but it is very similar. Some argue that the pluralism of a free society is best preserved through the vigilant tension that exists among organizations which are not themselves internally pluralistic. An organization that is pluralistic internally may be torn by internal division or even taken over by the enemies of freedom, thereby depriving society of the very institutions most necessary for its defense.[40] In contrast, others argue that a free society requires internally "free" institutions.

The justification for uniformity within institutions—namely, that unity is required in the face of a permanent external threat—is the same as the justification given for suppressing dissent in society as a whole. A long debate was waged in the West over whether society as a whole ought to be uniform and without dissent; the dissenters, the pluralists, won. A similar struggle goes on within the institutions in these societies, over whether these institutions ought to be uniform and without dissent.

This struggle over internal pluralism becomes more intense as one moves from economic to political to religious institutions, because the principles upon which each is founded demand increasing degrees of loyalty.[41] The struggles within religious institutions are perhaps the most intense, because they are fights over orthodoxy, the ideal of one truth.[42] In religious institutions, this struggle takes the form of a fight over which aspects of the faith are essential and therefore must be kept pure, and which are secondary.

The opposition between internally unified versus internally pluralist religious institutions parallels the contrast between sect and church. Yet a case can be made that either a sect *or* a church would resist a threat to freedom in society more successfully. In fact, the uniformity and resistance to internal dissent of the "sectarian" organization itself may *pose* a threat to freedom. This is not to suggest that it is always so, but rather to suggest that it simply is not useful to consider the effects on a free society of organizational form alone, divorced from a consideration of the content of what the organization is about.

COMPETITIVE RELIGIOUS PLURALISM — UNDER A CONSTITUTION

Competitive pluralism is an explicit ideal in economic and political matters and is an implicit practice in religious affairs. Why, then, is competitive religious pluralism so hard to stomach? Because religious institutions must try to explain the meaning of the most profound circumstances of human existence. Often they must play a role in justifying and motivating meaningful behavior in other spheres of social life as well.[43] To leave important "meaning" questions to the fickleness of the crowd seems to be trifling with sacred things.

Ultimately the justification for competitive religious pluralism is the same as the justification for competitive pluralism in other spheres: the world is founded on the Truth, and the Truth will out. As Lincoln said, you can't fool all of the people all of the time. *Vox populi, vox Dei.*

The example of Lincoln reminds us, though, of the great sociological necessity for rule by "the people" in a common system of order, a union under a constitution. Competitive pluralism depends upon rules which keep society civil. If the parties to a conflict do not keep themselves within those rules, then civil society is destroyed, and civil war ensues.[44] In this situation, pluralism is impossible, because pluralism depends upon a prior civil order. The civil order of any social institution is shaped by (though not produced by) its constitution.

In the United States, the Constitution creates, in very general terms, the form of order among the spheres of society, structuring the kind of pluralism that obtains in America. Likewise, within those spheres, the institutions have, more or less formally, their own "constitutions." These serve to structure the kind of pluralism that obtains within the institutions.

A constitutional order in society can prevent the disorder that the opponents of social pluralism fear. A constitutional order within institutions likewise can prevent the disorder that the opponents of institutional pluralism fear. The destructive pluralism that has beset so many institutions in the past generation, including the Presbyterian Church, is based upon an opposition to order and "hierarchy."[45] Constitutional pluralism, by contrast, allows for what Stephen Sykes has called "contained diversity," which is all that unity amounts to, given "the inconceivability of there ever being complete agreement about the identity of Christianity."[46] George Lindbeck's proposal that all doctrine is essentially a way of regulating religious discourse would be much more sociologically plausible if the relevant doctrines were understood to be institutionalized in the church's constitution.[47]

The prize to be won in intradenominational competition is control of the institutional machinery of the denomination. In the twentieth century, Protestant denominations increasingly have developed and rationalized their institutional structures, raising these competitive stakes.[48] Especially in the Presbyterian Church, the process of administrative centralization has gone along with the "theological decentralization"—that is, pluralism—that we have been considering.[49] In the one previous sociological study that specifically considers intradenominational competition, Mark Chaves found that institutional loyalists with ties to the developing agency structure beat competitors with strong (conservative) ideologies but weak institutional connections.[50]

Successful Competitors in the Presbyterian Church

The Presbyterian Church always has been a competitive and constitutional institution. The effect of the long struggle over pluralism, from Briggs to Machen, though, was to make competitive pluralism the manifest, rather than the latent, practice of the church. In the narrative of pluralism, there were three notably successful competitors in the church: Briggs's prosecutors, the Auburn Affirmationists, and the Special Commission of 1925.

The success of these competitors depended upon the detailed constitution of the Presbyterian Church and the commitment of the church as a whole to constitutionalism.[51] While intense struggles over diversity occurred in most American denominations from the end of the nineteenth century through the early decades of the twentieth, the battles in the Presbyterian Church were more severe and more obvious.[52] The constitution organized the denomination as a hierarchy of courts, which encouraged differences within the church to take the form of judicial proceedings.[53] The unusual intensity and articulation of the struggles in the Presbyterian Church make it a good place to study competitive pluralism.

The prosecution of Charles A. Briggs was the most enduring conservative success of the entire pluralism controversy, because it was the conservatives' best attempt at constitutional competition. Instead of public denunciations, polemical pamphlets, mass rallies, and General Assembly resolutions against liberal views (the conservative strategy in each subsequent stage of the controversy), the conservative party of the 1890s brought charges against Briggs himself in his presbytery. While, in the view of posterity, their victory remains tainted by procedural irregularities, it is almost certain that scrupulous due process would have produced the same result. Briggs's conservative prosecutors made their bid for the agreement of the loyalist center through a constitutional exposure of Briggs's liberal views, and they were rewarded with a massive victory in the greatest church trial in American history.

The competitive success of the conservatives was aided, of course, by the competitive failures of the liberals. Rather than competing with the conservatives for the loyalists, the Briggs liberals attempted a head-to-head conflict with the conservatives. The liberals demanded, in effect, that the loyalist majority swallow liberal views on the Bible, on reason, and, most damaging, on the desirability of dissolving the Presbyterian Church.

The liberal failure in the Briggs case is particularly ironic, since Charles Briggs is the only important figure in the entire story of Presbyterian pluralism—left, right, or center—who preached a vision of constitutional competition within the church. Of the dispute between Calvinism and Arminianism, for example, he wrote:

> I do not underrate the importance of the points of difference. I would not be willing to yield any position of historic Calvinism or to depart from the Puritan type of doctrine. But I see no reason why Calvinism could not maintain itself in the same ecclesiastical organization with Arminianism . . . I have such confidence in the principles of Calvinism that I believe they would have a better chance of overcoming Arminianism in a free and chivalrous contest in the same ecclesiastical organization, than . . . when shut off by themselves.[54]

Briggs's preaching, though, was the abstract vision of a church intellectual; Briggs himself never translated this view into a practical competitive program.

Liberals in the subsequent generation learned the lessons of the Briggs case and came back with their greatest success in this story, the Auburn Affirmation. Some liberals rejected the conservative "five points," but if they had publicly demanded that the church accept their position as legitimate, they would have gone the way of Charles Briggs. Instead, the liberal leadership successfully competed for loyalist support by meeting them more than half-way. The affirmation affirms the traditional doctrines; states with careful ambiguity that "many" of the signers actually agree with the "five points"; and, most importantly, grounds its plea for pluralism in specific Presbyterian constitutional procedures.

It is entirely possible that the "five points" would have been ratified by the presbyteries if they had been sent down. The fact that they were voted in by three different General Assemblies over a decade and a half suggests that there was considerable conservative sentiment in the denomination. Since the conservatives never did send the "five points" down to the presbyteries, however, they continuously had an exposed constitutional flank. In the period after 1910, the conservative leadership was passing to people, such as Machen, who were more committed to doctrine and less skilled in the affairs of the denomination. In contrast, with its leading intellectuals removed in the Briggs affair, the liberal leadership was opened to "life and work" ecumenists, such as Henry Sloane Coffin, who were active in denominational tasks. The future would lie with the denominational insiders.

By the mid-twenties, the liberal party was capable of successful competition. It convinced more than 10 percent of the church's ministers actually to sign the Affirmation, and it eventually was vindicated by the church as a whole. A measure of the liberals' success was that in 1943, after the long march of the Machenites out of the denomination, Henry Sloane Coffin, co-author of the Auburn Affirmation, was elected moderator of the church.

Conservative failures also contributed to the success of the affirmation. The conservatives constantly complained about it, without ever taking any constitutional action that the loyalists could sink their teeth into. The affirmation struggle was so successful for the liberals that, thereafter, they never again had to have a direct conflict with the conservatives. The competition had been the conservatives' to lose; since the conservatives had a conflictual, rather than competitive, ecclesiology, lose it they did.

The most successful competitors of all in the story of Presbyterian pluralism were the loyalists of the Special Commission of 1925. It is easy to forget that loyalist leaders are competitors, too; they must compete in order to mobilize their own half-formed party, as well as competing for liberal and conservative support. The Special Commission took a risk in staking out a constitutionally inclusive position. It indeed could have lost the struggle, if the conservatives, through the presbyteries, had launched a constitutional challenge to the commission's central contention that tolerance for diversity was an essential precept of the Presbyterian Church. The conservatives, though, failed to make a constitutional attack, sticking instead to the strategy of denouncing loyalist "indifferentism" and demanding as a right the ratification of the conservative position. The Special Commission's report was approved overwhelmingly, and the commission members themselves had an unprecedented series of successes in the competition for the church's highest office.

The extended struggle in the Presbyterian Church was won by those who competed legitimately within the constitution of the church. The effect of this struggle was to legitimize the diversity of groups competing under the constitution. The result of the Presbyterian struggle, therefore, was competitive pluralism under the constitution.

Chapter 14

PRESBYTERIAN PLURALISM
TODAY: A POSTSCRIPT

oday pluralism is officially institutionalized in the Presbyterian Church (U.S.A.).[1] At the highest levels, the church's bureaucracy is concerned with seeing that the denomination's diversity is represented in all official activities. There are even, at each level of the church, Committees on Representation specifically charged with this task. While these committees are most concerned with gender and "racial ethnic" representation, they also look out for theological minorities, although they are more attentive to the left positions than to the right ones.[2]

The church's official concern with pluralism has been driven, in the main, by the flowering of special interest groups within the Presbyterian communion. On the left, right, and center, groups such as Presbyterians for Gay and Lesbian Concerns, Presbyterians Pro-Life, and Presbyterians for Renewal have organized the denomination's parties for sustained pressure, especially on the church's bureaucracy. The existence of an influential loyalist group, Presbyterians for Renewal, which is conservative in theology but loyal to the denomination, is an important answer to those who see the church being torn apart by the broader "culture wars."[3]

In 1976, Dean Hoge, in *Division in the Protestant House,* offered a two-party analysis of conflict in the Presbyterian Church. In his account, progressive liberals and status-quo conservatives contended for the church, continuing a two-party system with roots in events at the beginning of the century. Hoge searched in vain for a third party of "independents," but he defined this party as those who would "oppose all forms of external mission . . . [who] hold opinions similar to those of the standard parties, but would probably hold them less intensely . . . [and who are not primarily theological, but] may instead be more intent on having their church serve functions such as support for home and family life and creation of friendships and community."[4] He did not search for a party of committed institutional loyalists and did not find one. Yet, amid the data that he does report is evidence of what he himself calls a "neo-orthodox" or "neo-traditionalist" group with a distinctively centrist theological position.[5]

In 1976, in response to one of the most active of the special interest groups, the conservative Presbyterian Lay Committee, the United Presbyterian Church in the U.S.A. created the Committee on Pluralism in the Church.[6] In 1988, the General Assembly amended the church's constitution, moving the rules governing special-interest organizations from the chapter dealing with governance and control to the chapter dealing with ministry and worship, on the grounds that the emergence of "special-interest organizations committed to specific ministries of service, nurture, or witness is one manifestation of the diversity of the church."[7]

The position of the Committee on Pluralism was that conflict in the church, when carried on within the terms of the constitution, may be reconciled creatively. As the first of the committee's "Guiding Principles" states, "The polity of the Church assumes that conflict will exist within the life of the Church and assumes further that conflict has both creative and destructive potential."[8] The Committee on Pluralism notes that, "when properly used, the polity of the church organizes conflict, encourages the contending parties to listen to one another, and greatly facilitates reconciliation."[9] In other words, the polity of the church encourages "conflict" to become "dialogue."

The "differences which naturally emerge" in the church are "responsible expressions of . . . diversity." Conflict, the committee allows, may "open up creative possibilities," and in fact the "presence of conflict means that something important to us is at stake. That is good." The group goes so far as to suggest that easy agreement in the church should cause "red flags" to go up, since agreement "always involves cutting off possibilities." To the 1978 General Assembly, the committee wrote, "The central thesis of this report has been the need to recognize the inevitability and value of conflict in pluralistic structures."[10]

This conception of the "inevitability and value of conflict" in the church, and indeed the conception of the church as a "pluralistic structure," is very far from the idea of one body united in the faith once delivered to the saints. The articulation, at the highest levels of the denomination, of this explicit conception of the church as an entity that contains and even benefits from diversity, represents a tremendous change in the self-conception of the Presbyterian Church. Note that what is at issue here is not whether there always has been diversity in the church (there has), but whether that diversity is viewed as acceptable and even valuable. This is true pluralism. This change in the Presbyterian Church is evident even in comparison with the 1930s; then, toleration in the church had won a victory, but pluralism had not yet been officially and explicitly accepted.

It is through the church's polity, its constitutional order, that continuity has been maintained between this pluralistic conception and the traditions of the Presbyterian Church. The Committee on Pluralism notes that the "assurance that conflicting viewpoints may be heard is safeguarded at several points in the *Book of Order* and in the *Manual of the General Assembly*." In fact, such safeguards for opposing, dissenting, and minority views are found throughout the rules of Presbyterian procedure.[11] The committee represents the view that the Presbyterian Church is a "denominated" part of the larger Christian Church, a denomination defined by its order. Thus, "the central elements of the faith of Presbyterians are all shared as well by other Christians. *It is the polity that contains the distinctive features*."[12] This is the constitutional conception of the church, as contrasted with the view that defines the church by its theological doctrines alone.

The concerns of the Committee on Pluralism were taken up by the "Task Force on Theological Pluralism within the Presbyterian Community of Faith," which made its final report to the General Assembly in 1988. Entitled *Is Christ Divided?*, the report continued the line taken by its predecessors in seeing diversity as inevitable and even valuable in promoting creativity and humility. The report recognized the existence of parties in the church and their struggle to gain control of the institutional life of the church.[13] The principal conclusion of the task force's report is that "[w]hat seems to characterize the Presbyterian Church today is less its theological diversity than its avoidance of the challenges of that diversity."[14] The principle recommendation of *Is Christ Divided?* is that the Presbyterian Church should deal with diversity through theological dialogue.

Since the adoption of the task force's recommendation by the General

Assembly, the problem of diversity has not diminished in the Presbyterian Church (U.S.A.). True, a notable minority of the church's leaders believe that "inclusivity" now is a distinctive attribute of Presbyterian culture.[15] On the other hand, many conservatives believe that pluralism in the denomination has been the cause of the latter's decline.[16] Furthermore, among the Baby Boom generation now taking control of the church, the loyalty of even active Presbyterians seems to be to mainline Protestantism in general, rather than to the Presbyterian Church specifically.[17]

The church's long-standing attempt to overcome diversity—and avoid theological dialogue—by retreating into the "life and work" or "unity in mission" of the church has failed.[18] The church's 1990 decision to remove from its constitution any official notice of the special-interest ("Chapter Nine") organizations is part of this same attempt to avoid theological conflict.[19] Theological dialogue has not been an effective way to overcome diversity, either, though, as the principal author of *Is Christ Divided?* has concluded since its publication.[20]

The experience of the Presbyterian Church in dealing with diversity both implicitly in the past and explicitly today suggests that competitive pluralism under the constitution is the most viable solution to the problem of diversity.

NOTES

INTRODUCTION

1. Jack Rogers, *Claiming the Center: Churches and Conflicting Worldviews* (Louisville, Ky.: Westminster/John Knox Press, 1995): xv.
2. For this idea and term, I am grateful to Donald A. Luidens and Roger J. Nemeth, "'Public' and 'Private' Protestantism Reconsidered: Introducing the 'Loyalists,'" *Journal for the Scientific Study of Religion* 26 (Dec. 1987): 450–64.
3. Albert O. Hirschman, *Exit, Voice, and Loyalty* (Cambridge, Mass.: Harvard Univ. Press, 1970).
4. James Davison Hunter, *Culture Wars: The Struggle to Define America* (New York: Basic, 1991); James Davison Hunter, *Before the Shooting Begins: Searching for Democracy in America's Culture Wars* (New York: Free Press, 1994); Robert Wuthnow, *The Restructuring of American Religion: Society and Faith Since World War II* (Princeton, N.J.: Princeton Univ. Press, 1988); Dean R. Hoge, *Division in the Protestant House: The Basic Reasons Behind Intra-Church Conflicts* (Philadelphia: Westminster Press, 1976).
5. Stephen R. Warner, "Work in Progress toward a New Paradigm for the Sociological Study of Religion in the United States," *American Journal of Sociology* 98 (Mar. 1993): 1044–93; Laurence R. Iannaccone, "The Consequences of Religious Market Structure: Adam Smith and the Economics of Religion," *Rationality and Society* 3 (Apr. 1991): 156–77; Mark Chaves and David E. Cann, "Regulation, Pluralism, and Religious Market Structure: Explaining Religious Vitality," *Rationality and Society* 4 (July 1992): 272–90; Roger Finke and Rodney Stark, *The Churching of America, 1776–1990: Winners and Losers in Our Religious Economy* (New Brunswick, N.J.: Rutgers Univ. Press, 1992).
6. The only partial exception is Mark Chaves, "Intraorganizational Power and Internal Secularization in Protestant Denominations," *American Journal of Sociology* 99 (July 1993): 1–48.

7. Lefferts Loetscher, *The Broadening Church: A Study of Theological Issues in the Presbyterian Church Since 1869* (Philadelphia: Univ. of Pennsylvania Press, 1954).

8. Mark Massa, *Charles Augustus Briggs and the Crisis of Historical Criticism* (Philadelphia: Fortress Press, 1989).

9. Bradley Longfield, *The Presbyterian Controversy: Fundamentalists, Modernists, and Moderates* (New York: Oxford Univ. Press, 1991).

10. Darryl G. Hart, *Defending the Faith: J. Gresham Machen and the Crisis of Conservative Protestantism in America* (Baltimore, Md.: Johns Hopkins Univ. Press, 1994).

11. Massa generally joins Loetscher in this liberal account; however, as a Jesuit, he is less interested than the Presbyterian authors in the intra-Presbyterian struggle and more concerned with historical criticism as a movement.

CHAPTER 1. THE PRESBYTERIAN CHURCH IN THE U.S.A. BEFORE THE BRIGGS CASE

1. Leonard J. Trinterud, *The Forming of an American Tradition: A Re-examination of Colonial Presbyterianism* (Philadelphia: Westminster Press, 1949).

2. Lefferts Loetscher, *A Brief History of the Presbyterians,* 4th ed. (Philadelphia: Westminster Press, 1978), 61–77.

3. Ibid., 64–65.

4. Although both the participants and outside observers usually use the terms *conservative* and *liberal*, these terms obscure how innovative the so-called conservatives actually are. Normally, the loyalist center is the most conservative, in the sense of traditional, static, and inert. This group is the most devoted to the Presbyterian Church *as it is*—to its history, unity, and rules of order. For this reason, the loyalists are sometimes called "moderate" conservatives, and those to their right are called "extreme" or "militant" conservatives.

5. Loetscher, *Brief History,* 69–70, 80, and 92–104; Trinterud, *Forming an American Tradition,* 95ff.

6. "[I]n the South the debates were short-lived, because dissent was simply not tolerated." George Marsden, *Fundamentalism and American Culture: The Shaping of Twentieth-Century Evangelicalism, 1840–1925* (Oxford, England: Oxford Univ. Press, 1980), 103.

7. George Marsden, *The Evangelical Mind and the New School Presbyterian Experience: A Case Study of Thought and Theology in Nineteenth-Century America* (New Haven, Conn.: Yale Univ. Press, 1970), 228.

8. Loetscher, *Broadening Church,* 54–55.

CHAPTER 2. 1890s: THE BRIGGS CASE AND ITS AFTERMATH

1. Channing Renwick Jeschke, "The Briggs Case: The Focus of a Study in Nineteenth-Century Presbyterian History" (Ph.D. diss., Divinity School, Univ. of

Chicago, 1966), 231, 271, 300; Carl Hatch, *The Charles A. Briggs Heresy Trial: Prologue to Twentieth-Century Liberal Protestantism* (New York: Exposition Press, 1969), 89; Richard L. Christensen, *The Ecumenical Orthodoxy of Charles Augustus Briggs (1841–1913)* (Lewiston, N.Y.: Mellen Univ. Press, 1995), 61ff. Loetscher, *Broadening Church,* 29–39. The Princeton editors were, in order, A. A. Hodge, Francis Patton, and B. B. Warfield.

2. Christensen, *Ecumenical Orthodoxy,* 84ff.

3. Loetscher, *Broadening Church,* 42; Jeschke, "Briggs Case," 286–87; see also these clippings in the Charles Briggs Papers at Union Theological Seminary: Francis Patton, quoted in "Articles of Faith," *New York Times,* Dec. 3, 1893; "The New Reformation," *New York Sun,* Dec. 11, 1889; Philip Schaff, quoted in "Dr. Schaff on the Creed," *New York Tribune,* Oct. 7, 1889. For Briggs's later assessment, see Charles A. Briggs, "Note Biographical, 1841–1889," typescript dated Apr. 1, 1889, in Briggs Papers, Box 44, Folder 33, 1; Charles A. Briggs, *The Defense of Professor Briggs Before the Presbytery of New York, 1893* (New York: Scribners, 1893), 88; Charles A. Briggs, "The Future of Presbyterianism in the United States of America," *North American Review* 157 (July 1893): 1–12, in Briggs Papers, Box 52, Folder 28; Max Gray Rogers, "Charles Augustus Briggs: Conservative Heretic" (Ph.D. diss., Columbia Univ., 1964), 382.

4. Charles A. Briggs, *The Authority of Holy Scripture: An Inaugural Address* (New York: Scribners, 1891; rpt. New York: Arno, 1972), 33–35, 43–45.

5. It later was charged that the conservatives pushed this motion through the presbytery meeting while the Union Seminary people, who would have opposed it, were at lunch; see Max Rogers, "Charles Augustus Briggs," 150.

6. John J. McCook, ed., *The Appeal in the Briggs Heresy Case before the General Assembly of the Presbyterian Church in the United States of America* (New York: John C. Rankin, 1893), 21.

7. Jeschke, "Briggs Case," 328.

8. Presbyterian Church in the U.S.A., *Minutes of the General Assembly,* 1893, 95–150; Jeschke, "Briggs Case," 330ff.

9. Presbyterian Church in the U.S.A., *Minutes of the General Assembly,* 1891, 93–105; Loetscher, *Broadening Church,* 55; Max Rogers, "Charles Augustus Briggs," 387.

10. Jeschke, "Briggs Case," 255; Max Rogers, "Charles Augustus Briggs," 403–4, 416, 430, 442–43; William R. Hutchison, *The Modernist Impulse in American Protestantism* (Cambridge, Mass.: Harvard Univ. Press, 1976), 178; Massa, *Briggs and Historical Criticism,* 126–35; Charles A. Briggs, "Memorial to Thomas Hastings," Apr. 1911, in Briggs Papers, Union Theological Seminary, Box 22, Folder 15, pp. 6–7.

11. Max Rogers, "Charles Augustus Briggs," 486–87; Robert Handy, *A History of Union Theological Seminary in New York* (New York: Columbia Univ. Press, 1987), 97–98.

12. Synod of New York and Philadelphia [Presbyterian], *Minutes of the Synod of New York and Philadelphia*, 1758, p. 286.
13. Loetscher, *Broadening Church*, 63–68.
14. George L. Prentiss, *The Union Theological Seminary in the City of New York: Its Design and Another Decade of Its History* (Asbury Park, N.J.: Pennypacker, 1899), 339; Loetscher, *Broadening Church*, 71–74; Max Rogers, "Charles Augustus Briggs," 41; Henry Sloane Coffin, *A Half-Century of Union Theological Seminary, 1896–1945: An Informal History* (New York: Scribners, 1954), 103.

CHAPTER 3. 1900s: BROADENING THE BASE

1. Edwin H. Rian, *The Presbyterian Conflict* (Grand Rapids, Mich.: Eerdmans, 1940), 18; see also Gary Scott Smith, *The Seeds of Secularization: Calvinism, Culture, and Pluralism in America, 1870–1915* (Grand Rapids, Mich.: Christian Univ. Press, 1985), 183, n. 2.
2. "Westminster Confession," chap. 25, sec. 6, cited in Loetscher, *Broadening Church*, 45.
3. "Westminster Confession," chap. 10, sec. 3. Charles Hodge, the eminent Old School theologian of Princeton Seminary, also had favored revision of this section.
4. This doctrine often is called "double" predestination, to distinguish it from the view that, while some are predestined to election, the fate of the others is not foreknown.
5. Presbyterian Church in the U.S.A., *Minutes of the General Assembly*, 1903, 15–17.
6. Rian, *Presbyterian Conflict*, 23–25.
7. Presbyterian Church (USA), *The Constitution of the Presbyterian Church (USA), Part One: The Book of Confessions* (Louisville, Ky.), 6.192.
8. The "Declaratory Statement" goes on to declare that the Confession text, "Elect infants, dying in infancy, are . . . saved by Christ through the Spirit" (chap. 10, sec. 3), is "not to be regarded as teaching that any who die in infancy are lost." It is a mistake, then, to infer that there are any unelect infants. Presbyterian Church (USA), *Constitution, Part 1: Book of Confessions*, 6.193.
9. Charles Evans Quirk, "The 'Auburn' Affirmation: A Critical Narrative of the Document Designed to Safeguard the Unity and Liberty of the Presbyterian Church in the U.S.A. in 1924" (Ph.D. diss., School of Religion, Univ. of Iowa, 1967), 20–24; Longfield, *Presbyterian Controversy*, 24.
10. Loetscher, *Broadening Church*, 96. The Cumberland minority that stayed out of the reunion may have been the more conservative part. See Dallas Roark, "J. Gresham Machen and His Desire to Maintain a Doctrinally True Presbyterian Church" (Ph.D. diss., State Univ. of Iowa, 1963), 102–3, n. 1.

11. Presbyterian Church U.S.A., *Minutes of the General Assembly*, 1906, 130–35; Massa, *Briggs and Historical Criticism*, 112.

Chapter 4. 1910s: Rhetorical Fundamentalism

1. Marsden, *Fundamentalism and American Culture*, 46 and 259, n.11.
2. "Most conservative Presbyterians . . . did not identify themselves completely with interdenominational fundamentalism at the double price of abandoning distinctive Calvinism and accepting premillenialism"; Loetscher, *Broadening Church*, 91.
3. John Hart, "The Controversy within the Presbyterian Church, USA, in the 1920s, with Special Emphasis on the Reorganization of Princeton Theological Seminary" (senior thesis, Princeton Univ., 1978), 20.
4. In addition to Machen, the other faculty members opposed were Oswald Allis, William B. Greene, C. W. Hodge, B. B. Warfield, and, somewhat surprisingly given later events, Stevenson's ally Charles Erdman; see Quirk, "Auburn Affirmation," 50. Stevenson himself later successfully opposed the plan in Baltimore Presbytery after he became convinced of its inadequacies, but Machen was not satisfied; see Ronald T. Clutter, "The Reorientation of Princeton Theological Seminary, 1925–1929" (Th.D. diss.: Dallas Theological Seminary, 1982), 190.
5. Rian, *Presbyterian Conflict*, 27.
6. In its report to the Thompson Committee, which investigated the tension in the seminary in 1926 (see below), the conservative majority dated the problems in the seminary back to the fight over the grand organic union plan; see Quirk, "Auburn Affirmation," 76.

Chapter 5. 1920s: Fundamentalists and Modernists Fight for the Center

1. Kenneth Cauthen, *The Impact of American Religious Liberalism* (New York: Harper and Row, 1962), 61–62.
2. Rian, *Presbyterian Conflict*, 29ff.
3. Marsden, *Fundamentalism and American Culture*, 172–73.
4. Quoted in Loetscher, *Broadening Church*, 112; Longfield, *Presbyterian Controversy*, 76.
5. See, e.g., J. Gresham Machen, "The Attack upon Princeton Seminary: A Plea for Fair Play," Dec. 1927 (pamphlet published by the author), 5. This misunderstanding is by no means a dead issue; see, e.g., Darryl Hart, *Defending the Faith*, 116. For an account which does grasp this point, see Randall Balmer and John Fitzmier, *The Presbyterians* (Westport, Conn.: Praeger, 1994), 88–89.
6. Henry Sloane Coffin and Robert Hastings Nichols, "An Affirmation," rpt. in *The*

Presbyterian Enterprise, ed. Maurice Armstrong, Lefferts Loetscher, and Charles Anderson (Philadelphia: Westminster, 1961), 287–88.

7. J. Gresham Machen, *Christianity and Liberalism* (1923; rpt. Grand Rapids, Mich.: Eerdmans, 1946), 27.

8. See J. N. D. Kelly, *Early Christian Doctrines* (New York: Harper and Row, 1978), 375ff.

9. Coffin and Nichols, "An Affirmation," 287.

10. Charles Hodge, "The Rights of Presbyteries Ought Not to Be Annulled" (New York: Anson D. F. Randall, 1896); see M. James Sawyer, *Charles Augustus Briggs and Tensions in Late-Nineteenth-Century American Theology* (Lewiston, N.Y.: Mellen Univ. Press, 1994), chap. 4.

11. Quirk, "'Auburn' Affirmation," 58, 177, 199–200, 382–83, 508, and 513–15.

12. Marsden, *Fundamentalism and American Culture,* 181; Quirk, "Auburn Affirmation," 157–58.

13. Quirk, "Auburn Affirmation," 242.

14. Presbyterian Church in the U.S.A., *Minutes of the General Assembly,* 1924, 195–96.

15. Rian, *Presbyterian Conflict,* 38. Fosdick remained an esteemed member of the Union Seminary faculty for years thereafter and went on to be the founding pastor of Riverside Church, across the street from Union. He was arguably the leading liberal preacher in America in the first half of this century. In the estimation of Henry Sloane Coffin, Fosdick was "the most eminent preacher of his time." See Coffin, *Half-Century of Union,* 62.

16. Presbyterian Church in the U.S.A., *Minutes of the General Assembly,* 1924, 198; Loetscher, *Broadening Church,* 123; Quirk, "Auburn Affirmation," 250–51.

17. Presbyterian Church in the U.S.A., *Minutes of the General Assembly,* 1924, 202.

18. See, e.g., Rian, *Presbyterian Conflict,* 55. Darryl Hart, *Defending the Faith,* 116, goes so far as to say that even the act of referring the overtures to committees was a trick of the "liberal lobby" used in "thwarting conservative advances through denominational red tape."

19. From a 1978 interview with Paul Woolley (a close Machen associate), cited in John Hart, "Reorganization of Princeton Seminary," 35.

20. Quirk, "Auburn Affirmation," 153, n. 43. In 1934, H. McAllister Griffiths, a Machen ally, tried to bring charges against the Affirmationists in Philadelphia Presbytery, but that body ruled that the time limit for such charges had passed; see Quirk, "Auburn Affirmation," 321.

21. D. Clair Davis, "Evangelicals and the Presbyterian Tradition: An Alternative Perspective," *Westminster Theological Journal* 42 (Fall 1979): 155–56.

22. Loetscher, *Broadening Church,* 128.

23. Quirk, "Auburn Affirmation," 297.

24. Norman Furniss, *The Fundamentalist Controversy, 1918–1931* (New Haven, Conn.: Yale Univ. Press, 1954), 137–38.

25. Furniss, *Fundamentalist Controversy*, 134; Presbyterian Church (USA), *Minutes of the General Assembly*, 1927, 61; Loetscher, *Broadening Church*, 134.

CHAPTER 6. 1929: THE BATTLE FOR PRINCETON SEMINARY

1. Machen, "Attack on Princeton Seminary," 16.
2. Allyn Russell, *The Voices of American Fundamentalism: Seven Biographical Studies* (Philadelphia: Westminster Press, 1976), 152.
3. J. Ross Stevenson, "Address to the General Assembly," 1926, manuscript in J. Ross Stevenson, "Confidential Letters and Documents," Speer Library, Princeton Theological Seminary, Princeton, N.J.
4. Machen, "Attack upon Princeton Seminary," 10.
5. Quoted in Rian, *Presbyterian Conflict*, 70.
6. John Hart, "Princeton Seminary," 75; Ronald T. Clutter, "The Reorganization of Princeton Theological Seminary Reconsidered," *Grace Theological Journal* 7 (1986): 188.
7. Clutter, "Reorientation of Princeton Seminary," 70.
8. Ned B. Stonehouse, *J. Gresham Machen: A Biographical Memoir* (Grand Rapids, Mich.: Eerdmans, 1954), 219.
9. Clutter, "Reorientation of Princeton Seminary," 100–103.
10. Paul Martin, secretary to the Princeton Seminary faculty, noted that Machen, a commissioner to the General Assembly in which Stevenson proposed the union, was grieved "almost to tears" by the proposal; Paul Martin to William O. Thompson, Dec. 23, 1926, in "Correspondence Regarding Machen Case, 1925–1927," Speer Library, Princeton Theological Seminary, Princeton, N.J.
11. Rian, *Presbyterian Conflict*, 78; John Hart, "Reorganization of Princeton Seminary," 62–63.
12. Rian, *Presbyterian Conflict*, 25.
13. See, e.g., Machen, "Attack upon Princeton Seminary," 20.
14. Allis did not write this editorial but appears to have instigated it, as Erdman suspected. Allis affirmed to the Thompson Committee in 1929 that he *still* thought the editorial correct in linking Erdman with the "rationalism of the University." Presbyterian Church in the U.S.A., "Report of the Special Committee to Visit Princeton," 147.
15. Quoted in Rian, *Presbyterian Conflict*, 72.
16. Stevenson, "Address to 1926 General Assembly."
17. Quoted in Russell, *Voices of Fundamentalism*, 155. Furniss, *Fundamentalist Controversy*, 140, reports that Erdman tried to "prevent open debate on the nomination to save Machen from sharp criticism by the liberals."
18. This division paralleled the distinction in local Presbyterian congregations between the session and the trustees.

19. Statement of the faculty "Majority," quoted in the report of the Thompson Committee, in Presbyterian Church in the U.S.A., *Minutes of the General Assembly,* 1929, 87.
20. See, e.g., Stevenson's claims that he was a "fundamentalist" and a "conservative Presbyterian" and that all of Princeton Seminary was loyal to the standards of the church. J. Ross Stevenson, "The Greetings of a Conservative Presbyterian to the Methodist League for Faith and Life," speech delivered in Philadelphia, Feb. 8, 1926, Formal Address no. 202, Papers of J. Ross Stevenson, Speer Library, Princeton Theological Seminary, Princeton, N.J.
21. Presbyterian Church in the U.S.A., *Minutes of the General Assembly,* 1929, 87.
22. John Hart, "Reorganization of Princeton Seminary," 84.
23. Ibid., 88.
24. Ibid., 89, 101; Stonehouse, *J. Gresham Machen,* 437.
25. A proposed change in the governance of the seminary was supposed to sit before the church for a year before it could be acted upon. Machen argued that, while the Thompson Committee had brought in a *general* plan for reorganizing the seminary boards more than the required year before, the proper period had not elapsed for its *specific* plan.
26. Russell, *Voices of Fundamentalism,* 155.

CHAPTER 7. 1930s: MACHEN AND THE CONSERVATIVE SEPARATION

1. The merger eventually was accomplished in 1958. See Loetscher, *Brief History,* 155; Rian, *Presbyterian Conflict,* 118.
2. Presbyterian Church in the U.S.A., *Minutes of the General Assembly,* 1934, 159, 242.
3. Darryl Hart, *Defending the Faith,* 203, n. 35.
4. Presbyterian Church in the U.S.A., *Minutes of the General Assembly,* 1933, 28.
5. Two other overtures were sent that were critical of the Foreign Missions Board, as well as four overtures commending it. Ibid., 154.
6. Ibid., 1934, 71.
7. Ibid., 72.
8. Ibid., 1933, 159.
9. Ibid., 159–60.
10. There is some question about whether he could have found any "modernists" in the mission field. In 1923, Machen's ally on the Princeton Seminary faculty, Robert Dick Wilson, had approved the theological soundness of Far Eastern missionaries he visited; see James A. Patterson, "Robert E. Speer, J. Gresham Machen, and the Presbyterian Board of Foreign Missions," *American Presbyterians* 64 (1986): 59. As late as 1935, Donald Barnhouse, the well-known conservative Presbyterian minister from Philadelphia, toured the missions and brought back

an enthusiastic report, calling them 98% orthodox. Machen's newspaper, *The Presbyterian Guardian*, did not dispute these figures but said that "symptoms" were more important than numbers; see Roark, "J. Gresham Machen and His Desire to Maintain a Doctrinally True Presbyterian Church," 125, n. 1.

11. Rian, *Presbyterian Conflict*, 96.

12. Presbyterian Church in the U.S.A., *Minutes of the General Assembly*, 1934, 72.

13. Wayne Headman, "A Critical Evaluation of J. Gresham Machen" (M. Theol. thesis, Princeton Theological Seminary, 1974), 158.

14. Presbyterian Church in the U.S.A., *Minutes of the General Assembly*, 1934, 112.

15. Ibid., 115–16.

16. Rian, *Presbyterian Conflict*, 173, 175, 178–82.

17. Ibid., 184.

18. "Dr. Machen Defies Presbytery in N. J.," *Philadelphia Evening Bulletin*, Sept. 26, 1934.

19. Presbyterian Church in the U.S.A., Presbytery of New Brunswick, "Action of the Presbytery of New Brunswick, Apr., 1935," typescript in Record Group 7, Box 1, Folder 3, Dept. of History, Presbyterian Church (USA), 4–6. See also Rian, *Presbyterian Conflict*, 184.

20. Rian, *Presbyterian Conflict*, 173–84; Presbyterian Church in the U.S.A., *Minutes of the General Assembly*, 1936, 101.

21. Presbyterian Church in the U.S.A., Publicity Dept., "Statement," n.d., in Record Group 20, Box 1, Folder 9, Dept. of History, Presbyterian Church (USA), n.p.; Presbyterian Church in the U.S.A., *Minutes of the General Assembly*, 1936, 99–100.

22. Rian, *Presbyterian Conflict*, 219.

23. Ibid., 229.

24. Ibid., 260–65. On Macartney's background, see Longfield, *Presbyterian Controversy*, 106.

25. Roark, "J. Gresham Machen and His Desire to Maintain a Doctrinally True Presbyterian Church," 138.

26. Rian, *Presbyterian Conflict*, 103, 242.

27. Ibid., 234.

28. Mark A. Noll, "The Pea Beneath the Mattress—Orthodox Presbyterianism in America," *Reformed Journal* 36 (Oct. 1986): 15.

29. Russell, *Voices of Fundamentalism*; Richard Hofstadter, *Anti-Intellectualism in American Life* (New York: Knopf, 1963), 132.

CHAPTER 8. THE LIBERAL: CHARLES A. BRIGGS

1. Jeschke, "Briggs Case," 135; Max Rogers, "Charles Augustus Briggs," 7; Massa, *Briggs and Historical Criticism*, 27.

2. Sawyer, *Briggs and Tensions*, 14ff; Prentiss, *Union Theological Seminary*, 313;

Jeschke, "Briggs Case," 136; Max Rogers, "Charles Augustus Briggs," 6; Massa, *Briggs and Historical Criticism,* 28.

3. Massa, *Briggs and Historical Criticism,* 35–36.
4. Sawyer, *Briggs and Tensions,* 18–19; Massa, *Briggs and Historical Criticism,* 36–43; Jeschke, "Briggs Case," 104, 139; Hatch, *Briggs Heresy Trial,* 23.
5. Massa, *Briggs and Historical Criticism,* 44–45; Jeschke, "Briggs Case," 131.
6. Charles A. Briggs, "The Advance Toward Church Unity," *The Independent,* Jan. 1, 1891, p. 1; in Briggs Papers, Union Theological Seminary, Box 52, Folder 1.
7. Charles A. Briggs, *American Presbyterianism: Its Origin and Early History* (New York: Scribners, 1885), 18, 79, xiii.
8. Charles A. Briggs, *Church Unity: Studies of Its Most Important Problems* (New York: Scribners, 1909), 16.
9. Briggs, *American Presbyterianism,* 140 and xii–xiii. Charles A. Briggs, *Whither? A Theological Question for the Times* (New York: Scribners, 1889), 88. Briggs, "Future of Presbyterianism," n.p.
10. Briggs, *Whither?,* x.
11. Sawyer, *Briggs and Tensions,* 47, n. 90.
12. Ibid., 22, n. 55.
13. Charles A. Briggs to Francis Brown, Nov. 8, 1888, quoted in Max Rogers, "Charles Augustus Briggs," 81.
14. Charles A. Briggs, "Union of Northern and Southern Presbyterians," *The Independent,* Apr. 26, 1888, n.p., in Briggs Papers, Union Theological Seminary, Box 53, Folder 46. Briggs makes specific reference to the Woodrow case, in which a southern seminary professor was treated unjustly, according to Briggs and many northern critics, for his "advanced" views on evolution.
15. Briggs, *Church Unity,* 4.
16. Briggs, *American Presbyterianism,* 18.
17. Briggs, *Defense of Professor Briggs,* 2.
18. Briggs, *Whither?,* 6.
19. Briggs, *Defense of Professor Briggs,* 3–4
20. Ibid., 17.
21. Charles A. Briggs, *The Ethical Teachings of Jesus* (New York: Scribners, 1904), 50–51.
22. Charles A. Briggs, *Biblical Study: Its Principles, Methods and History* (New York: Charles Scribner's Sons, 1887), 36–37; quoted in Hutchison, *Modernist Impulse,* 92.
23. Briggs, *Whither?,* 15–16.
24. Ibid., 16–17.
25. Charles A. Briggs, *The Bible, the Church, and the Reason: The Three Great Fountains of Divine Authority,* 2d ed. (New York: Scribners, 1893), 29–30.
26. Briggs, *Whither?,* 274.
27. Ibid., 247–48.

28. Briggs, *American Presbyterianism*, 288–89.
29. Ibid., 373.
30. Charles A. Briggs, "The Alienation of Church and People," *Forum* 74 (Nov. 1893): 374.
31. Briggs, *Church Unity*, 449.
32. Charles A. Briggs, "Terms of Christian Union," *Christian Union*, May 12, 1887, in Briggs Papers, Union Theological Seminary, Box 53, Folder 41.
33. Briggs, *Whither?*, 297.
34. Briggs, *Church Unity*, 15.

CHAPTER 9. THE CONSERVATIVE: J. GRESHAM MACHEN

1. Russell, *Voices of Fundamentalism*, 134–35, 139; J. Gresham Machen, "Christianity in Conflict," in *Contemporary American Theology*, ed. Vergilius Ferm (New York: Roundtable Press, 1932), 1:248; Darryl Hart, *Defending the Faith*, 5; Longfield, *Presbyterian Controversy*, 31ff.
2. Russell, *Voices of Fundamentalism*, 135.
3. J. Gresham Machen, quoted in Russell, *Voices of Fundamentalism*, 135.
4. Machen, "Christianity in Conflict," 254–55.
5. Ibid., 255–57.
6. Russell, *Voices of Fundamentalism*, 138; Machen, "Christianity in Conflict," 264.
7. Darryl Hart, *Defending the Faith*, 85.
8. Russell, *Voices of Fundamentalism*, 144–45; Marsden, *Fundamentalism and American Culture*, 174–75.
9. See, e.g., Machen, "Attack upon Princeton Seminary," 5.
10. See, e.g., William Masselink, *Professor J. Gresham Machen: His Life and Defense of the Bible* (N.p.: [1938?]); Henry W. Coray, *J. Gresham Machen: A Silhouette* (Grand Rapids, Mich.: Kregel Publishers, 1981); W. Stanford Reid, "J. Gresham Machen," in *The Princeton Theology*, ed. David Wells, 93–112 (Grand Rapids, Mich.: Baker Book House, 1989); and Darryl Hart, *Defending the Faith*, 108ff, 154. Hart claims that Machen was expelled for his combative personality and his orthodoxy, rather than for the violations of church order with which he was charged.
11. Presbyterian Church in the U.S.A., Presbytery of Philadelphia, "Minutes," Mar. 5 and Apr. 2, 1934, in Record Group 7, Box 1, Folder 3, Dept. of History, Presbyterian Church (USA). See also Rian, *Presbyterian Conflict*, 172.
12. Later in the trial, the clerk of the Presbytery of Philadelphia, possibly at the prompting of the defense, sent the "coupon" in question. The prosecution argued that this demonstrated nothing about the legal state of Machen's reception but was, on all evidence, the unilateral action of the clerk, without authorization by the presbytery.
13. Presbyterian Church in the U.S.A., *Minutes of the General Assembly*, 1936, 97.

14. Machen, *Christianity and Liberalism*, 20.
15. One of the few treatments of Machen's theology is John C. Vander Stelt, *Philosophy and Scripture: A Study in Old Princeton and Westminster Theology* (Marleton, N.J.: Mack Publishing, 1978). This work avoids any consideration of polity and ecclesiology. In fact, for Machen, church government seems long to have been a weak point; of his ministerial licensure examination in 1914, Machen wrote, "My examination in church government was not passed very brilliantly, but when I could not answer the questions[,] the examiner answered them for me." Quoted in Stonehouse, *J. Gresham Machen*, 194–95.
16. J. Gresham Machen, "Statement" [to the Thompson Committee, appointed by the General Assembly of 1926 to study Princeton Theological Seminary], Nov. 23, 1926, printed together with "Documents Appended to a Statement" and "Additional Statement" (Privately "printed, not published"), 13–14. This idea is repeated many times in Machen's writings.
17. J. Gresham Machen, "The Responsibility of the Church in Our New Age" (1932), in *What Is Christianity?*, ed. Ned B. Stonehouse (Grand Rapids, Mich.: Eerdmans, 1951), 284.
18. Ibid., 283–84.
19. Machen, *Christianity and Liberalism*, 167–69.
20. J. Gresham Machen, "Relations Between Christians and Jews," speech delivered to the Fellowship of Reconciliation, Oct. 29, 1924, in Stonehouse, *What Is Christianity?*, 112.
21. J. Gresham Machen, "The Apostolic Church and the Church of To-day," *Rapid Survey of the Literature and History of New Testament Times* no. 6 (Philadelphia: Publication Dept., Board of Christian Education, Presbyterian Church in the U.S.A., 1915), 224.
22. See, e.g., Machen, *Christianity and Liberalism*, 34; J. Gresham Machen, "The Present Issue in the Church," sermon delivered at First Presbyterian Church, Princeton, N.J., Dec. 30, 1923, n.p., pamphlet in Machen Papers, Westminster Theological Seminary, Philadelphia, Pa.; J. Gresham Machen, "Prophets True and False" (1926), in *Best Sermons, 1926*, ed. Joseph Fort Newton (New York: Harcourt, Brace, 1926), 129.
23. Machen, *Christianity and Liberalism*, 2.
24. Machen, *What Is Faith?*, 41.
25. Machen, *Christianity and Liberalism*, 46–47.
26. J. Gresham Machen, "My Idea of God," in *My Idea of God: A Symposium of Faith*, ed. Joseph Fort Newton (Boston: Little, Brown, 1926), 40–41. Machen seems to have had Harry Emerson Fosdick in mind as the exemplar of this liberal position.
27. Machen, *What Is Faith?*, 130.
28. Machen, *Christianity and Liberalism*, 40.

29. Longfield, *Presbyterian Controversy*, 173. For a critique of Machen's Common Sense Realist view of history, see George Marsden, "J. Gresham Machen, History, and Truth," *Westminster Theological Journal* 42 (Fall 1979): 157–75.
30. Machen, *Christianity and Liberalism*, 160.
31. J. Gresham Machen, "Anti-Christian in Ten Years," Mar. 2, 1932, quoted in Headman, "Critical Evaluation," 42.
32. Machen to Clarence Macartney, May 5, 1936, in Machen Papers, Montgomery Library, Westminster Theological Seminary, Philadelphia, Pa.
33. J. Gresham Machen to S. M. Robinson, Sept. 1, 1933, quoted in Headman, "Critical Evaluation," 167.
34. Headman, "Critical Evaluation," 133.
35. J. Gresham Machen to C. L. Richards, Apr. 11, 1934; quoted in Headman, "Critical Evaluation," 164.
36. J. Gresham Machen to Arthur Machen, Dec. 12, 1934, quoted in Headman, "Critical Evaluation," 197.
37. Headman, in reporting Macartney's account of this exchange, goes on to say, "No traces of such correspondence could be found by this student [that is, Headman]"; in an interview, "[Paul] Woolley [Machen's ally] suggested that such a Machen response, if made, was probably done in jest." Headman, "Critical Evaluation," 193. Machen's letter does exist, however; as the quotation from the letter shows, he definitely was not speaking in jest. J. Gresham Machen to Clarence Macartney, May 9, 1936, p. 2, in Machen Papers, Montgomery Library, Westminster Theological Seminary.
38. J. Gresham Machen to James E. Bennett, Oct. 1, 1934; quoted in Headman, "Critical Evaluation," 193.
39. Machen, "Attack upon Princeton Seminary," 9–10, 17.
40. Ibid., 10–11.
41. Machen, "Statement," 42.
42. Machen, "Attack upon Princeton Seminary," 18.
43. Presbyterian Church in the U.S.A., "Presbyterian Church in the USA, complainant, versus J. Gresham Machen, accused, before the Special Judicial Commission of the Presbytery of New Brunswick," 1935, typed transcript of proceedings, in Machen Papers, Westminster Theological Seminary, 356–60.
44. Machen, "Attack upon Princeton Seminary," 17.
45. Machen, *Christianity and Liberalism*, 49–51.
46. J. Gresham Machen, editorial, "Can Christian Men Enter the Ministry of the Presbyterian Church in the U.S.A.?" *Presbyterian Guardian*, Feb. 2, 1936, p. 143, quoted in "The American Council of Christian Churches: A Study of Its Origin, Leaders, and Characteristic Positions," by John Albert Stroman (Th.D. diss., School of Theology, Boston Univ., 1966), 88.
47. Darryl Hart, *Defending the Faith*, 164.

CHAPTER 10. THE LOYALISTS:
THE SPECIAL COMMISSION OF 1925

1. Presbyterian Church in the U.S.A., *Minutes of the General Assembly,* 1926, 62; Presbyterian Church in the U.S.A., "Minutes of the Special Commission of 1925," Sept. 22–24, 1925, typescript in Box M13.5 P92, Historical Dept., Presbyterian Church (USA), 1.
2. Quirk, "Auburn Affirmation," 284.
3. Information in this section comes from the biographical ("H5") files on each man in the Historical Dept., Presbyterian Church (USA).
4. See Theodore A. Gill, Jr., "American Presbyterians in the Global Ecumenical Movement," in *The Diversity of Discipleship: Presbyterians and Twentieth-Century Christian Witness,* ed. Milton J. Coalter, John M. Mulder, and Louis B. Weeks (Louisville, Ky.: Westminster/John Knox Press, 1991), 139.
5. No file on Nathan Moore exists in the Presbyterian Church archives; this information was supplied by Carol R. Kelm and James Siler, Oak Park (Ill.) Historical Society, June 30 and July 14, 1992. "Nathan G. Moore, Distinguished Resident, Dies," *Oak Leaves,* Oak Park, Ill., Nov. 16, 1939, 72.
6. Speer also was tied to Princeton Seminary through Camp Diamond in New Hampshire, where the Speer family and Charles Erdman's family spent their summers; see William R. Hutchison, "Protestantism as Establishment," in *Between the Times: The Travail of the Protestant Establishment in America, 1900–1960,* ed. William R. Hutchison (Cambridge, England: Cambridge Univ. Press, 1989), 9.
7. John H. Mackay, "Robert Elliott Speer, a Man of Yesterday and Tomorrow," pamphlet prepared for the Speer centennial celebration at Princeton Theological Seminary, 1967, in Robert Speer folder, H5, Historical Dept., Presbyterian Church (USA), 8.
8. Dr. Ezra P. Giboney and Agnes M. Potter, *The Life of Mark A. Matthews, "Tall Pine of the Sierras"* (Grand Rapids, Mich.: Eerdmans, 1943), 93.
9. Presbyterian Church (USA), Special Commission of 1925, "Minutes," Sept. 22 to 24, 1925, 1, 6.
10. This position was argued forcefully by Machen, esp. in *Christianity and Liberalism.*
11. Presbyterian Church in the U.S.A., Special Commission of 1925, "Report of the Committee on Causes of Unrest and Possibilities of Relief," in Box M13.5 P92, Dept. of History, Presbyterian Church (USA), 9.
12. Ibid., 8.
13. Ibid., 5.
14. Ibid., 6–7.
15. Ibid., 6.
16. Presbyterian Church in the U.S.A., Special Commission of 1925, "Report of the

Committee on Constitutional Procedure," in Box M13.5 P92, Dept. of History, Presbyterian Church (USA), 22.

17. Ibid., 27–28.
18. Presbyterian Church in the U.S.A., Special Commission of 1925, "Minutes," Mar. 11 and 12, 1926.
19. Presbyterian Church in the U.S.A., Special Commission of 1925, "Report of the Special Commission of 1925," 19–20.
20. For examples of this error (which seems to be based on a misreading of the more careful statements of Loetscher in *Broadening Church*), see Bradley J. Longfield and George M. Marsden, "Presbyterian Colleges in Twentieth-Century America," in *The Pluralistic Vision,* ed. Milton J. Coalter, John M. Mulder, and Louis B. Weeks (Louisville, Ky.: Westminster/John Knox Press, 1992), 106; Jack B. Rogers and Donald K. McKim, "Pluralism and Policy in Presbyterian Views of Scripture," in *The Confessional Mosaic,* ed. Milton J. Coalter, John M. Mulder, and Louis B. Weeks (Louisville, Ky.: Westminster/John Knox Press, 1991), 38; and Milton J. Coalter, John M. Mulder, and Louis B. Weeks, *The Re-Forming Tradition* (Louisville, Ky.: Westminster/John Knox Press, 1991), 125.

Chapter 11. Princeton and Union: The Dialogue of Pluralism

1. For an excellent treatment of the subsequent triumph of neo-orthodoxy throughout the Presbyterian seminaries, see John M. Mulder and Lee A. Wyatt, "The Predicament of Pluralism: The Study of Theology in Presbyterian Seminaries Since the 1920s," in Coalter, Mulder, and Weeks, *Pluralistic Vision,* 43–57.
2. This account of Princeton's early history relies on Lefferts Loetscher, *Facing the Enlightenment and Pietism: Archibald Alexander and the Founding of Princeton Theological Seminary,* Presbyterian Historical Society Contributions to the Study of Religion, no. 8 (Westport, Conn.; Greenwood Press, 1983).
3. This philosophy had been brought from Scotland to the College of New Jersey in the eighteenth century by John Witherspoon, who taught Alexander's teacher, William Graham; ibid., 1–15, 138, 164–65.
4. Ibid., 76–77.
5. Ibid., 160.
6. Ibid., 76–77.
7. Ibid., 92, 242; Marsden, *Evangelical Mind,* 227.
8. A. A. Hodge, *The Life of Charles Hodge* (New York: Charles Scribner's Sons, 1880), 503.
9. Ibid., 521.
10. Marsden, *Fundamentalism and American Culture,* 112.
11. William D. Livingstone, "The Princeton Apologetic as Exemplified by the Work

of Benjamin B. Warfield and J. Gresham Machen: A Study in American Theology, 1880–1930" (Ph.D. diss., Yale Univ., 1948), 331–32.

12. Paul Martin to William O. Thompson, Dec. 23, 1926, p. 6, in "Correspondence Regarding the Machen Case," Speer Library, Princeton Theological Seminary, Princeton, N.J.

13. Clutter, "Reorientation of Princeton Theological Seminary," 57.

14. John Hart, "Controversy within the Church," 153.

15. Clutter, "Reorientation of Princeton Theological Seminary," 90.

16. Beach to Stevenson, July 12, 1914, in J. Ross Stevenson, "Confidential Letters and Documents," Speer Library, Princeton Theological Seminary, Princeton, N.J.

17. John Hart, "Controversy within the Church," 25, 50, 153. Not only were almost all of the faculty graduates of the seminary, but also many of them were related to one another. Several generations of Hodges served on the faculty, as well as several Alexanders and Breckenridges.

18. Clutter, "Reorientation of Princeton Seminary," 100.

19. This story is told more fully in John Hart, "Controversy within the Church," and Clutter, "Reorientation of Princeton Seminary."

20. Mulder and Wyatt, "Predicament of Pluralism," 43–47; John Hart, "Controversy within the Church," 162.

21. Westminster Theological Seminary, *Catalogue, 1986–1988*, 6–7, describes its heritage thus: "In the days of . . . [B. B. Warfield and J. Gresham Machen], a movement designed to bring to an end the adherence of Princeton to the scriptural theology which had made her great began to gain ground increasingly. Finally, in 1929, a coalition of modernist and indifferentist forces in the Presbyterian Church in the U.S.A. accomplished the reorganization of Princeton Seminary. . . . Almost immediately after the reorganization, . . . Westminster Theological Seminary was founded in Philadelphia and . . . [it] continued the exposition and defense of that great body of biblical truth which the old Princeton had loved."

22. Livingstone, "Princeton Apologetic," 6. Puzzlingly, this author also says that Warfield and Machen fought this fight "until the whole struggle died down in the early twenties" (8). Although Machen gets equal billing with Warfield in the title of this work, he is barely mentioned in the text, suggesting that this research was cut off before a planned study of the decisive events of 1926–29 actually was completed.

23. Paul Martin to William O. Thompson, Dec. 23, 1926, in "Correspondence Regarding Machen Case, 1925–1927," Speer Library, Princeton Theological Seminary, Princeton, N.J., 6; Clutter, "Reorientation of Princeton Seminary," 230–31.

24. George L. Haines, "The Princeton Theological Seminary, 1925–1960," (Ph.D. diss., New York Univ., 1966), 3.

25. See also Hutchison, *Modernist Impulse*, 93.

26. Coffin, *Half-Century of Union*, 5, 13.

27. Ibid., 70.
28. Thomas Hastings to John Crosby Brown (board chairman), July 15, 1901, in John Crosby Brown Papers, Burke Library, Union Theological Seminary, New York, quoted in Max Rogers, "Charles Augustus Briggs," 413–14.
29. Max Rogers, "Charles Augustus Briggs," 458–59.
30. Handy, *History of Union,* notes that, half a century after Briggs's trials, "the seminaries related to the [Presbyterian] General Assembly were teaching as a matter of course positions similar to and often more extreme than those for which Briggs had been repudiated" (91).
31. After Coe came Robert Hume, Congregationalist; Harry E. Fosdick, Baptist; Foakes Jackson, Anglican; etc. See Coffin, *Half-Century of Union,* 59, 71.
32. Handy, *History of Union,* 112.
33. Coffin, *Half-Century of Union,* 183–84, 103.
34. McGiffert, like his predecessor, had an earned doctorate, unusual for a seminary professor at that time. Both had been students of Briggs, and neither had been pastors. Handy, *History of Union,* 120, 155–57.
35. Coffin, *Half-Century of Union,* 39, 188.
36. Handy, *History of Union,* 162.
37. Longfield, *Presbyterian Controversy,* 81.
38. Handy, *History of Union,* 162.
39. Morgan Phelps Noyes, "The Coffin Years," in Coffin, *Half-Century of Union,* 123.
40. Coffin, *Half-Century of Union,* 26–27.
41. Cauthen, *Impact of Religious Liberalism,* 41–43.
42. Henry P. Van Dusen, "The Liberal Movement in Theology," in *The Church Through Half a Century: Essays in Honor of William Adams Brown,* ed. Samuel M. Cavert and Henry P. Van Dusen (New York: Scribners, 1936), 74.
43. Ibid., 77. Emphasis in original.
44. Ibid., 81.
45. Anonymous former student, quoted in Coffin, *Half-Century of Union,* 29.
46. See Cauthen, *Impact of Religious Liberalism,* 27–30.
47. Handy, *History of Union,* 44, 51.
48. Coffin, *Half-Century of Union,* 26–27.
49. Cauthen, *Impact of Religious Liberalism,* 61. This congregation became the Riverside Church, built across the street from Union Seminary.
50. Coffin, *Half-Century of Union,* 224.
51. Van Dusen, in "Liberal Movement," notes that many students of liberal theology find it "natural to divide their accounts into roughly four periods—the beginnings in the eighties and nineties, the nineties to the World War, the War to the Depression, and the present situation. Those divisions might be characterized: 'the evangelical impact', 'pre-War optimism', 'disillusionment and uncertainty', 'self-examination and new beginnings'" (83).

52. Coffin, *Half-Century of Union*, 149.
53. Handy, *History of Union*, 189.
54. Ibid., 61, 121.
55. Then called the College of New Jersey. Loetscher, *Facing Enlightenment and Pietism*, 138.
56. Henry P. Van Dusen, "Liberal Movement," went so far as to say that "America had known only one theological movement of consequence—the New England Theology" (68). This would have surprised the proponents of "Princeton Theology."
57. For the early establishment of the ties between New York Presbyterianism and New England, see Trinterud, *Forming of an American Tradition*, 47, 75, 212.
58. Marsden, *Evangelical Mind*, 137.
59. Philip Schaff, quoted in Handy, *History of Union*, 92.
60. Marsden, *Evangelical Mind*, 217.
61. Roark, "J. Gresham Machen and His Desire to Maintain a Doctrinally True Presbyterian Church," 67, n. 1.
62. J. Gresham Machen, quoted in Stonehouse, *J. Gresham Machen*, 221–22.
63. Marsden, *Evangelical Mind*, 160.
64. Livingstone, "Princeton Apologetic," 65.
65. Ibid., p. 7, 93n, and p. 258.
66. Clutter, "Reorientation of Princeton Seminary," 90.
67. Coffin, *Half-Century of Union*, 35.
68. Cauthen, *Impact of Religious Liberalism*, 127.
69. John T. McNeill, *The History and Character of Calvinism* (New York: Oxford Univ. Press, 1954), 409.
70. Quirk, "Auburn Affirmation," 27.
71. George Marsden, *Understanding Fundamentalism and Evangelicalism* (Grand Rapids, Mich.: Eerdmans, 1991), 200–201, n. 30.
72. Handy, *History of Union*, 199–201.
73. Robert L. Kelly, *Theological Education in America* (New York: Geo. Doran, 1924); see also Haines, "Princeton Seminary," 45.
74. Prentiss, *Union Theological Seminary*, 342.
75. Clair Davis of Westminster Seminary, though generally sympathetic to the Princeton "majority" position, concluded that the problem with Princeton then was that it was not trying to train aggressive pastors, but had become "a holding operation for the intellectual upper middle class"; see Davis, "Evangelicals and the Presbyterian Tradition," 156.
76. Coffin, *Half-Century of Union*, 94.
77. Russell, *Voices of Fundamentalism*, 146–48.
78. Handy, *History of Union*, 149.
79. Coffin, *Half-Century of Union*, 186–87.
80. Handy, *History of Union*, 191–92.

81. Henry Sloane Coffin, quoted in ibid., 194.

CHAPTER 12. PARTIES IN THE PRESBYTERIAN CHURCH

1. Loetscher, *Broadening Church*, 59.
2. Marsden, *Fundamentalism and American Culture*, 180–81.
3. Quirk, "Auburn Affirmation," 55–58; Mulder and Wyatt, "Predicament of Pluralism," 39. This three-party view of the Presbyterian Church in this period is supported by Martin Marty, *Modern American Religion*, vol. 2: *The Noise of Conflict, 1919–1941* (Chicago: Univ. of Chicago Press, 1991), 176–84; Roark, "J. Gresham Machen and His Desire to Maintain a Doctrinally True Presbyterian Church," 130, 210, 214; John Hart, "Controversy within the Church," 2; Russell, *Voices of Fundamentalism*, 155; and Clutter, "Reorientation of Princeton Seminary," 47.
4. Hirschman, *Exit, Voice, and Loyalty.*
5. Jeschke, "Briggs Case"; Hatch, *Briggs Heresy Trial*; Max Rogers, "Charles Augustus Briggs"; and Massa, *Briggs and Historical Criticism*. William Livingstone, likewise, did not class Briggs among the "Modernists," but rather as "quite within the evangelical tradition"; Livingstone, "Princeton Apologetic," 239. Sawyer, *Briggs and Tensions*, 179–86, partially dissents because he defines "conservative" as "Princetonian," but even he essentially agrees with the above assessment.
6. Briggs, "Future of Presbyterianism," n.p.
7. Israel J. Hathaway, "Speech to the Detroit General Assembly, 1891, on the Briggs Case," quoted in Max Rogers, "Charles Augustus Briggs," 168.
8. Simon J. McPherson, "Hunting Heretics and Saving Men: A Sermon Preached Sunday Morning, January 8, 1893, in Second Presbyterian Church, Chicago" (Chicago: Knight, Leonard, 1893), n.p.
9. James S. Ramsay, "A Discourse," sermon delivered at Harlem Presbyterian Church, New York City, June 21, 1891 (Privately "published by request"), n.p.
10. Machen, "Attack upon Princeton Seminary," 9. The internal quotation is not attributed to anyone, a practice common in Machen's polemical writings.
11. Roark, "J. Gresham Machen and His Desire to Maintain a Doctrinally True Presbyterian Church," 2, n. 1; 7; and 213.
12. The one exception was Pearl S. Buck, whom he did not actually prove was a modernist, but simply forced to resign before an inquiry was held. He continued to make general charges of modernism in the missions after her removal, although he did not offer specifics.
13. Machen, *What Is Faith?*, 18–19.
14. Headman, e.g., noted that the Princeton directors were "strongly conservative," while the trustees were "more mainstream"; no party to that struggle was "liberal." Headman, "Critical Evaluation," 95; see also Clutter, "Reorganization of Princeton Theological Seminary," 179–81.

15. J. Ross Stevenson, "Greetings of a Conservative Presbyterian," 1.

16. Paul Martin to William O. Thompson, Dec. 23, 1926, in "Correspondence Regarding Machen Case, 1925–1927," Speer Library, Princeton Theological Seminary, Princeton, N.J., 7.

17. Well before 1936, however, he issued some surprising broadsides, as in his claims that the Young Men's Christian Association was "overwhelmingly on the anti-Christian side," that the northern Methodist Church was "overwhelmingly against the gospel," and that the revered missionary leader John R. Mott was no Christian because he had some connection with Union Seminary. This latter institution Machen called the "chief center of anti-Christian propaganda in the religious life of this country." These aspersions all appeared in a letter from Machen to James Cannon, Mar. 18, 1925, cited by J. Ross Stevenson in a speech before the directors of Princeton Seminary, 1925; in J. Ross Stevenson, "Confidential Letters and Documents," Speer Library, Princeton Theological Seminary, Princeton, N.J.

18. Machen, "Honesty and Freedom in the Christian Ministry," *Moody Bible Monthly* 24 (Mar. 1924): 357.

19. Machen, "Attack upon Princeton Seminary," 36.

20. Machen, "Additional Statement" to the Thompson Committee, Nov. 23, 1926, printed together with "Statement" and "Documents Appended to a Statement" (Privately "printed, not published," 1926), 17. This sentence probably was a veiled criticism of Charles Erdman.

21. Machen, "Christian Scholarship and Evangelism" (1932), in Stonehouse, *What Is Christianity?*, 130–31.

22. Headman, "Critical Evaluation," 127.

23. Ibid., 210.

24. J. Gresham Machen, *New Testament Greek for Beginners* (New York: Macmillan, 1923); F. Brown, A. Driver, and C. A. Briggs, *Hebrew and English Lexicon of the Old Testament* (Oxford, England: Oxford Univ. Press, 1906).

25. Charles Erdman, quoted in Longfield, *Presbyterian Controversy*, 147.

26. Marsden, *Fundamentalism and American Culture*, 180.

27. Longfield, *Presbyterian Controversy*, 50–51.

28. Presbyterian Church in the USA, "Studies in the Constitution of the Presbyterian Church in the U.S.A.," in Presbyterian Church in the U.S.A., *Minutes of the General Assembly*, 1934, 73–74.

29. Ibid., 76–77.

30. Ibid., 98.

31. See also Headman, "Critical Evaluation," 185.

32. Presbyterian Church in the USA, "Presbyterian Church in the USA, complainant, versus J. Gresham Machen, accused, before the Special Judicial Commission of the Presbytery of New Brunswick," 1935, transcript of proceedings, in Machen Papers, Westminster Theological Seminary, Philadelphia, Pa., 32–36.

33. Ibid., 259.
34. Ibid., 63–64, 67.
35. Ibid., 268–70.
36. Gary Scott Smith, *Seeds of Secularization,* 6–7.
37. Richard Lovelace, "Evangelical Revivals and the Presbyterian Tradition," *Westminster Theological Journal* 42 (Fall 1979): 144–45.
38. D. Clair Davis, quoted in ibid., 155–56. Davis, who also did his graduate work at Westminster Seminary, was part of a congregation that had switched its affiliation from the Machen-founded Orthodox Presbyterian Church to the newer Presbyterian Church of America. Telephone conversation with Philip Monroe, Montgomery Library, Westminster Theological Seminary, Philadelphia, Pa., July 7, 1992.
39. Marsden, *Evangelical Mind,* 245; emphasis added.
40. Editorial, Edmund B. Chaffee "Suspend Machen from Ministry," *Christian Century* 53 (June 17, 1936): 878, quoted in Stroman, "American Council of Christian Churches," 76.
41. See, e.g., Darryl Hart's claim, in *Defending the Faith,* that "the controversy surrounding Machen and its resolution illustrate a larger point about twentieth-century church life: public relations and image control have often been more effective than confessional standards and church order for settling rifts within America's largest Protestant denominations" (110).
42. Edwin H. Rian, "Why I Am Re-entering the Ministry of the Presbyterian Church (USA)," in Quirk, "Auburn Affirmation," Appendix I, 282–90.

CHAPTER 13. COMPETITIVE PLURALISM

1. See Bernard Lonergan, *Doctrinal Pluralism* (Milwaukee, Wisc.: Marquette Univ. Press, 1971), 53.
2. Jay Newman, *Foundations of Religious Tolerance* (Toronto, Ont., Canada: Univ. of Toronto Press, 1982), 13–14.
3. On incoherence and the threat of social crises, see Jürgen Habermas, *Legitimation Crisis,* trans. Thomas McCarthy (1973; rpt. Boston: Beacon Press, 1975).
4. Hoge, *Division in the Protestant House,* 126–27.
5. This problem is underscored in George Forell, *The Proclamation of the Gospel in a Pluralistic World* (Philadelphia; Fortress, 1973), 2–3. See also Gustav Mensching, *Tolerance and Truth in Religion,* trans. H.-J. Klimkeit (1955; rpt. Tuscaloosa, Ala.: Univ. of Alabama Press, 1971), esp. 11–12.
6. I am grateful to R. Stephen Warner for raising this point.
7. Charles McCoy, *When Gods Change: Hope for Theology* (Nashville, Tenn.: Abingdon, 1980), 48. See also Brigitte Berger and Peter Berger, *The War Over the Family: Capturing the Middle Ground* (Garden City, N.Y.: Anchor/Doubleday, 1983), 63.

8. For a similar spectrum (from "imperialism" to "syncretism"), see Paul Knitter, *No Other Name? A Critical Survey of Christian Attitudes Toward the World Religions* (Maryknoll, N.Y.: Orbis, 1985), 9. For a parallel political spectrum, see Stanislaw Ehrlich, *Pluralism On and Off Course* (New York: Pergamon, 1982), xi–xiii. For a similar treatment of ideologies, see John Barnsley, *The Social Reality of Ethics* (London: Routledge and Kegan Paul, 1972) 11.

9. Wilfred Cantwell Smith sometimes stretches pluralism to the point of relativism; see his *Religious Diversity,* ed. Willard Oxtoby (New York: Harper and Row, 1976), 12–13, 151.

10. For an excellent treatment of the early development of the idea of religious freedom, see Quentin Skinner, *The Foundations of Modern Political Thought* (Cambridge, England: Cambridge Univ. Press, 1978), 2: 246ff and vol. 2, passim. For the Presbyterian role in this struggle, see Franklin Palm, *Calvinism and the Religious Wars* (New York: Holt, Rinehart, and Winston, 1932; rpt. New York: Howard Fertig, 1971) 50; and Paul Woolley, "Calvin and Toleration," in *The Heritage of John Calvin,* ed. J. Bratt, 137–57 (Grand Rapids, Mich.: Eerdmans, 1973).

11. For an important debate between universalists and their critics, see John Hick and Paul F. Knitter, eds., *The Myth of Christian Uniqueness* (Maryknoll, N.Y.: Orbis Books, 1987); and the reply volume, Gavin D'Costa, ed., *Christian Uniqueness Reconsidered* (Maryknoll, N.Y.: Orbis Books, 1990). For the position that all religions are equally *invalid,* see Val J. Peter, "A Primer on Pluralism," *Communio: International Catholic Review* (Spokane, Wash.) 10 (1983): 144.

12. Jay Newman, *Foundations of Religious Tolerance,* 21.

13. Benjamin Mariante, *Pluralistic Society, Pluralistic Church* (Washington D.C.: University Press of America, 1981), proposes a third two-party method of fighting diversity, through a "theology of counter-ecclesial institutions . . . [which] provides a basis for a pluriform ecclesiology." Church and counter-church would channel diversity into separate institutions, each of which could maintain its authority (110–13). This method of schism or separation, however, only displaces the problem of diversity to a higher level—from the level on which there is diversity within a church to the level on which there is diversity between church and counter-church.

14. See John Cobb, "The Meaning of Pluralism for Christian Self-Understanding," in *Religious Pluralism,* ed. Leroy Rouner, 161–79 (Notre Dame, Ind.: Univ. of Notre Dame Press, 1984); and David Tracy, *Plurality and Ambiguity: Hermeneutics, Religion, Hope* (San Francisco: Harper and Row, 1987). Franklin Littell, in his influential *From State Church to Pluralism: A Protestant Interpretation of Religion in America* (Garden City, N.Y.: Anchor/Doubleday, 1962), promotes a pluralism of dialogue among those churches which have a "consciousness of calling" to pluralism and voluntaryism (xiii). In contrast, Richard John Neuhaus is a contemporary advocate of a pluralism of conflict; see Neuhaus, *The Naked Public Square* (Grand Rapids, Mich.: Eerdmans, 1984), esp. 125ff.

15. In their thoughtful conclusion to the massive "Presbyterian Presence" series, Coalter, Mulder, and Weeks contend that, while theological pluralism has brought "unquestioned benefits" to the Presbyterian Church, it is "inherently unstable as a foundation for Christian identity and denominational mission." They admit that dialogue probably will not solve the "predicament of pluralism," but they can offer no better alternative; Coalter, Mulder, and Weeks, *Re-Forming Tradition*, 140–43.

16. A leading contemporary proponent of this view is Raimundo Panikkar; see, e.g., his "Religious Pluralism: The Metaphysical Challenge," in Rouner, *Religious Pluralism*, 97–115. This was the view of Reinhold Niebuhr, who regarded the appearance of freedom and tolerance in Western society as due to the providence of God; see Niebuhr, "A Note on Pluralism," in *Religion in America*, ed. John Cogley (New York; Meridian, 1958), 43–44. For other examples, see Charles McCoy, *When Gods Change*, on the benefits of a "challenging diversity" (62); and Benjamin Mariante, *Pluralistic Society, Pluralistic Church*, who proposed understanding the "nature of diversity as gifts of grace" (117). An unusually thoughtful treatment of the inevitability and sometime benefits of disagreement within the church is Stephen Sykes, *The Identity of Christianity: Theologians and the Essence of Christianity, from Schleiermacher to Barth* (Philadelphia: Fortress Press, 1984).

17. See George Lindbeck, *The Nature of Doctrine: Religion and Theology in a Postliberal Age* (Philadelphia: Westminster, 1984).

18. Hunter, *Culture Wars*, 304–6.

19. Mayer N. Zald and Michael A. Berger, "Social Movements in Organizations: Coup d'Etat, Insurgency, and Mass Movements," *American Journal of Sociology* 83 (1978): 855.

20. There also exists a kind of status quo in which there is not even conflict or dialogue. David Tracy, *The Analogical Imagination: Christian Theology and the Culture of Pluralism* (New York: Crossroads, 1981), identifies the unfortunate possibilities of this position as, on the one hand, "a repressive tolerance where all is allowed because nothing is finally taken seriously," or, on the other, a cover for a "genial confusion" (xi). See also Neuhaus, *Naked Public Square*, 23.

21. Georg Simmel, "Conflict," in *Conflict and the Web of Group-Affiliations*, by Georg Simmel, trans. Kurt Wolf and Reinhard Bendix (New York: Free Press, 1955), 57; orig. pub. in Georg Simmel, *Soziologie* (1908).

22. Ibid., 58–60. This conception of the benefits of competition for society as whole is like Adam Smith's. The larger question of the beneficial effects of conflict for society has been explored by Lewis Coser, *The Function of Social Conflict* (New York: Free Press, 1956).

23. Simmel, "Conflict," 63–64.

24. Georg Simmel, *The Sociology of Georg Simmel*, trans. and ed. Kurt Wolff (New York: Free Press, 1950), 144.

25. Simmel, "Conflict," 69.

26. James Reichley, *Religion and American Public Life* (Washington, D.C.; Brookings Institution Press, 1985), 288.

27. Some have seen a virtue in competition if it causes people deliberately to choose their faith, as opposed to being simply "born into it." Note, though, that this is claimed to be a virtue not because a chosen faith is more likely to be true, but because people are more likely to be committed to a faith they have chosen. See Jay Newman, *Foundations of Religious Toleration,* 86.

28. For the development of this idea in a particular case, see William J. Weston, "Michael Novak's Pluralist Religion," *This World* 19 (Fall 1987), 14–26, esp. the section on John Courtney Murray. See also Raymond Hock, "The Pluralism of John Courtney Murray, S.J., and Its Relation to Education" (Ph.D. diss.: School of Education, Stanford Univ., 1964).

29. See Hunter, *Culture Wars.*

30. See Daniel Bell, *The Cultural Contradictions of Capitalism* (New York: Basic, 1976); and Michael Novak, *The Spirit of Democratic Capitalism* (New York: American Enterprise Institute and Simon and Schuster, 1982).

31. See, e.g., John Maurice Clark's oft-cited *Competition as a Dynamic Process* (Washington, D.C.: Brookings Institution, 1961).

32. Richard John Neuhaus, using an analysis similar to the one proposed here, contends that "[t]here is an inherent and necessary relationship between democracy and pluralism." Neuhaus, *Naked Public Square,* 84.

33. See Ehrlich, *Pluralism On and Off Course*; Peter Henrici, "The Church and Pluralism," *Communio: International Catholic Review* 10 (1983), 133–48.

34. Mariante, *Pluralistic Society, Pluralistic Church,* 93; William Newman, *American Pluralism: A Study of Minority Groups and Social Theory* (New York: Harper and Row, 1973), 115–17, 169–70.

35. The classic source of this idea is Ernst Troeltsch, *The Social Teachings of the Christian Churches,* 2 vols., trans. Olive Wyon (1911; English translation published Chicago, 1931; University of Chicago Press, 1981). Other important (and more recent) works on this subject are Bryan Wilson, *Religious Sects: A Sociological Study* (New York: McGraw-Hill, 1970); and Werner Stark, *The Sociology of Religion,* 5 vols. (New York: Fordham Univ. Press, 1963–71).

36. Not coincidentally, much of the leading work on the denomination has been done by American scholars. See esp. H. Richard Niebuhr, *The Social Sources of Denominationalism* (New York: Holt, 1929), and Winthrop Hudson, "Denominationalism as a Basis for Ecumenicity: A Seventeenth-Century Conception," *Church History* 24 (1955): 32–50, and the essays in Russell Richey, ed., *Denominationalism* (Nashville, Tenn.: Abingdon, 1977).

37. Gregory Baum, *Religion and Alienation: A Theological Reading of Sociology* (New York: Paulist, 1975), 149–51.

38. Hirschman, *Exit, Voice, and Loyalty,* although he does not apply these terms to religious competition.

39. Warner, "New Paradigm for the Sociological Study of Religion"; Finke and Stark, *Churching of America*; Iannaccone, "Consequences of Religious Market Structure"; and Chaves and Cann, "Regulation, Pluralism, and Religious Market Structure."
40. This argument has been made to me by Juan J. Linz. See also Lindbeck, *Nature of Doctrine*, 77–78.
41. Hirschman, *Exit, Voice, and Loyalty*, 78–79.
42. Stephen Sykes, *Identity of Christianity*, observes that "[i]t would . . . be extremely difficult to think that easy toleration of diversity of opinion . . . [comes] naturally to a mind formed . . . upon the teaching of the New Testament. If controversy is inevitable it is also serious. There are choices to be made about what to believe, to say and to do, and these choices matter, because it is possible to go seriously wrong" (25).
43. On the "transfer of scarce meaning" from the cultural (including the religious) sphere to the other spheres, see Habermas, *Legitimation Crisis*.
44. This is the meaning of the functionalist distinction between "conflict within the system" and "conflict about the system"; for a discussion, see William Newman, *American Pluralism*, 118ff.
45. Barbara Brown Zikmund, "The Values and Limits of Pluralism and Representation in the Church," in Coalter, Mulder, and Weeks, *Pluralistic Vision*, 327–48.
46. Sykes, *Identity of Christianity*, 11. See also Frederick Sontag, "New Minority Religions as Heresies," in Rouner, *Religious Pluralism*, 38.
47. Lindbeck, *Nature of Doctrine*, esp. 32ff.
48. Peter Takayama, "Administrative Structures and Political Processes in Protestant Denominations," *Publius: The Journal of Federalism* 4 (1974): 5–37; K. Peter Takayama, "Formal Polity and Changes of Structure: Denominational Assemblies," *Sociological Analysis* 36 (Spring 1975): 17–28; K. Peter Takayama and Lynn Weber Cannon, "Formal Polity and Power Distribution in American Protestant Denominations," *Sociological Quarterly* 20 (Summer 1979): 321–32.
49. James Moorhead, "Presbyterians and the Mystique of Organizational Efficiency, 1870–1936," in *Reimagining Denominationalism: Interpretive Essays,* ed. Robert Bruce Mullin and Russell Richey (New York: Oxford Univ. Press, 1994): 264–87.
50. Chaves, "Intraorganizational Power and Internal Secularization."
51. Marsden, *Fundamentalism and American Culture,* 116
52. Furniss, *Fundamentalist Controversy,* 127, 171.
53. Hutchison, *Modernist Impulse,* 115; Marsden, *Fundamentalism and American Culture,* 109.
54. Briggs, *Whither?*, 243–44.

Chapter 14. Presbyterian Pluralism Today: A Postscript

1. In 1958, the Presbyterian Church in the USA, the "northern Presbyterians" treated

in this study, merged with the United Presbyterian Church of North America, a descendent of several smaller Scottish bodies, to create the United Presbyterian Church in the USA. In 1983, this body merged with the Presbyterian Church in the United States, the "southern Presbyterians," to create the current Presbyterian Church (USA). Prior to the merger, the southern Presbyterians also had gone through a "pluralizing" restructuring and a conservative secession; see Richard W. Reifsnyder, "Managing the Mission: Church Restructuring in the Twentieth Century," in *The Organizational Revolution: Presbyterians and American Denominationalism,* ed. Milton J. Coalter, John M. Mulder, and Louis B. Weeks (Louisville, Ky.: Westminster/John Knox Press, 1992), 75–78; also David B. McCarthy, "The Emerging Importance of Presbyterian Polity," in Coalter, Mulder, and Weeks, *Organizational Revolution,* 279–306.

2. Coalter, Mulder, and Weeks, *Re-Forming Tradition,* 141.
3. For examples of such critics, see Wuthnow, *Restructuring of American Religion;* Hunter, *Culture Wars;* and Hoge, *Division in the Protestant House.* For evidence of continuing loyalist strength in the Presbyterian Church, see Gary S. Eller, "Special-Interest Groups and American Presbyterianism," in Coalter, Mulder, and Weeks, *Organizational Revolution,* 268ff; and Jack B. Rogers and Donald K. McKim, "Pluralism and Policy in Presbyterian Views of Scripture," in Coalter, Mulder, and Weeks, *Confessional Mosaic,* 57.
4. Hoge, *Division in the Protestant House.* 83.
5. Ibid., 43–46, 78–82.
6. The Committee on Pluralism was a sub-unit of the Advisory Council on Discipleship and Worship. Much of the information in this chapter comes from Elizabeth Villegas, then associate director of the council, conversation on Aug. 1, 1986.
7. The Advisory Council on Discipleship and Worship, which recommended this change, argued that, since these organizations are not official agencies of the church, "they may express views contrary to those of the governing bodies in the same way that individual members may." "Proposed Change in *Book of Order* Would Affect Ch. 9 Organizations," *Presbyterian Outlook* 170 (Jan. 18, 1988): 6.
8. United Presbyterian Church in the U.S.A., Advisory Council on Discipleship and Worship, Committee on Pluralism, "Criteria for the Limits of Dissent," unpub. internal document, 1979, p. 1, available from the Advisory Council on Discipleship and Worship. This document is a compilation of statements made by several official bodies of the Presbyterian Church and includes the "Report of the Committee on Pluralism," as it was received by the General Assembly in 1978.
9. Ibid., p. 1.
10. Ibid., 1–2, 21.
11. Ibid., 3–8.
12. Ibid., 21. This statement is quoted from the "Proposal to Revise the Confessional Position of the United Presbyterian Church in the USA," in Presbyterian Church

in the USA, Advisory Council on Discipleship and Worship, Committee on Pluralism, "Report of the Committee on Pluralism to the 1978 General Assembly," 296. The emphasis has been added by the committee.

13. Presbyterian Church (USA), Advisory Council on Discipleship and Worship, Committee on Pluralism, *Is Christ Divided? A Report Approved by the 200th General Assembly (1988), Presbyterian Church (USA)* (Louisville, Ky.: Office of the General Assembly, 1988), 2, 41, 46ff.

14. Ibid., 7.

15. Louis B. Weeks, "Presbyterian Culture: Views from the 'Edge,'" in *Beyond Establishment: Protestant Identity in a Post-Protestant Age,* ed. Jackson Carroll and Wade Clark Roof (Louisville, Ky.: Westminster/John Knox Press, 1993), 315.

16. Longfield, *Presbyterian Controversy,* 4.

17. Dean Hoge, Benton Johnson, and Donald Luidens, *Vanishing Boundaries: The Religion of Mainline Protestant Baby Boomers.* (Louisville, Ky.: Westminster/John Knox Press, 1994), 118–21.

18. Presbyterian Church in the (USA), Advisory Council on Discipleship and Worship, Committee on Pluralism, *Is Christ Divided?,* 8.

19. For an account, see Eller, "Special-Interest Groups and American Presbyterianism," in Coalter, Mulder, and Weeks, *Organizational Revolution,* 260–61.

20. Conversation with Rev. Joseph Small, associate director for theology and worship, Presbyterian Church (USA), Louisville, Ky., June 24, 1992.

BIBLIOGRAPHY

Armstrong, Maurice, Lefferts Loetscher, and Charles Anderson, eds. *The Presbyterian Enterprise.* Philadelphia: Westminster, 1961.

"Articles of Faith." *New York Times,* Dec. 3, 1889; in Briggs Papers, Union Theological Seminary, Box 57, Folder 3.

Balmer, Randall, and John Fitzmier. *The Presbyterians.* Westport, Conn.: Praeger, 1994.

Barnsley, John. *The Social Reality of Ethics.* London: Routledge and Kegan Paul, 1972.

Baum, Gregory. *Religion and Alienation: A Theological Reading of Sociology.* New York: Paulist Press, 1975.

Beach, Sylvester. Letter to J. Ross Stevenson, July 12, 1914. In J. Ross Stevenson, "Confidential Letters and Documents," Speer Library, Princeton Theological Seminary, Princeton, New Jersey.

Bell, Daniel. *The Cultural Contradictions of Capitalism.* New York: Basic, 1976.

Berger, Brigitte, and Peter Berger. *The War Over the Family: Capturing the Middle Ground.* Garden City, N.Y.: Anchor/Doubleday, 1983.

Bratt, John, ed. *The Heritage of John Calvin.* Grand Rapids, Mich.: Eerdmans, 1973.

Briggs, Charles A. "The Advance toward Church Unity." *The Independent,* Jan. 1, 1891; in Briggs Papers, Union Theological Seminary, Box 52, Folder 1.

———. "The Alienation of Church and People." *Forum* 74 (Nov. 1893): 366–78; in Briggs Papers, Union Theological Seminary, Box 52, Folder 2.

———. "The American Idea of Church and State." *New York Evangelist,* Mar. 22, 1888; in Briggs Papers, Union Theological Seminary, Box 52, Folder 3.

———. *American Presbyterianism: Its Origin and Early History.* New York: Scribners, 1885.

———. *The Authority of Holy Scripture: An Inaugural Address.* New York: Scribners, 1891; rpt. New York: Arno, 1972.

———. *The Bible, the Church and the Reason: The Three Great Fountains of Divine Authority.* 2d ed. New York: Scribners, 1893.

————. *Biblical Study: Its Principles, Methods, and History.* New York: Scribners, 1887.

————. "Biblical Theology." *Presbyterian Review* 3 (July 1882): 503–20.

————. "Catholic—The Name and the Thing." *American Journal of Theology* 7 (1903): 417–42.

————. "Christian Unity." *Christian Union,* June 12, 1890; in Briggs Papers, Union Theological Seminary, Box 52, Folder 13.

————. *Church Unity: Studies of Its Most Important Problems.* New York: Scribners, 1909.

————. "A Critical Study of the History of Higher Criticism with Special Reference to the Pentateuch." *Presbyterian Review* 4 (Jan. 1883): 69–130.

————. "Defects of American Presbyterianism." *New York Evangelist,* Apr. 19, 1888; in Briggs Papers, Union Theological Seminary, Box 52, Folder 20.

————. *The Defense of Professor Briggs before the Presbytery of New York, 1893.* [Published together with Charles A. Briggs, *The Authority of Holy Scripture,* cited above, 2d ed.] New York: Scribners, 1893.

————. "Elias Neau, the Confessor and Catechist of Negro and Indian Slaves." Paper read before the Society for the Propagation of the Gospel, Apr. 18, 1889; in Briggs Papers, Union Theological Seminary, Box 52, Folder 25.

————. *The Ethical Teaching of Jesus.* New York: Scribners, 1904.

————. "Federation." *Churchman,* June 21, 1890; in Briggs Papers, Union Theological Seminary, Box 52, Folder 27.

————. *The Fundamental Christian Faith: The Origin, History and Interpretation of the Apostles' and Nicene Creeds.* New York: Scribners, 1913.

————. "The Future of Presbyterianism in the United States of America." *North American Review* 157 (July 1893): 1–12, in Briggs Papers, Union Theological Seminary, Box 52, Folder 28.

————. "The Future of Religion in America." *Review of the Churches,* July 15, 1892; in Briggs Papers, Union Theological Seminary, Box 52, Folder 29.

————. "The Historic Episcopate as a Basis of Reunion." *Christian at Work,* May 3, 1888; in Briggs Papers, Union Theological Seminary, Box 52, Folder 41.

————. *History of the Study of Theology.* 2 vols. Ed. Emilie Grace Briggs. New York: Scribners, 1916.

————. "Is Rome an Ally, an Enemy, or Both?" *Christian at Work,* Apr. 12, 1888; in Briggs Papers, Union Theological Seminary, Box 52, Folder 45.

————. "Memorial to Thomas Hastings." Typescript, Apr. 1911; in Briggs Papers, Union Theological Seminary, Box 22, Folder 15.

————. "Note Biographical, 1841–1889." Typescript, Apr. 1, 1889; in Briggs Papers, Union Theological Seminary, Box 44, Folder 33.

————. "A Plea for an American Alliance of the Reformed Churches." *Presbyterian Review* 9 (Apr. 1888): 306–9 in Briggs Papers, Union Theological Seminary, Box 53, Folder 15.

————. "Presbyterianism and Catholicity." *New York Evangelist,* May 28, 1885; in Briggs Papers, Union Theological Seminary, New York, Box 53, Folder 18.

————. "The Relation of the Church to Social Reform." Typescript, n.d. [ca. 1896]; in Briggs Papers, Union Theological Seminary, Box 29, Folder 14.

————. "Subscription and Revision." *Christian Union,* Dec. 12, 1889; in Briggs Papers, Union Theological Seminary, Box 53, Folder 37.

————. "Terms of Christian Union." *Christian Union,* May 12, 1887; in Briggs Papers, Union Theological Seminary, Box 53, Folder 41.

————. *Theological Symbolics.* Ed. Emilie Grace Briggs. New York: Scribners, 1914.

————. "Theses on Religious Instruction in Public Schools." Typescript, 1903; in Briggs Papers, Union Theological Seminary, Box 32, Folder 4.

————. "Union of Northern and Southern Presbyterians." *The Independent,* Apr. 26, 1888; in Briggs Papers, Union Theological Seminary, Box 53, Folder 46.

————. *Whither? A Theological Question for the Times,* New York: Scribners, 1889.

Briggs, Charles A., Francis Brown, and S. R. Driver. *Hebrew and English Lexicon of the Old Testament.* Oxford, England: Oxford University Press, 1906.

Cadier, Jean, ed. *John Calvin.* Grand Rapids, Mich.: Eerdmans, 1966.

Calvin, John. *Institutes of the Christian Religion.* Translated by Ford Lewis Battles from the edition of 1559. Library of the Christian Classics, vol. 21. Philadelphia: Westminster Press, 1960.

Carroll, Jackson, and Wade Clark Roof, eds. *Beyond Establishment: Protestant Identity in a Post-Protestant Age.* Louisville, Ky.: Westminster/John Knox Press, 1993.

Cauthen, Kenneth. *The Impact of American Religious Liberalism.* New York: Harper and Row, 1962.

Cavert, Samuel McCrea, and Henry Pitney Van Dusen, eds. *The Church through Half a Century: Essays in Honor of William Adams Brown.* New York: Scribners, 1936.

Chaves, Mark. "Intraorganizational Power and Internal Secularization in Protestant Denominations." *American Journal of Sociology* 99 (July 1993): 1–48.

Chaves, Mark, and David E. Cann. "Regulation, Pluralism, and Religious Market Structure: Explaining Religious Vitality." *Rationality and Society* 4 (July 1992): 272–90.

Christensen, Richard L. *The Ecumenical Orthodoxy of Charles Augustus Briggs (1841–1913),* Lewiston, N.Y.: Mellen Univ. Press, 1995.

Clark, John Maurice. *Competition as a Dynamic Process.* Washington, D.C.: Brookings Institution Press, 1961.

Clutter, Ronald T. "The Reorganization of Princeton Theological Seminary Reconsidered." *Grace Theological Journal* 7 (1986): 179–201.

————. "The Reorientation of Princeton Theological Seminary, 1925–1929." Th.D. diss.: Dallas Theological Seminary, 1982.

Coalter, Milton J., John M. Mulder, and Louis B. Weeks. *The Re-Forming Tradition: Presbyterians and Mainstream Protestantism.* Louisville, Ky.: Westminster/John Knox Press, 1992.

————, eds. *The Confessional Mosaic: Presbyterians and Twentieth-Century Theology*. Louisville, Ky.: Westminster/John Knox Press, 1990.

————. *The Diversity of Discipleship: Presbyterians and Twentieth-Century Christian Witness*. Louisville, Ky.: Westminster/John Knox Press, 1991.

————. *The Mainstream Protestant "Decline": The Presbyterian Pattern*. Louisville, Ky.: Westminster/John Knox Press, 1990.

————. *The Organizational Revolution: Presbyterians and American Denominationalism*. Louisville, Ky.: Westminster/John Knox Press, 1992.

————. *The Pluralistic Vision: Presbyterians and Mainstream Protestant Education and Leadership*. Louisville, Ky.: Westminster/John Knox Press, 1992.

————. *The Presbyterian Predicament: Six Perspectives*. Louisville, Ky.: Westminster/John Knox Press, 1990.

Cogley, John, ed. *Religion in America*. New York: Meridian, 1958.

Coffin, Henry Sloane. *A Half-Century of Union Theological Seminary, 1896–1945: An Informal History*. New York: Scribners, 1954.

Coray, Henry W. *J. Gresham Machen: A Silhouette*. Grand Rapids, Mich.: Kregel Publishers, 1981.

Coser, Lewis. *The Function of Social Conflict*. New York: Free Press, 1956.

[Coyle, John P.] "The Main Issue: A Straight Question to Dr. Briggs." Anonymous pamphlet. Saratoga Springs, N.Y.: Walden and Crawley, 1890.

Davis, D. Clair. "Evangelicals and the Presbyterian Tradition: An Alternative Perspective." *Westminster Theological Journal* 42 (Fall 1979): 152–56.

D'Costa, Gavin, ed. *Christian Uniqueness Reconsidered*. Maryknoll, N.Y.: Orbis Books, 1990.

Dennison, Charles, ed. *The Orthodox Presbyterian Church, 1936–1986*. Philadelphia: Committee for the Historian of the Orthodox Presbyterian Church, 1986.

"Dr. Machen Defies Presbytery in N.J." *Philadelphia Evening Bulletin*, Sept. 26, 1934.

"Dr. Schaff on the Creed," *New York Tribune*, Oct. 7, 1889; Briggs Papers, Union Theological Seminary, Box 57, Folder 30.

Ehrlich, Stanislaw. *Pluralism On and Off Course*. New York: Pergamon Press, 1982.

Ehrlich, Stanislaw, and Graham Wootton, eds. *Three Faces of Pluralism*. Westmead, England: Gower, 1980.

Farand, S. A. "The Other Side: A Review of the Trial of Rev. Charles A. Briggs, D.D." Pamphlet. New York: A. D. F. Randolph, [1897?].

Finke, Roger, and Rodney Stark. *The Churching of America, 1776–1990: Winners and Losers in Our Religious Economy*. New Brunswick, N.J.: Rutgers University Press, 1992.

Forell, George W. *The Proclamation of the Gospel in a Pluralistic World: Essays on Christianity and Culture*. Philadelphia: Fortress Press, 1973.

Fry, John. *The Trivialization of the United Presbyterian Church*. New York: Harper and Row, 1975.

Furniss, Norman. *The Fundamentalist Controversy, 1918–1931*. New Haven, Conn.: Yale University Press, 1954.

Giboney, Ezra P., and Agnes M. Potter. *The Life of Mark A. Matthews, "Tall Pine of the Sierras."* Grand Rapids, Mich.: Eerdmans, 1943.

Habermas, Jürgen. *Legitimation Crisis*. Translated by Thomas McCarthy. 1973; rpt. Boston: Beacon Press, 1975.

Haines, George L. "The Princeton Theological Seminary, 1925–1960." Ph.D. diss., New York University, 1966.

Haller, William. *Liberty and Reformation in the Puritan Revolution*. New York: Columbia University Press, 1955.

Handy, Robert. *A History of Union Theological Seminary in New York*. New York: Columbia University Press, 1987.

Hart, Darryl G. *Defending the Faith: J. Gresham Machen and the Crisis of Conservative Protestantism in America*. Baltimore, Md.: Johns Hopkins University Press, 1994.

Hart, John. "The Controversy within the Presbyterian Church, U.S.A., in the 1920s, with Special Emphasis on the Reorganization of Princeton Theological Seminary." Senior thesis in history, Princeton Univ., Princeton, New Jersey, 1978.

Hatch, Carl. *The Charles A. Briggs Heresy Trial: Prologue to Twentieth-Century Liberal Protestantism*. New York: Exposition Press, 1969.

Headman, Wayne. "A Critical Evaluation of J. Gresham Machen." M. Theol. thesis, Princeton Theological Seminary, 1974.

Henrici, Peter. "The Church and Pluralism." *Communio: International Catholic Review* 10 (1983): 133–48.

Hick, John, and Paul F. Knitter, eds. *The Myth of Christian Uniqueness*. Maryknoll, N.Y.: Orbis Books, 1987.

Hirschman, Albert O. *Exit, Voice, and Loyalty*. Cambridge, Mass.: Harvard Univ. Press, 1970.

Hock, Raymond. "The Pluralism of John Courtney Murray, S.J., and Its Relation to Education." Ph.D. diss., School of Education, Stanford University, 1964.

Hodge, A. A. *The Life of Charles Hodge*. New York: Charles Scribner's Sons, 1880.

Hodge, Charles. *The Constitutional History of the Presbyterian Church in the United States of America*. 2 parts. Philadelphia: Presbyterian Board of Publications and Sabbath School Work, 1851.

———. "The Rights of Presbyteries Ought Not to Be Annulled." Pamphlet. New York: Anson D. F. Randall, 1896.

Hofstadter, Richard. *Anti-Intellectualism in American Life*. New York: Knopf, 1963.

Hoge, Dean R. *Division in the Protestant House: The Basic Reasons Behind Intra-Church Conflicts*. Philadelphia: Westminster Press, 1976.

Hoge, Dean, Benton Johnson, and Donald Luidens. *Vanishing Boundaries: The Religion of Mainline Protestant Baby Boomers*. Louisville, Ky.: Westminster/John Knox Press, 1994.

Hudson, Winthrop. "Denominationalism as a Basis for Ecumenicity: A Seventeenth-Century Conception." *Church History* 24 (1955): 32–50.

Hunt, Anne. "No Other Name? A Critique of Religious Pluralism." *Pacifica: Australian Theological Studies* 3 (Feb. 1990): 45–60.

Hunter, James Davison. *Before the Shooting Begins: Searching for Democracy in America's Culture Wars.* New York: Free Press, 1994.

———. *Culture Wars: The Struggle to Define America.* New York: Basic, 1991.

Hutchison, William R. *The Modernist Impulse in American Protestantism.* Cambridge, Mass.: Harvard University Press, 1976.

Hutchison, William R., ed. *Between the Times: The Travail of the Protestant Establishment in America, 1900–1960.* Cambridge, England: Cambridge University Press, 1989.

Iannaccone, Laurence R. "The Consequences of Religious Market Structure: Adam Smith and the Economics of Religion." *Rationality and Society* 3 (Apr. 1991): 156–77.

Jeschke, Channing Renwick. "The Briggs Case: The Focus of a Study in Nineteenth-Century Presbyterian History." Ph.D. diss., Divinity School, University of Chicago, 1966.

Kelly, J. N. D. *Early Christian Doctrines.* New York: Harper and Row, 1978.

Kelly, Robert L. *Theological Education in America.* New York: Geo. Doran, 1924.

Knitter, Paul. *No Other Name? A Critical Survey of Christian Attitudes Toward the World Religions.* Maryknoll, N.Y.: Orbis, 1985.

[Laidlaw, R. J.]. *The Trial of Dr. Briggs before the General Assembly: A Calm Review of the Case,* by a Stranger. New York: Anson Randolph, 1893.

Leith, John. *Introduction to the Reformed Tradition.* Atlanta, Ga.: John Knox Press, 1977.

Lindbeck, George. *The Nature of Doctrine: Religion and Theology in a Postliberal Age.* Philadelphia: Westminster Press, 1984.

Littell, Franklin H. *From State Church to Pluralism: A Protestant Interpretation of Religion in American History.* Garden City, N.Y.: Anchor/Doubleday, 1962.

Livingstone, William D. "The Princeton Apologetic, as Exemplified by the Work of Benjamin B. Warfield and J. Gresham Machen: A Study in American Theology, 1880–1930." Ph.D. diss., Yale University, 1948.

Loetscher, Lefferts. *A Brief History of the Presbyterians.* 4th ed. Philadelphia: Westminster Press, 1978.

———. *The Broadening Church: A Study of Theological Issues in the Presbyterian Church since 1869.* Philadelphia: University of Pennsylvania Press, 1954.

———. *Facing the Enlightenment and Pietism: Archibald Alexander and the Founding of Princeton Theological Seminary.* Presbyterian Historical Society Contributions to the Study of Religion, No. 8. Westport, Conn.: Greenwood Press, 1983.

Lonergan, Bernard. *Doctrinal Pluralism.* Milwaukee, Wisc.: Marquette University Press, 1971.

Longfield, Bradley. *The Presbyterian Controversy: Fundamentalists, Modernists, and Moderates.* New York: Oxford University Press, 1991.

Lovelace, Richard. "Evangelical Revivals and the Presbyterian Tradition." *Westminster Theological Journal* 42 (Fall 1979): 130–51.

Luidens, Donald A., and Roger J. Nemeth. "'Public' and 'Private' Protestantism Reconsidered: Introducing the 'Loyalists.'" *Journal for the Scientific Study of Religion* 26 (Dec. 1987): 450–64.

McCook, John J., ed. *The Appeal in the Briggs Heresy Case before the General Assembly of the Presbyterian Church in the United States of America.* New York: John C. Rankin, 1893.

McCoy, Charles. *When Gods Change: Hope for Theology.* Nashville, Tenn.: Abingdon, 1980.

McNeill, John T. *The History and Character of Calvinism.* New York: Oxford University Press, 1954.

McPherson, Simon. "Hunting Heretics and Saving Men: A Sermon Preached Sunday Morning, Jan. 8, 1893, in Second Presbyterian Church, Chicago." Chicago: Knight, Leonard, 1893.

Machen, J. Gresham. "The Apostolic Church and the Church of To-day." *A Rapid Survey of the Literature and History of New Testament Times* no. 6. Philadelphia: Publication Dept., Board of Christian Education, Presbyterian Church in the U.S.A., 1915.

———. "The Attack upon Princeton Seminary: A Plea for Fair Play." Pamphlet published by the author, Dec. 1927.

———. "Can Christian Men Enter the Ministry of the Presbyterian Church in the U.S.A.?" *Presbyterian Guardian,* Feb. 2, 1936.

———. *Christian Faith in the Modern World.* New York: Macmillan, 1936.

———. *Christianity and Liberalism.* 1923; rpt. Grand Rapids, Mich.: Eerdmans, 1946.

———. "Christianity in Conflict." In *Contemporary American Theology,* ed. Vergilius Ferm, 1: 245–74. New York: Roundtable Press, 1932.

———. "An Earnest Plea for Christian Freedom—and Honesty!" *Lookout,* Mar. 2, 1923.

———. "A Future for Calvinism in the Presbyterian Church?" *Banner,* Apr. 4, 1930.

———. "The Good Fight of Faith." Sermon delivered at Chapel, Princeton Theological Seminary. *The Presbyterian,* Mar. 28, 1929.

———. "Honesty and Freedom in the Christian Ministry." *Moody Bible Monthly* 24 (Mar. 1924): 355–57.

———. "Is Christianity True?" *Bible Today* 17 (May 1923): 197–99.

———. Letter to Clarence Macartney, May 9, 1936. In "General Correspondence, 1935–1936," Machen Papers, Westminster Theological Seminary, Philadelphia, Pa.

———. Letter to Edwin Rian, Nov. 1, 1935. In "General Correspondence, 1935–1936," Machen Papers, Westminster Theological Seminary, Philadelphia, Pa.

————. Letter to Maitland Alexander, Sept. 27, 1935. In "General Correspondence, 1935–1936," Machen Papers, Westminster Theological Seminary, Philadelphia, Pa.

————. "The Mission of the Church." *Presbyterian and Herald and Presbyter,* Apr. 8, 1926.

————. "Modernism and the Board of Foreign Missions of the Presbyterian Church in the U.S.A." Pamphlet published by the author, 1933.

————. "My Idea of God." In *My Idea of God: A Symposium of Faith,* ed. Joseph Fort Newton, 37–50. Boston: Little, Brown, 1926.

————. *New Testament Greek for Beginners.* New York: Macmillan, 1923.

————. *The Origin of Paul's Religion.* 1921; rpt. New York: Macmillan, 1923.

————. "The Parting of the Ways." *The Presbyterian,* Apr. 17, 1924.

————. "The Present Issue in the Church." Sermon delivered at First Presbyterian Church, Princeton, N.J., Dec. 30, 1923. Pamphlet in Machen Papers, Westminster Theological Seminary, Philadelphia, Pa.

————. "The Present Situation in the Presbyterian Church." *Christianity Today* 1 (May 1930): 5–7.

————. "Prophets False and True." In *Best Sermons of 1926,* ed. Joseph Fort Newton, 115–23. New York: Harcourt, Brace, 1926.

————. "The Separateness of the Church." Sermon delivered at Chapel, Princeton Theological Seminary, Mar. 8, 1925. Pamphlet in Machen Papers, Westminster Theological Seminary, Philadelphia, Pa.

————. "Shall the General Assembly Represent the Church?" *The Presbyterian,* Mar. 5, 1925.

————. "Statement" [to the Thompson Committee, appointed by the General Assembly of 1926 to study Princeton Theological Seminary], Nov. 23, 1926. Printed together with "Documents Appended to a Statement" and "Additional Statement." Privately "printed, not published," Princeton, N.J.

————. *The Virgin Birth of Christ.* New York: Harper and Brothers, 1930.

————. *What Is Christianity? and Other Addresses.* Ed. Ned B. Stonehouse. Grand Rapids, Mich.: Eerdmans, 1951.

————. *What Is Faith?* 1925; rpt. New York: Macmillan, 1927.

Mackey, John H. "Robert Elliott Speer, a Man of Yesterday and Tomorrow." Pamphlet prepared for the Speer centennial celebration at Princeton Theological Seminary, 1967.

Mariante, Benjamin. *Pluralistic Society, Pluralistic Church.* Washington, D.C.: University Press of America, 1981.

Marsden, George. *The Evangelical Mind and the New School Presbyterian Experience: A Case Study of Thought and Theology in Nineteenth-Century America.* New Haven, Conn.: Yale University Press, 1970.

————. *Fundamentalism and American Culture: The Shaping of Twentieth-Century Evangelicalism, 1840–1925.* Oxford, England: Oxford University Press, 1980.

————. "J. Gresham Machen, History and Truth." *Westminster Theological Journal* 42 (Fall 1979): 157–75.

————. *Understanding Fundamentalism and Evangelicalism*. Grand Rapids, Mich.: Eerdmans, 1991.

————. "Understanding Fundamentalist Views of Society." In *Reformed Faith and Politics,* ed. Ronald H. Stone, 65–76. Washington, D.C.: University Press of America, 1983.

Martin, Paul. Letter to W. O. Thompson, Dec. 23, 1926. In "Correspondence Regarding the Machen Case, 1925–1927," Speer Library, Princeton Theological Seminary, Princeton, N.J.

Marty, Martin. *Modern American Religion,* vol. 2: *The Noise of Conflict, 1919–1941.* Chicago: University of Chicago Press, 1991.

Massa, Mark. *Charles Augustus Briggs and the Crisis of Historical Criticism.* Philadelphia: Fortress Press, 1990.

Masselink, William. *Professor J. Gresham Machen: His Life and Defense of the Bible.* N.p.: [1938?].

Mensching, Gustav. *Tolerance and Truth in Religion.* Translated by H.-J. Klimkeit. 1955; rpt. Tuscaloosa, Ala.: University of Alabama Press, 1971.

Moore, J. Laurence. *Religious Outsiders and the Making of Americans.* New York: Oxford University Press, 1986.

Mullin, Robert Bruce, and Russell Richey, eds. *Reimagining Denominationalism: Interpretive Essays.* New York: Oxford University Press, 1994.

"Nathan G. Moore, Distinguished Resident, Dies." *Oak Leaves,* Oak Park, Ill., Nov. 16, 1939.

Neuhaus, Richard. *The Naked Public Square.* Grand Rapids, Mich.: Eerdmans, 1984.

Newman, Jay. *The Foundations of Religious Tolerance.* Toronto, Ont., Canada: University of Toronto Press, 1982.

Newman, William. *American Pluralism: A Study of Minority Groups and Social Theory.* New York: Harper and Row, 1973.

"The New Reformation." *New York Sun,* Dec. 11, 1889; in Briggs Papers, Union Theological Seminary, Box 58, Folder 1.

Niebuhr, H. Richard. *The Social Sources of Denominationalism.* New York: Holt, 1929.

Noll, Mark A. "The Pea Beneath the Mattress—Orthodox Presbyterianism in America." *Reformed Journal* 36 (Oct. 1986): 11–16.

Novak, Michael. *The Spirit of Democratic Capitalism.* New York: American Enterprise Institute and Simon and Schuster, 1982.

Palm, Frederick C. *Calvinism and the Religious Wars.* New York: Holt, Rinehart, and Winston, 1932; rpt. New York: Howard Fertig, 1971.

Patterson, James A. "Robert E. Speer, J. Gresham Machen, and the Presbyterian Board of Foreign Missions." *American Presbyterians* 64 (1986): 58–68.

Peter, Val J. "A Primer on Pluralism." *Communio: International Catholic Review* 10 (1983): 128–32.

Prentiss, George L. *The Union Theological Seminary in the City of New York: Its Design and Another Decade of Its History.* Asbury Park, N.J.: Pennypacker, 1899.

Presbyterian Church in the U.S.A. *Minutes of the General Assembly.* 3rd Series. Philadelphia: Office of the General Assembly, Presbyterian Church in the U.S.A. Issued annually.

———. "Presbyterian Church in the U.S.A., complainant, versus J. Gresham Machen, accused, before the Special Judicial Commission of the Presbytery of New Brunswick." 1935. Transcript of proceedings, in Machen Papers, Westminster Theological Seminary, Philadelphia, Pa.

———. "Report of the Special Committee to Visit Princeton Theological Seminary [Thompson Committee]." Pamphlet, 1927.

———. "Studies in the Constitution of the Presbyterian Church in the U.S.A." In *Minutes of the General Assembly,* 1934.

Presbyterian Church in the U.S.A. Presbytery of New Brunswick. "Action of the Presbytery of New Brunswick, Apr. 1935." Typescript; Record Group 7, Box 1, Folder 3, Dept. of History, Presbyterian Church in the U.S.A.

Presbyterian Church in the U.S.A. Publicity Dept. "Statement." Record Group 20, Box 1, Folder 9, Dept. of History, Presbyterian Church in the U.S.A., n.d. [ca. June 1936].

Presbyterian Church in the U.S.A. Special Commission of 1925. Minutes and reports (typescript). Box M13.5 P92, Historical Dept., Presbyterian Church in the U.S.A., Philadelphia.

Presbyterian Church (USA). Advisory Council on Discipleship and Worship. Committee on Pluralism. "Criteria for the Limits of Dissent." Unpublished internal document, 1979.

———. *Is Christ Divided? A Report Approved by the 200th General Assembly (1988), Presbyterian Church (U.S.A.).* Louisville, Ky.: Office of the General Assembly, 1988.

———. *The Constitution of the Presbyterian Church (USA), Part One: The Book of Confessions.* Louisville, Ky.: Office of the General Assembly, 1994.

"Proposed Change in *Book of Order* Would Affect Ch. 9 Organizations." *Presbyterian Outlook* 170 (Jan. 18, 1988): 60.

Quirk, Charles Evans. "The 'Auburn' Affirmation: A Critical Narrative of the Document Designed to Safeguard the Unity and Liberty of the Presbyterian Church in the United States of America in 1924." Ph.D. diss., School of Religion, University of Iowa, 1967.

Ramsay, James S. "A Discourse." Sermon delivered at Harlem Presbyterian Church, New York City, June 21, 1891. Privately "published by request."

Reichley, A. James. *Religion in American Public Life.* Washington, D.C.: Brookings Institution Press, 1985.

Rian, Edwin H. *The Presbyterian Conflict.* Grand Rapids: Eerdmans, 1940.

Richey, Russell, ed. *Denominationalism.* Nashville, Tenn.: Abingdon, 1977.

Roark, Dallas. "J. Gresham Machen and His Desire to Maintain a Doctrinally True Presbyterian Church." Ph.D. diss., State University of Iowa, 1963.

Roberts, David E., and Henry P. Van Dusen, eds. *Liberal Theology: An Appraisal: Essays in Honor of Eugene Lyman.* New York: Scribners, 1942.

Rogers, Jack. *Claiming the Center: Churches and Conflicting Worldviews.* Louisville, Ky.: Westminster/John Knox Press, 1995.

Rogers, Max Gray. "Charles Augustus Briggs: Conservative Heretic." Ph.D. diss., Columbia University, 1964.

Rouner, Leroy, ed. *Religious Pluralism.* Notre Dame, Ind.: Univ. of Notre Dame Press, 1984.

Russell, C. Allyn. *The Voices of American Fundamentalism: Seven Biographical Studies.* Philadelphia: Westminster Press, 1976.

Sawyer, M. James. *Charles Augustus Briggs and Tensions in Late Nineteenth-Century American Theology.* Lewiston, N.Y.: Mellen University Press, 1994.

Simmel, Georg. *Conflict and the Web of Group-Affiliations.* Translated by Kurt Wolff and Reinhard Bendix. 1908, 1922; English translation published New York: Free Press, 1955.

———. *The Sociology of Georg Simmel.* Translated and ed. Kurt Wolff. New York: Free Press, 1950.

Skinner, Quentin. *The Foundations of Modern Political Thought.* Vol. 2. Cambridge, England: Cambridge University Press, 1978.

Smith, Gary Scott. *The Seeds of Secularization: Calvinism, Culture, and Pluralism in America, 1870–1915.* Grand Rapids, Mich.: Christian University Press, 1985.

Smith, Wilfred Cantwell. *Religious Diversity.* Ed. Willard G. Oxtoby. New York: Harper and Row, 1976.

Stark, Werner. *The Sociology of Religion.* 5 volumes: New York: Fordham University Press, 1963–71.

Stevenson, J. Ross. "Address to the General Assembly." 1926. In J. Ross Stevenson, "Confidential Letters and Documents," Speer Library, Princeton Theological Seminary, Princeton, New Jersey.

———. "The Greetings of a Conservative Presbyterian to the Methodist League for Faith and Life." Speech delivered in Philadelphia, Feb. 8, 1926. Formal Address no. 202, Papers of J. Ross Stevenson, Speer Library, Princeton Theological Seminary, Princeton, New Jersey.

———. "Speech to the Directors." Speech delivered at Princeton Theological Seminary, 1925. In J. Ross Stevenson, "Confidential Letters and Documents," Speer Library, Princeton Theological Seminary, Princeton, New Jersey.

Stonehouse, Ned B. *J. Gresham Machen: A Biographical Memoir.* Grand Rapids, Mich.: Eerdmans, 1954.

Stroman, John Albert. "The American Council of Christian Churches: A Study of Its Origin, Leaders, and Characteristic Positions." Th.D. diss., School of Theology, Boston University, 1966.

Sykes, Stephen. *The Identity of Christianity: Theologians and the Essence of Christianity, from Schleiermacher to Barth.* Philadelphia: Fortress Press, 1984.

Synod of New York and Philadelphia [Presbyterian]. *Minutes of the Synod of New York and Philadelphia.* Philadelphia; issued annually to 1787.

Takayama, K. Peter. "Administrative Structures and Political Processes in Protestant Denominations." *Publius: The Journal of Federalism* 4 (1974): 5–37.

———. "Formal Polity and Changes of Structure: Denominational Assemblies." *Sociological Analysis* 36 (Spring 1975): 17–28.

Takayama, K. Peter, and Lynn Weber Cannon. "Formal Polity and Power Distribution in American Protestant Denominations." *Sociological Quarterly* 20 (Summer 1979): 321–32.

Tracy, David. *The Analogical Imagination: Christian Theology and the Culture of Pluralism.* New York: Crossroads Press, 1981.

———. *Plurality and Ambiguity: Hermeneutics, Religion, Hope.* San Francisco: Harper and Row, 1987.

Trinterud, Leonard J. *The Forming of an American Tradition: A Re-examination of Colonial Presbyterianism.* Philadelphia: Westminster Press, 1949.

Troeltsch, Ernst. *The Social Teachings of the Christian Churches.* 2 volumes. Translated by Olive Wyon. 1911; English translation published Chicago, 1931; Chicago: University of Chicago Press, 1981.

Vander Stelt, John C. *Philosophy and Scripture: A Study in Old Princeton and Westminster Theology.* Marleton, N.J.: Mack Publishing, 1978.

Warner, R. Stephen. "Work in Progress toward a New Paradigm for the Sociological Study of Religion in the United States." *American Journal of Sociology* 98 (Mar. 1993): 1044–93.

Weber, Max. *From Max Weber: Essays in Sociology.* Translated and ed. Hans Gerth and C. Wright Mills. New York: Oxford University Press, 1946.

———. *The Protestant Ethic and the Spirit of Capitalism.* Translated by Talcott Parsons. 1904–5; English translation published New York: Scribners, 1958.

Wells, David, ed. *The Princeton Theology.* Grand Rapids, Mich.: Baker Book House, 1989.

Westminster Theological Seminary. *Catalog, 1986–1988.* Philadelphia: Westminster Theological Seminary, 1986.

Weston, William J. "Michael Novak's Pluralist Religion." *This World* 19 (Fall 1987): 14–26.

Wilson, Bryan. *Religious Sects: A Sociological Study.* New York: McGraw-Hill, 1970.

Woodhouse, H. F. "The Limits of Pluralism." *Scottish Journal of Theology* 34 (1981); 1–15.

Woolley, Paul. *The Significance of J. Gresham Machen Today.* Nutley, N.J.: Presbyterian and Reformed Publishing, 1977.

Wuthnow, Robert. *The Restructuring of American Religion: Society and Faith Since World War II.* Princeton, N.J.: Princeton University Press, 1988.

Zald, Mayer N., and Michael A. Berger. "Social Movements in Organizations: Coup d'Etat, Insurgency, and Mass Movements." *American Journal of Sociology* 83 (1978): 823–61.

INDEX

Adopting Act, 4
Alexander, Maitland, 26, 103
Allis, Oswald, 33, 35, 149n, 151n
American Revolution, 3, 15
Arminianism, 12, 15
Armstrong, William Park, 33
"Auburn Affirmation," 22–25, 26, 27,
    43, 61, 78, 91, 107, 112, 115; as
    successful competition, 137–38
Auburn Theological Seminary, 25, 91

Balmer, Randall, 149n
Baptists, 15, 21, 26
Barnsley, John, 166n
Baum, Gregory, 168n
Beach, Sylvester, 160n
Bell, Daniel, 168n
Berger, Brigitte, 165n
Berger, Michael, 167n
Berger, Peter, 165n
Bible, 4, 6, 7, 10, 27, 54, 64, 79, 83,
    109; inerrancy of, 8, 18, 83, 85;
    Higher Criticism of, 6, 7, 8
Birch, George, 10; as successful
    competitor, 136–37
Boston Evening Transcript, 67
Briggs, Charles A., xiii, xiv, 5, 6–9, 85,
    88, 97, 147n, 154n, 155n, 163n,
    164n, 169n; biographical sketch,
    49–50; broad church ecclesiology,

50–58; and ecumenism 9, 15, 51–
57, 89; in Episcopal Church, 9, 53;
inaugural address ("The Authority
of Holy Scripture"), 7; compared to J.
Gresham Machen, 104–10; suspension from the ministry 8–9, 27, 89,
100
Briggs, Emilie Grace, 9
Broadening Church, xiii, 102
Bryan, William Jennings, 22, 27, 29, 61
Buck, Pearl S., 40, 163n

Calvinism, 7, 15, 32, 84–85, 88, 95,
    117, 120, 149n
Cann, David, xii, 145n, 169n
Cannon, Lynn Weber, 169n
Cauthen, Kenneth, 149n, 161n, 162n
"Chapter IX" organizations. *See* Special
    Interest Groups
Chaves, Mark, xii, 136, 145n, 169n
Chester, Presbytery of, 26
Choice, in religion, 129–30
Christ, 18, 24, 28, 79, 89
Christensen, Richard, 147n
Church union. *See* Ecumenism
Cincinnati, Presbytery of, 10, 26
Civil War, 4, 16
Clark, John Maurice, 168n
Clergy, 3
Clutter, Ronald, 149n, 151n, 160n,